Trust and Organizations

Trust and Organizations
Confidence across Borders

Edited by

Marta Reuter, Filip Wijkström,
and
Bengt Kristensson Uggla

TRUST AND ORGANIZATIONS

First published in 2013 by
PALGRAVE MACMILLAN®
in the United States—a division of St. Martin's Press LLC,
175 Fifth Avenue, New York, NY 10010.

Where this book is distributed in the UK, Europe and the rest of the world, this is by Palgrave Macmillan, a division of Macmillan Publishers Limited, registered in England, company number 785998, of Houndmills, Basingstoke, Hampshire RG21 6XS.

Palgrave Macmillan is the global academic imprint of the above companies and has companies and representatives throughout the world.

Palgrave® and Macmillan® are registered trademarks in the United States, the United Kingdom, Europe and other countries.

ISBN: 978–1–137–37074–7

Library of Congress Cataloging-in-Publication Data

Trust and organizations : confidence across borders / edited by Marta Reuter, Filip Wijkström, and Bengt Kristensson Uggla.
    pages cm
    Includes bibliographical references and index.
    ISBN 978–1–137–37074–7 (hardback)
    1. Organizational sociology. 2. Organizational behavior—Moral and ethical aspects. 3. Trust. I. Reuter, Marta. II. Wijkström, Filip. III. Uggla, Bengt Kristensson.

HM791.T78 2013
302.3'5—dc23   2013025368

A catalogue record of the book is available from the British Library.

Design by Newgen Knowledge Works (P) Ltd., Chennai, India.

First edition: December 2013

D 10 9 8 7 6 5 4 3 2

Contents

Figures

Acknowledgments

The work on this book has been a truly collaborative effort. First and foremost to be thanked are the contributors, many of whom we now count among our friends and not only as esteemed colleagues. But the book would never have happened without the persistent and strong support from Åke Danielsson, former partner with PwC Sweden. He and PwC Sweden have for a long time collaborated with us to create bridges spanning the traditional gulfs between academia and the many worlds outside of our ivory towers. Åke encouraged us to take on the challenge of addressing a number of issues of importance for organizational life in general and for certain "trust industries" in particular, when looking at the greater map of the role of trust in society. Through generous support from PwC Sweden and also the guidance of their senior partner Henrik Steinbrecher, we were able to have an earlier set of manuscripts translated into English, thanks also to the efforts of Kathleen C. Anderson.

At a very early stage of this book's life, Dr. Ilinca Benson, currently director of research at the Swedish Centre for Business and Policy Studies, was instrumental in shaping some of the crucial ideas carrying the book forward. At a public seminar at the School of Business, University of Stockholm, in November 2012, Ilinca and Professor Apostolis Papakostas from Södertörn University were also kind enough to offer us their comments on how we could develop our work further.

At a later stage in the process, we were fortunate enough to work with the efficient team of Dr. Linda Portnoff, Olle Grundin, and Tobias Nielsen at Volante, who helped us in the process of midwifing the book into the world. Finally, our sincere thanks goes to Leila Campoli, Sarah Lawrence, and Charlotte Maiorana at Palgrave Macmillan for their smooth and encouraging support in the process of producing and publishing the book.

The editors, Stockholm,
October 2013

CHAPTER 1

Trust Contextualized: Confidence in Theory and Practice

Bengt Kristensson Uggla, Marta Reuter, and Filip Wijkström

What is the role of social trust in society and in organizational life? Does trust, as many imagine, function as a sort of a web that holds together the entire machinery of society, as a lubricant that oils the wheels of exchange and transactions? Or is it, in reality, a loose but sticky glue that produces inertia and slowness of reaction, hampering mobility and change? What mechanisms have developed in modern society to create, manage, maintain, and convey trust, not only in such different organizational settings as corporations, agencies of public administration, and civil society organizations, but also across these boundaries and other settings? What happens in the transition zone between different societal contexts, when trust is being recontextualized in diverse institutions and cultures? And—perhaps of particular importance today—what can we learn from the logic of de- and recontextualization of trust, in situations where public confidence is shattered?

Questions related to the fundamental conditions and functions of social trust have probably always been important to people. It is fairly uncontroversial to postulate that trust is an inevitable prerequisite for all kinds of human interactions, regardless of time and place. If the way in which we relate to each other and to our institutions were characterized only by distrust and lack of confidence, hardly any of us would dare to take our car on to the roads, take the bus to work, leave our children in kindergarten, or drop them off at school. Nor would we take the risk to prepare the food that we have purchased at the supermarket, go to our neighbors for dinner, or eat from the menu at a restaurant, although we seem to do this in very different ways in different countries, as shown by Kjærnes, Harvey, and Warde (2007) in their book *Trust in Food*. Neither would we, which brings us to the main concern of this book, dare to strike complex business deals, care to reach out to create a European Union, or, indeed, share rich flows of information between different types of organizations.

For good reasons, in many situations we have to take for granted that we can trust other people. Although most of us realize that it would be naive to approach fellow human beings with a form of blind trust that does not include some degree of skepticism, we can, nevertheless, not escape the fact that some kind of mutual confidence has to be in place for all of us to be able to live our daily lives together. This is true in the case of close dialogical relationships as well as more institutionalized and formalized contexts in today's organization society. However, when making the transition between (informal) dialogues and (formal) institutions, as well as between different organizational, institutional, and cultural settings, we are confronted with a complexity of trust matters that asks for our attention as social scientists.

The above applies in particular to the realms of economy and politics; arguably, nothing would work in these spheres if people did not trust one another and the institutions in place. The frequently heard reference to particular fields of these realms as *trust industries* has thus a lot of truth to it. In today's world, it is no longer possible to reduce trust to a "soft" issue, in comparison with more tangible phenomena such as money and legal structures. In fact, many of the profound challenges and urgent problems that we experience in our time, ranging from democratic deficits and economic crises to the lack of self-esteem in many peoples' everyday life, become more comprehensible if we understand them as a spectrum of a trust and confidence crisis (Reuter, Wijkström, and Kristensson Uggla 2012). Such a reading of our contemporary world and the human condition opens up for more fruitful strategies to tackle the dilemmas that our societies face today, no matter if they are dressed in the language of governance (Ostrom 1990; Anheier 2013), social capital (Putnam 1993; Coleman 1996), or framed as an interplay between trust and distrust (Hardin 2004; Papakostas 2012), just to mention a few possible approaches. This applies not the least to the economic predicament dominating the European news at the time of writing and publishing this book. There are, in our view, good reasons to interpret the crippling debt and currency crisis that currently affects Europe as a crisis of trust, and that this particular diagnosis should guide the actions taken in order to cope with the situation.

Trust and Organizations

For the purposes of this book, we have assembled a number of social science scholars from different disciplines, and asked them to reflect on the intricate relationship between social trust and organizational life, as well as on the ways in which these two constitute and shape each other. It is nowadays almost a truism to say that we live in an *organization society*; at the same time, many of us are probably not even aware of the degree to which organizing and organizations pervade the late modern world, governing, structuring, and framing most, if not all, societal activities, processes, and exchanges (see, e.g., Ahrne 1994 and Brunsson 2010). In this increasingly organization-based web of societal relations, trust plays a number of pivotal roles, which, however, have so far not been satisfactorily explored by the social sciences.

Our point of departure in this anthology is the conviction that the idea of trust holds one important key to the understanding of matters related to the existence, functioning, and behavior of organizations, and that this has become even more evident in postindustrial societies. At the most basic level, trust could be seen as the key ingredient holding organizations and institutions together; after all, what are these if not imaginary creations of the human mind, sustained only by our sheer belief—or confidence—in their existence, stability, and operational capacity? If the elemental trust of citizens, in the workings of the organizational and institutional system that we all are embedded in, were at some point withdrawn, that system would crumble to dust within moments. From this point of view, all organizational structures and governance practices are fundamentally dependent on a degree of trust, no matter how different its empirical form in different contexts. At the same time, however, the reverse is also true; in the late modern world, characterized by an increasingly impersonal nature of human relations, organizations and institutions themselves can be understood as instruments or vehicles that help create, relay, and administer basic trust across geographical, cultural, and social distances. As some of the chapters in this book will illustrate, organizational practices that aim at confidence building can, however, also be a potent instrument in processes that ultimately call into question and/or undermine trust, creating spirals of mutually reinforcing need for control and lack of confidence.

This interdependent and context-bound nature of the relationship between trust and organizations is the focus of the present volume. Strangely enough, the importance of trust and confidence—two related concepts that, despite the nuanced difference in meaning, will be used interchangeably in the book—has become a major theme in the social sciences only in the recent decades. Despite the growing interest in this subject, however, the common tendency to think of trust in a univocal, rather simplistic way, has generated a situation where the concrete trust-related practices developed in the spectrum of different contexts have been given scant attention. As a result, a contextual approach to trust is largely missing in the social science literature. Here, the chapters and authors of this book make a valuable contribution, and hopefully also open up a more nuanced scholarly conversation about the context-bound nature of trust and confidence in organizational and social life. The texts assembled in the volume offer a rich variety of perspectives that may contribute to a better understanding of the potential conflicts and dilemmas arising when trust is constantly being (re)contextualized in ever-new organizational, institutional, and cultural settings.

In order to understand how differently trust can be expressed in different contexts, the best place to start may be from firsthand experience. Several years ago, one of us editors participated in a Swedish delegation visiting a top-ranked university in the United States, with the purpose of initiating cooperation between that university and our Swedish institution. The discussions during our meetings went well, and there seemed to be no real complications in the negotiations with our American colleagues. A feeling of mutual understanding and trust arose surprisingly quickly, and after a few intense days, during which pleasant meetings had been interspersed with social activities, our delegation returned to Sweden with high expectations in terms of possible future cooperation between the two institutions.

Shortly after returning, we received a follow-up email from the American partners with many kind words—and an attachment. As we opened and read the attachment, however, our mood changed completely: suddenly, it was as if all of the trust that had emerged during the visit in the United States had been taken away, and the enthusiasm disappeared. Why? The reason may, at the first sight, seem trivial. The attachment contained an extensive draft of a contract, where each paragraph in detail regulated the obligations and commitments to the project. Every single part the delegation had discussed could be found in the document—but the information was now presented in a dry, dense legalese that immediately produced a feeling of confusion on our part. What had happened? Did the American friends get cold feet about the collaboration? Did they no longer trust us? Time passed and the email remained lying in the in-box, without any replies from us Swedes. The motivation to follow up the initiative seemed literally crushed, and we felt as if this entire ambitious project, with all its positive energy, had with one blow run out of steam.

After some time, we received a phone call. It was our American colleagues who, from across the Atlantic, sounded somewhat surprised and confused, wondering what had happened to us. Why didn't we respond to their enthusiasm? Had something dramatic happened and changed the scene since we had parted ways? Why had we not responded to their email in order to continue with our cooperation? Their disappointment was evident.

Only then did it dawn upon us, what we undoubtedly had known in theory, but in practice, and in a rush, had forgotten: contracts and formalizations are assigned very different meanings and functions in Sweden and the United States. While we, in our informal Swedish everyday life, usually tend to view a handshake as the ultimate sign of trust—and a contract, in contrast, as a signal of lack of confidence, due to the fact that some form of "insurance" is required to trust the counter party—on the other side of the Atlantic, a contract actually manifests a tangible expression of mutual trust.

The Complexity of Trust and Organizations: The Importance of the Context

Misunderstandings in interorganizational interactions that arise from cultural differences are naturally not a new object of interest for social scientists. However, within the academic debate on trust and its role in human and organizational relations, the importance of the context has not received enough attention. The above-described experience of how the prerequisites for trust and reliance can change when entering into new settings discloses a complexity far beyond the instrumental logic of those who attempt to portray trust as a capital easy to manage. Thus, this example may serve as an appropriate starting point for a conversation about the fundamental conditions of trust in different organizational, institutional, and cultural contexts.

First, we can learn something about how complicated it is, in terms of trust, to move between theory and practice when trust is being contextualized, because in this transition a number of unpredictable transformations take place—transitions in both directions—which reinforce the conviction that trust is not something simple and univocal.

Second, the above anecdote demonstrates that a "trust capital" cannot be treated as an abstract and universal asset that may simply be transferred and used in new situations, because trust can only exist as something strongly contextualized and situation dependent. Furthermore, the prerequisites for the distribution and organization of trust also differ distinctively between different countries, cultures, organizations, and institutions.

Third, we can learn something about the profound ironic logic of formalization. In the transition between theory and practice, and boundary transgression between different settings, the occurrence of not only control systems, rules, and institutionalizations, such as the contract in our story above, but also different kinds of auditing, have a fundamentally ambiguous effect on trust. These kinds of institutionalizations and follow-up mechanisms can in some contexts strengthen, but in other contexts weaken, the capital of trust.

Fourth, and indirectly laying the foundations for this book, the anecdote says something about our embeddedness—as social scientists but first and foremost as humans—in our own institutional (in this case Northern European) trust culture. The above-described incident illustrates the need for an autoreflexive stance—a skeptical attitude toward one's own assumption about trust and its workings, if you wish—in any discussion of trust as a societal phenomenon that aspires to relevance beyond the present particular cultural context. We will return to the implications of this ambition for the present volume further in this chapter.

Finally, in a list that certainly could be made longer, the story above points toward the need to take the role and complexity of trust in interorganizational relations seriously. This is of extraordinary importance in a world characterized by increasingly transnational relationships and by an increasingly global information logic. In today's society, trust-related challenges are not limited to a local or national specificity, as we are all confronted, on a daily basis, not the least due to the new digital information system, with the most diverse organizational, institutional, and cultural logics, and constantly forced to face our counterparts across the many increasingly blurry boundaries in the globalizing world.

Trust across Borders

The last of the above reflections serves, in fact, as the main departure point for most of the contributions in this book. In a recent analysis of the interplay of trust and distrust in society, the sociologist Apostolis Papakostas (2012) draws attention to the role of boundaries—spatial, social, and organizational—in the creation and management of trust and of its counterpart, distrust. Sharing this perspective, the research presented in most of the chapters in this volume is grounded in the realization that trust-related dilemmas are at their most pronounced at broadly understood junction points, where established boundaries between organizations, institutions, and/or geographical/cultural settings are being put into question, stretched, or crossed. Indeed, one of the main conclusions that can be drawn from the empirical studies presented in this volume is that when we move between distinct geographical, institutional, and organizational contexts and differing social practices, trust itself undergoes a series of profound transformations.

Most of the contributions in the book revolve in one way or another around the question of how trust logics play out—and, frequently, are instrumentalized—across organizational, institutional, or national borders; these three dimensions of boundary crossing form a sort of a font for the discussion that runs as a red thread through the individual chapters. In some of the texts, this may mean investigating what happens to trust and its prerequisites in interactions and exchanges between individual organizations and their distinct organizational cultures. For others, it may entail enquiring how trust is affected, transformed, and used—but also what role(s) it plays itself—in the meeting between different institutional logics (cf. Friedland and Alford 1991), or when societal actors operate across the border between different institutional spheres. Finally, in yet other chapters, it can involve exploring the ways in which trust is used, managed, reproduced, and recreated in the world of increasingly ubiquitous transnational interactions. Notably, these three dimensions are certainly not mutually exclusive; on the contrary, as the texts in this book illustrate, the significance of trust and the complexity of the trust-related societal dynamics and mechanisms become even more acutely visible when these dimensions overlap—as they most often do in real life.

Trust in Theory and Practice

Today, a comprehensive range of international literature, both academic and more popular in tone, addresses trust and confidence in depth, linking often the challenges and dilemmas associated with trust to related concepts, such as social capital (see, e.g., Putnam 1993; Fukuyama 1995; Hardin 2004 and 2006; Cook, Hardin, and Levi 2005; Trägårdh

2009). We do not intend to repeat here the insights from this meritorious literature, although several of the contributions to this anthology build upon and refer to some of the theories and concepts developed there. Neither do we have the ambition of developing a theory of trust of our own. The aim of this publication is, instead, to illustrate and shed light on the richness of the organizational and institutional contexts in which the complexity of trust—and the dilemmas related to trust management—manifest themselves.

As several of the book's chapters show, the issue of trust and distrust at the societal level is intimately linked to issues of control and monitoring, key concepts in governance literature. Today's organization society is, however, less characterized by micromanagement and hierarchical delegation, and increasingly dominated by self-organizing and self-reporting systems, regulated by objective-based management, decentralization, and local autonomy in the form of a kind of control "from within." These trends have led to the emergence of a generalized accounting and control culture that is becoming increasingly pervasive in our societies, giving rise to concepts such as "audit society" (Power 1999). The "control addiction," which according to critics such as Power emerges as a result of the excesses of the audit society, is characterized, among others, by the ironic development logic also characterizing other addictions: although there are short-term profits, in the long run, more trust-related problems are created than solved.

In this context, it is important to recall that the opposite of trust is not suspicion or distrust. Just as it would be both naive and devastating for the concept of trust if we, in all situations, blindly trusted others, it seems a simplification to identify institutions solely with distrust. As the chapters in this book illustrate, trust and distrust are rather intricately intertwined with and feeding into each other in our institutions, and criticism, control, and auditing can be understood as integral parts of the complex dialectic of our "trust industries."

In the present volume, as an alternative to the more dystopian perspectives that see potential conspiracies lurking behind such headings as "audit society" or "regulation society," we have chosen to focus on the fundamentally ambiguous nature, as well as on the multidimensional meanings, of trust in relation to practices such as accounting and auditing. Through our selection of empirical case studies we explore and illuminate how, on the one hand, strong trust capital seems to require control, auditing, follow-up processes, review, and so on; while on the other hand, these activities, despite the best of intentions, can contribute to undermining that very same capital. One of the lessons that may be drawn from some of the studies presented here, is thus that even when the purpose is to inspire confidence, the growing number of institutionalized systems for inspection and evaluation may lead, over time, to a hollowing-out of public trust as well as of interpersonal relationships in general.

Trust Seen through a Nordic Lens

The character of the contributions to this publication is multidisciplinary, as the dilemmas related to trust for, in, and between organizations clearly transcend the horizons of a single academic discipline. Our ambition has also been to illustrate the universality and ubiquitousness of the importance of trust through the broad range of organizational and institutional settings that are in focus in the individual chapters. While some of the texts focus on corporations and on the workings of trust in commercial activities, others discuss the ways in which trust matters to—and is utilized by—civil society organizations, both at the national and at the global level. Dilemmas surrounding the public's confidence in political and public administration projects and the measures taken to instill such confidence are the focus of yet other contributions to this volume. Some of the chapters take also an explicit aim at the borderland between these different societal spheres and sectors, exploring what happens to trust when organizational practices and activities combine commercial and public as well as civic logics and rationales.

This diversity of perspectives notwithstanding, the approaches used and the analyses developed here are inevitably influenced by the Northern European—specifically Swedish—background of the collection's authors. While the research discussed here displays a very broad empirical range, from studies of the European currency and commercial certification systems to local Indonesian trade union negotiations and the dilemmas of local welfare service provision in Swedish municipalities, the scholars analyzing and reflecting upon these empirical settings are all firmly embedded in the Swedish institutional context, and thus susceptible to relating to trust in a rather particular way. This cultural background inevitably constitutes a very particular lens through which we regard trust and distrust. This is illustrated poignantly by the final chapter of this book, where the historian Lars Trägårdh reflects upon how, and suggests why, Sweden stands out from most other societies when it comes to its exceptionally high degree of social trust, as expressed in people's confidence both in fellow citizens and in the public institutions.

The "Nordic perspective" that permeates this book is, however, characterized not only by the presumable influence of the wider cultural Nordic view of trust on the book's contributors. More importantly (from a theoretical point of view), it is also characterized, on the one hand, by a strong interest common among Swedish organization scholars for institutions and institutional analysis (see Brunsson and Jacobsson 2000 on standardization as a good example of this so-called Scandinavian new institutionalism); and on the other hand, by a strong critical and constructivist current within Swedish organization studies (see, e.g., Czarniawska and Sévon 2005). Although the contributions in our volume stretch across many disciplines and several different approaches, we argue that these trends in the Swedish organization studies give also an echo here. In most chapters, an explicit or implicit interest in institutions as the normative and governing structures in which organizations are embedded—and as important conveyer belts and manipulators of social trust—is apparent. At the same time, our common focus on the ambiguous, multidimensional, and double-edged nature of trust, and our somewhat questioning attitude toward many of the trust-building organizational practices and strategies prevalent in different organizational fields, position us close to the critical Scandinavian tradition in management and organization theory (for a contribution in this tradition dealing explicitly with the matter of trust in organizational analysis, see Furusten and Werr [2005]).

Contents of the Book

There is in today's public debate, in spite of the increased insight into the critical significance of trust, a recurring tendency to view trust-related issues as somewhat flimsy, as a luxury, and, therefore, as a challenge not particularly urgent. In order to illustrate that it is not possible to marginalize these issues, by reducing trust to a "soft" concept, we have chosen to start our book with a text that goes right to the center of the severe financial crisis that has hit the world in general, and Europe in particular, in several shockwaves since 2008. Johan Fornäs's chapter, "Currency for Europe: Monetary Solidity, Trust, and Identification across National Borders" addresses the trust component associated with the European currency, which, second only to the European Union (EU) flag, stands out as the most important symbol of the EU project. The symbolism of the European currency—as a coin with two sides—is not only expected to engender confidence in the currency, but also in the overall EU project.

Fornäs shows how currency, in addition to serving as a means of payment, also ties people and societies together: the currency communicates meaning and cultural identity to the same degree as it serves as a means for transactions. Through the interaction between the motifs on the front and reverse sides of the coins, the designers have chosen to manifest the motto "United in diversity," which is fully in line with the salad bowl metaphor characterizing the EU (in contrast to the American melting pot metaphor). This construction makes it possible for the common currency to be included in national contexts by offering varying interpretations for different countries—at the same time as these interpretations are redefined as being European. Thus, the trust-building project identified by Fornäs in his research on the symbolism of the European currency appears far from unambiguous. The EU project, rather, attempts to actively balance the national and the transnational, the cultural and the financial, the symbols' abstract cultural expression and the concrete institutionalized everyday practices, the individual and the collective, the local and the global. As the author notes, "it is in this fascinating borderland that trust is expressed and created."

The common currency could be viewed as an example of an elaborate attempt to create an institution, whose aim it is to evoke and maintain the general public's trust in a specific political and financial project. According to many sociologists, such confidence does not arise on its own, but is utterly dependent on well-functioning social institutions generating trust for the entire social unit. One such institution is the audit. Maria Gustavson and Bo Rothstein's contribution to the anthology, "Can Auditing Generate Trust? The Organization of Auditing and the Quality of Government," sheds light on one of the main aims of auditing: to secure the general public's trust in the public administration. At the same time, the chapter problematizes the complex relationship between the audit institution and social trust. Auditing has existed, in some form, for as long as we have had organized societies, and the need of such an institution can be derived from the question of the extent to which citizens are able to trust the complex social agreements in modern society. The authors highlight an interesting interrelationship between auditing and trust: auditing is necessary to assure the quality of public administration and to increase citizens' confidence that public authorities function as they are supposed to. At the same time, the audit institution is itself ultimately dependent on citizens' trust in audit activities and in the auditors' impartiality; without such trust, auditing becomes meaningless. The chapter addresses the points of reference for each of these two dimensions and the dilemmas generated. Moreover, the authors expand the scope of their discussion from Western societies and pose the question of whether the relationship between auditing and trust can take a similar form in other contexts, especially in societies where trust in public administration is claimed to be based on values other than those found in the Western world. Is it possible to speak about different types of "trust regimes"? Gustavson and Rothstein's discussion on the conditions of auditing in African countries indicates that we should be careful in assigning too much significance to cultural patterns and differing values. Doing so, we risk missing the increasingly transnational normative driving forces and their significance for society's development. One such driving force is, for example, the logic of the professional identity, which results in audit professionals outside the Western world tending to identify themselves with the values and the practices that, according to the authors of this chapter, have the potential to generate social trust.

Niklas Egels-Zandén's contribution, "From Global Consumer Power to Local Worker Power," also touches upon the transnational dimension of trust moving across boundaries, reconfigured in different contexts. This chapter focuses on how trust is constructed in the relationship between process and result, based on empirical research into how global consumer power is "converted" or "translated" into local worker power by civil society actors operating at the international level. The background is the global interrelation between, on the one hand, Western consumers and multinational companies with strong brands; and on the other hand, employers and employees at the local level, in this case Indonesia. The chapter sheds light on the relational complexity that emerges both between various levels in production chains, with numbers of intermediaries between local factories in the "South" and the global brands in the Western world, and between many different types of actors (such as trade unions, consumer rights organizations, nongovernmental organizations [NGOs], large global companies, local producers, etc.) which, in the case of Indonesia, appear at different levels.

Against this background, it is possible to understand the puzzle why local producers and factories in Indonesia, who were previously not at all interested in or dependent on the requirements of the relatively weak local trade unions, still find themselves negotiating with these unions. The "currency" that has made this situation possible is trust. The author illustrates how a threat directed at Western consumers' trust in global brands strategically connects these consumers, organizations in the transnational civil society, and Indonesian trade unions. Civil society actors can use the trust of consumers in brands and their *power to take their money elsewhere* as a "hovering hand" over the global companies, and thereby make the latter force their local suppliers to participate in negotiations with trade unions. The relational link that the author reveals between global trust processes and local power struggles is definitely worth attention.

The discussion in the next chapter in the anthology revolves also around the question of the public's trust in brands and producers, although the authors follow a different path and focus on the tools used to create and maintain trust in a society flooded with brands and products. In the chapter "The Certification Paradox: Monitoring as a Solution and a Problem," Ingrid Gustafsson and Kristina Tamm Hallström highlight the phenomenon of "third-party certification" and the issues regarding trust and control that it evokes. The chapter sheds light on the increasingly complex transnational chain of control measures that has emerged in the area of certification and the regulations surrounding this seemingly deregulated field. In recent times, a comprehensive market for standards and certification has developed: instruments aimed at helping the general public to navigate the jungle of products and services and to create trust in producers and their products and services. The purpose of third-party certification is to certify that companies comply with specific standards and the certification mark or diploma signals that the certified product or service is trustworthy. At the same time, certification is in itself a commercial service, implying a dilemma similar to that discussed by Gustavson and Rothstein: how can those who have been assigned to control others, be controlled themselves? In this chapter, the authors approach this dilemma as a "trust problem in the market for trust," and pose the question whether it is rather not *distrust* that is the actual focus of such certification activities.

Several chapters in the anthology raise the question of organizations' dependency on the public's trust for their survival. In many cases, this trust is generated and conveyed by one of late modern society's most powerful actors: the mass media. Two of the chapters explore how organizations' reputations, and thus also the public's trust, is mediated and shaped by their image as constructed in the media. Lars Strannegård reflects in his chapter, "The Triumph of Feelings: On the Power of Imagery in Business," upon the significance of reputation, rumor, and the public image in late modern and postmodern societies. With the current research about the mediatization of politics and economy as a starting point, and taking aim at the media logic that governs both the shape of politics and its contents in an increasingly evident manner, Strannegård discusses the organizational phenomena and practices that emerge around the public image of an organization. Today's trends toward increasing transparency, comparability, control, and standardization of organizational life may easily give rise to the idea that "hard" facts and different types of documented figures should be sufficient in order to create clear lines of separation between well-performing and underperforming actors. However, according to the author, this idea is misleading. Since the human being is governed by emotions, our perception of the surrounding world—including the organizations in it—is based more on impressions, feelings, and associations, rather than rational reasoning based on facts. This is where communication enters the scene, together with the communicators: there is an entire market for activities where facts and figures are put into a context and manipulated to give a certain image of an actor, an activity, or an event. The presentation and image are, thus, important tools for organizations who, in order to win the public trust they need for their survival, have to be seen as legitimate at all costs.

Pernilla Petrelius Karlberg, Maria Grafström, and Karolina Windell also raise the issue of the mass media's power over public trust in organizations in modern society; in this case a major nonprofit, voluntary organization. Their chapter, "The Creation of a Crisis of Confidence: A Study of the Mediatization of the Red Cross," gives the reader an insight into the drama that publicly unfolded in spring 2010, when the Swedish Red Cross ran the gauntlet in the media, in the wake of the revelation of the fraud committed by the communications director, John af Donner, and of the heated discussion surrounding the remuneration paid to the chairman, Bengt Westerberg. The authors portray an image of two competing institutional logics impacting our image of, and trust for, the organizations found in civil society. On the one hand, there is the traditional logic and rationality of classical popular movements and member organizations, prevalent in Swedish civil society during most of the twentieth century; on the other hand, we have the ascending logic of charities and fundraising organizations, inspired by the outlook and structure of civil society in the Anglo-Saxon countries. The organizational practices and activities that are to be regarded as legitimate, and thus also deserve the trust of the public, depend on which of these two logics is applied as the starting point, and, above all, which of them is currently being adopted by the media. The chapter describes the collision between the two logics in the case of the Red Cross scandal, and the manner in which the mass media, by emphasizing one of them, also contributed to the formation of the organization's own view on how to regain the public's trust.

The chapter contributed by Eva Hagbjer, Johnny Lind, and Ebba Sjögren focuses on the fundamental challenges to upholding citizens' trust in publicly financed services, when the services are subcontracted to profit-driven companies in the emerging private market for health care. Such trust is necessary, if for nothing else, to maintain the general public confidence in the welfare system as such. As with many other texts in this book, this chapter, "Trust in the Monitoring of Publicly

Funded Services: A Case Study of Two Outsourced Care Homes for the Elderly," develops a kind of dialectic approach to trust, which deviates from the otherwise prevalent tendency of viewing trust as an unambiguous concept. As their point of reference, the authors use the distinction between "mechanical objectivity" (based on the application of predetermined standards) and "disciplinary objectivity" (achieved through using professional knowledge and judgment). In their investigations of the relationship between a municipality and two commercial service providers, the authors find a clear dominance of the use of mechanical objectivity, in line with predetermined reporting requirements. However, the follow-up processes do not automatically lead to a better examination and also appear to have an ambiguous function. The authors indicate a possible conflict between the general trust in systems and the more particularist trust in actors in relation to the contents of a specific operation. Moreover, the room for interpretation that always exists in the application of standards has an important role to play in this respect; this room for interpretation, however, becomes invisible when the results are reported with the precision and comparability required by the standards for mechanical objectivity. In sum, mechanical objectivity and disciplinary objectivity produce two difference types of knowledge that may serve as the foundation for trust, and the authors advocate that both methods are necessary in a well-functioning follow-up system.

In the next chapter, "The Grammar of Trust as Ethical Challenge," Bengt Kristensson Uggla reflects upon the trust-related challenges and the multidimensionality of trust that become apparent in different societal contexts. Two empirical cases serve as a font for the discussion: a scandal associated with the revelation of improper intimacy between a high-rank Swedish official and a political reporter, and the publishing of an ethical conduct instruction by a Swedish public agency. The departure point of the discussion is the reflection that what might be viewed as virtue in dialogical relationships (friendships) might simultaneously be viewed as corruption in public institutions and vice versa: that fairness as an institutional virtue can hardly be said to be sufficient to maintain dialogical confidence. As there is no simple, unambiguous solution to this dilemma, it is necessary, the author argues, to develop a dialectic conceptual model—a *grammar of trust*, inspired by the hermeneutical philosophy of Paul Ricoeur—which would account for the multidimensionality of confidence, and thereby also for its transformations in the transition between theory and practice.

There are, as indicated in these different chapters, many ways in which trust or confidence can be created, both as regards the individual actors, and as regards the society in general. But what are the reasons that some specific societies show a larger degree of trust between people than other societies? In the final chapter in the book, "The Historical Incubators of Trust in Sweden: From the Rule of Blood to the Rule of Law," the author Lars Trägårdh rises above the organizational focus that characterizes the other texts, and instead takes aim at the larger questions prompted by the apparent and considerable international variations in the degree of social trust in the population from a historical perspective. For a long time, many have believed that modernity, with its individualism—some would perhaps say "atomism"—and liberation from the traditions and premodern social ties, has had a negative impact on the degree of individuals' trust in each other and, ultimately, in social institutions. The source and origin of trust has, in this tradition, been sought in tight communities based on ties of blood, ethnicity, and religious affiliation or on ideological beliefs.

The most recent generation of research in these areas, however, shows a surprising international pattern which, to a large extent, contradicts this conventional view: the Nordic countries—which are often seen as an outpost of modernity and which also differ radically (especially in the case of Sweden) from most other societies as regards the degree of the individual's liberation from traditional ties—are also the societies that show the highest degree of social trust and confidence in other people. While previous observers have reflected on a possible relationship between the strong social trust in Sweden and the other Nordic countries, on the one hand, and the comprehensive social welfare systems and "welfare collectivism" presumably developed in these countries on the other hand, Trägårdh directs attention toward other distinctive characteristics of the Swedish society, which he opines might have served as the breeding ground for not only the remarkably strong but also "cool"—that is rational, individualized, and not particularly sensitive—trust prevalent in the Swedish society. He seeks the origin of this atypical trust in specific historical and institutional factors that have formed the Swedish mindset, and that have led to the situation where a mix of an impersonal, but broad, social trust, a deeply embedded individual independence, and at the same time a certain sense of loneliness, have all come to be considered as features of Swedish society.

In sum, the contributions to this book are intended to serve as a series of contextualizations, through which the multidimensional and ambiguous nature of social trust in the organization society is illuminated.

Various types of institutional contexts, as well as various spheres or sectors in society and cultures from distinctive parts of the world form a framework for the manifold manifestations of trust, and, simultaneously, actively contribute to the latter's continuous metamorphoses. When moving from theory to practice, as when moving between distinctive cultures, institutions, and organizations, one needs to pay attention to how the conditions of and prerequisites for trust change—sometimes dramatically.

References

Ahrne, Göran. 1994. *Social Organizations: Interaction Inside, Outside, and Between Organizations.* London: Sage.

Anheier, Helmut K. 2013. *The Governance Report 2013.* Hertie School of Governance. Oxford, UK: Oxford University Press.

Brunsson, Nils. 2010. "Vad är företagsekonomi?" In *Företagsekonomins frågor,* edited by Nils Brunsson, 10–21. Stockholm: SNS.

Brunsson, Nils, and Bengt Jacobsson. Eds. 2000. *A World of Standards.* Oxford, UK: Oxford University Press.

Cook, Karen S., Russell Hardin, and Margaret Levi. 2005. *Cooperation without Trust?* New York: Russel Sage Foundation.

Coleman, James S. 1996. *Foundations of Social Theory.* Cambridge, MA: Belknap Press of Harvard University Press.

Czarniawska, Barbara, and Guje Sévon. Eds. 2005. *Global Ideas. How Ideas, Objects and Practices Travel in the Global Economy.* Copenhagen: Liber and Copenhagen Business School Press.

Friedland, Roger, and Robert R. Alford. 1991. "Bringing Society Back In: Symbols, Practices, and Institutional Contradictions." In *The New Institutionalism in Organizational Analysis,* edited by Walter W. Powell and Paul J. DiMaggio, 232–263. Chicago: University of Chicago Press.

Fukuyama, Francis. 1995. *Trust: The Social Virtues and Creation of Prosperity.* New York: Free Press.

Furusten, Staffan, and Andreas Werr. Eds. 2005. *Dealing with Confidence. The Construction of Need and Trust in Management Advisory Services.* Copenhagen: Copenhagen Business School Press.

Hardin, Russell. Ed. 2004. *Distrust.* New York: Russell Sage Foundation.

———. 2006. *Trust.* Cambridge, UK: Polity Press.

Kjærnes, Unni, Mark Harvey, and Alan Warde. Eds. 2007. *Trust in Food. A Comparative and Institutional Analysis.* Houndmills: Palgrave Macmillan.

Ostrom, Elinor. 1990. *Governing the Commons: The Evolution of Institutions for Collective Action.* Cambridge, UK: Cambridge University Press.

Papakostas, Apostolis. 2012. *Civilizing the Public Sphere—Distrust, Trust and Corruption.* New York: Palgrave.

Power, Michael. 1999. *The Audit Society: Rituals of Verification.* Oxford, UK: Oxford University Press.

Putnam, Robert D. 1993. *Making Democracy Work. Civic Traditions in Modern Italy.* Princeton, NJ: Princeton University Press.

Reuter, Marta, Filip Wijkström, and Bengt Kristensson Uggla. Eds. 2012. *Vem i hela världen kan man lita på? Förtroende i teori och praktik.* Lund: Studentlitteratur.

Trägårdh, Lars. Ed. 2009. *Trust in Modern Sweden: The Dumb Swede and Other Mysteries.* Stockholm: SNS Förlag.

CHAPTER 2

Currency for Europe:
Monetary Solidity, Trust, and
Identification across National Borders

Johan Fornäs

The clinking of coins in your pocket and the rustling of notes as you take them from your wallet. Metal shining like gold and the refined security features of the banknotes, vouching for a value on which you can always rely. But then you find yourself in a different place, or at a different time, and you suddenly have to familiarize yourself with new symbols and denominations. Instead of the familiar krona to which you have grown so accustomed, you curiously weigh this unknown currency in your hand. The visual design confidently communicates the entity safeguarding its value. Every coin and every banknote signals both its denomination and the issuing country.

However, here, I am not referring to any nation-state but to the European Union (EU). The year is 2002 and I find myself in a European metropolis. Accompanied by other cultural researchers, I am exploring the manner in which local, national, and European identities cross-fertilize in different medial contexts. It suddenly strikes me how the euro has made Europe into a living, concrete fact of life for its citizens. And I next discover that the reverse sides of the euro coins are adorned with embossments of European icons: a German eagle, a Celtic harp, a Greek ship . . . Europeanness takes on a new meaning—at the same time both commonplace and profound. As a Swede, I belong to a country that has not changed from its krona to the euro, which seems today like a financially sound decision, but on a symbolical level, I envy those who are allowed to have this experience of European belonging. Being European but not fully able to take part in its symbols perhaps motivates my curiosity in how such significant tokens identify the continent to which I belong: being in this way ambivalently positioned in a kind of symbolic borderland is a productive starting point for exploring the signifying processes involved here.

Eight years later, this same euro has been shaken by an unexpected crisis of confidence. The crisis started in Greece, regarded by many as the cradle of European civilization—not least by the EU, who chose for its currency the name "euro" and the symbol "€." The latter, consciously designed to remind its users of Europe's Greek roots, had been an attempt to further strengthen the credibility of the EU by means of historical continuity. The euro crisis has heralded a period of turbulence, during which there has even been talk of the risk of the EU dissolving, and the solidity of the euro has been questioned. Scandinavian supporters of the krona feel they have strengthened their case and are relieved that they did not embark upon the euro journey. In such a manner, monetary and geopolitical affairs are woven together in an intricate pattern.

Everyone uses money, and even if only a few numismatists study currency in detail, ordinary citizens are exposed, on a daily basis, to the symbolic images circulating on banknotes and coins. Here, I will look at the manner in which currency and other symbols have been and are employed in attempts to bolster confidence in Europe as a common transnational project.[1] Trust is usually based on some degree of familiarity with that which is to be trusted. As for Europe, the distance between individual citizens and the transnational institutions in which they are supposed to have confidence, including the euro, is immensely larger than for any one of its nation-states. Also, being composed of highly diverse nation-states, the continent by necessity has a particularly complex internal structure, which further makes the development of trust even more precarious. This applies horizontally to the mutual trust needed between citizens in different regions, for instance, between Germany and Greece, in order to legitimize solidarity between Europe's nations, but also vertically between citizens and pan-European institutions such as the euro. It is, therefore, interesting how this new currency has been designed in order to meet such high demands and makes efforts to offer symbols that invite people to place trust in it.

Europe's Trust Project

Currency is a lot more than a technical means of payment. As a tool of exchange, money ties people and societies together, and serves as the means of circulation for civilizations linked by the exchange of goods. As a measure of value, it functions as a great equalizer, enabling the abstraction and measurement of wealth across all walks of society—even if some insist that there are, in fact, values that cannot be quantified in monetary terms.

At the same time, currency, in its many forms, must necessarily also function as a medium for communicating meaning. The recently developed electronic currency has reduced this communication to an absolute minimum, with the focus simply on the currency designations, for example, £, $, €, or ¥, or abbreviations, such as SEK, GBP, USD, or EUR. With traditional coins and banknotes, the capacity for symbolism is much greater, and here it is a question of confidence-building design on two mutually dependent levels. On the one hand, this is a matter of building confidence in the currency itself, as a bearer of value. A number of security features that are difficult to counterfeit, distinguish real currency from the copies used for fun in toys and games. On the other hand, the symbolism is a matter of assuring the user that the issuer of the currency is financially sound and has the ability to withstand the most severe tests and crises without wavering. Here, the currency design is used to symbolize the identity of the issuing institution or entity, thereby providing a visual suggestion as to how citizens can identify with their nation—or, in this case, with Europe as a transnational community.[2]

In the EU, the euro appears to be seen at least as much a matter of cultural identity as a tool for value transactions. In the 2004 draft treaty establishing a constitution for Europe, currency was not primarily referred to as an economic means of payment but, instead, as a symbol denoting European identity. This witnesses the symbolic power of money and perhaps also something of the way in which the economy has become culturalized, in that symbolic features are so evident at the heart of what is unashamedly materialistic in nature.

In the draft Constitutional Treaty, five key symbols for Europe were specified:

The flag of the Union shall be a circle of twelve golden stars on a blue background.

The anthem of the Union shall be based on the Ode to Joy from the Ninth Symphony by Ludwig van Beethoven.

The motto of the Union shall be: United in diversity.

The currency of the Union shall be the euro.

9 May shall be celebrated throughout the Union as Europe day.[3]

It is true that these symbols were among the first to disappear when the constitution had to be revised after defeat in the French and Dutch referenda on the issue. Nevertheless, when the Treaty of Lisbon was finally adopted, 16 of EU's member states attached a solemn declaration of loyalty to those symbols:[4]

> Belgium, Bulgaria, Germany, Greece, Spain, Italy, Cyprus, Lithuania, Luxemburg, Hungary, Malta, Austria, Portugal, Romania, Slovenia and the Slovak Republic declare that the flag with a circle of twelve golden stars on a blue background, the anthem based on the "Ode to Joy" from the Ninth Symphony by Ludwig van Beethoven, the motto "United in diversity," the euro as the currency of the European Union and Europe Day on 9 May will, for them, continue as symbols to express the sense of community of the people in the European Union and their allegiance to it.

All five symbols continue to be used, despite the fact that they are not included in the current constitution; they had each previously also been accepted by both the Council of Europe and the EU. The flag, the anthem, the motto, and the celebration day continue to be used to identify Europe. And the same applies to the euro, although only some 20 countries have adopted it. Not even the aftermath of the Southern European financial crisis from 2009 onward appears, thus far, to have been able to sink the euro project.

Throughout the various phases of the integration process, the Council of Europe and the EU institutions have eloquently championed the importance of unifying symbols. Time after time, hopes have been raised that a set of officially legitimized symbols would be able to strengthen the citizens' confidence in, and their identification with, the unifying project of the European community by conveying an emotionally anchored, as well as emotionally reinforcing, image of its underlying values.

A large number of public documents from this process are easily accessible on the website Centre Visuel de la Connaissance sur l'Europe (CVCE; www.cvce.eu), together with explanatory background texts by the Italian lawyer, Carlo Curti Gialdino. He argued that political symbols crystallize and maintain collective identities, express the citizens' common values, and create loyalty toward such values, thus acting as a unifying force:

> The political symbols of a State (flag, emblem, motto, anthem, currency, national public holiday) . . . crystallize national identity by making it tangible; in other words, they codify the subjective nature of the nation. The nation is an invisible concept and, therefore, needs to be symbolized if it is to be seen and acclaimed, if it is to be loved. It is precisely in this

way that the symbol provides identity: it shows citizens what is theirs and generates loyalty, *affectio societatis*, to the sign representing the nation. The use of symbols, therefore, has a unifying and federating power.

When they sing the same anthem, honor the same flag, use the same currency, or celebrate the same public holiday, citizens are all sharing a common sentiment. Every political symbol is a tangible sign of identity codifying the shared values that the symbol represents and that are generally detailed in a constitution.

As in the case of nations, political symbols serve an identifying function for the EU as well. They are the external signs of that constitutional patriotism—as defined by Jürgen Habermas, to be precise—through which European citizens, aware of their belonging, can be influenced to set aside their differences and act in the common public good and, therefore, to perceive the EU as their home or *Heimat*.

In this sense, symbols may help to consolidate the fledgling European *demos*. They should undoubtedly not do so in opposition to national *demoi* but as a distillation of the specific shared values of a highly integrated area such as the EU. The community methods and participative democracy launched by the Constitutional Treaty could help the EU to emerge as a new postnational political system based precisely on shared values, where the national interest coincides with the European interest. Political symbols such as the flag, the anthem, the motto, the currency, and Europe Day may therefore contribute, by creating emotive images and rites, even subliminally, toward making the EU more legitimate in the eyes of its citizens and help them to identify with the plan for a common destiny. In other words, they help to construct a political identity, so that a set of values that identifies us as belonging to the same community are felt to be binding.[5]

In this manner, proponents of European unification express a need and a wish to make use of the legitimizing function of collective symbols, inherited from nation-states but now to be applied on a much larger and more heterogeneous scale, which puts much greater strain on these symbols, as they have to be felt to be binding across so many geographical, linguistic, and cultural borders, and must also be balanced toward their still valid national counterparts.

The integration project was originally initiated as a means of putting an end to centuries of European warfare. Since 1985, the Schuman Declaration has been commemorated each year on May 9. It was the French politician Robert Schuman who, in 1950, had proposed the establishment of a union between the old archrivals, France and Germany, on the basis of precisely those coal and steel industries that had been a source both of competition and of its mortal weapons. Schuman argued that peace was required in order to build prosperity and power, and thus, out of the ruins of a continent brutally desolated in World War II, there was created what would, in time, become the EU. "O friends, not these tones!" the deep bass voice of Beethoven had urged, using the words of Schiller to express the dreams of common joy ("Joy, bright spark of divinity") and universal fraternity ("all men become brothers"). The song was first heard in 1824—in the aftermath of the Napoleonic Wars and the Congress of Vienna—and was sung to a catchy melody inspired by the popular style of the French Revolution. Some 150 years later, it was deemed an appropriate European anthem, first by the Council of Europe in 1972, then by the EU in 1985, although, in the end, the lyrics were omitted in order to avoid the problem of choosing one single language and because it was, strangely, regarded as being too universal to serve to identify something specifically European. A flag was designed and adopted by the Council of Europe in 1955 and by the EU in 1986. With its symmetrical circle of stars, and the number 12, the flag was meant to represent perfect harmony, and was also, in the spirit of Schiller and Beethoven, seen as conveying a Promethean view of Europe's states, cultures, and citizens striving to reach the heavens and to become the equals of the gods. Thus, the circle of stars achieves the same exalting effect as a saint's halo. On the one hand, the empty circle can, perhaps a little maliciously, be interpreted as expressing the lack of a core in the European identity. But, on the other hand, the empty space comprises a type of open agora allowing shifting actors to make a symbolic entrance into a public space in which everyone is of equal value. When the emblem of the flag is used in different contexts, it has often been tempting to add another symbol in the empty space between the stars, for example, a symbol for another institution with whom the EU cooperates. Gay activists have created a version in which the stars are colored with the colors of the rainbow and the EU, itself, has commissioned Rem Kohlhaas's company to design an alternative EU logo in the form of a bar code with colors from the national flags of the growing number of member states. It is clear that there are many who struggle to introduce some expression of diversity into European unity. In this spirit, the motto "United in diversity" became the little brother of EU symbols in 2000, intended to emphasize the respect for diversity guaranteed by the principle of subsidiarity: the inner division existing between the continent's regions, in terms of languages, cultures, and nations, would in this manner be transformed from an obstacle to integration into a valuable resource. This was also in line with the reevaluation of diversity and multiculturalism that developed not the least in Central and Eastern Europe following the fall of the Berlin Wall.

The euro, introduced in 2002, became the crowning glory: a physically active mechanism that, at the same time, could be designed in a symbolically cogent manner, with the intention to consolidate and develop the recognition of what is European, as well as further strengthening identification with these European values. The different symbols have had a somewhat varied success. Europe Day is, it is true, celebrated in a number of countries, not the least in Eastern Europe where the concept of Europe has been linked to newfound independence. However, in some countries, for example Sweden, the date receives virtually no attention, partly due to the fact that the Council of Europe has insisted on instead celebrating its own formation on May 5, which only contributes to the confusion. The anthem has, indeed, its strong points, while at the same time, it is regarded by many as being rather too ceremonious and highbrow. This refers, in particular, to the official version arranged by Herbert von Karajan, with a much slower tempo than by Beethoven, and with lyrics omitted, which makes it difficult to sing. The motto is known by few, but echoes in the background of a number of political documents and has, therefore, a not entirely insignificant concealed life. The flag is well known and has acquired an integral position in all projects financed by the EU, as well as on the number plates of cars and on the web. Last but not least, the euro seems to be here to stay.

As a combined project for peace and prosperity, and with an ambiguous mix of altruistic-universal and egoistic-Eurocentric motives, the EU started by constructing stable economic and, in time, also political institutions for cooperation across national borders. Certain social activities were also coordinated; although in the cultural area, national and regional autonomy was emphasized. Gradually, however, many joined Jürgen Habermas and others, who worried about the lack of some form of shared public sphere through which to foster a collective will. This required not only a common language, but also at least some fundamental constituents of a shared culture and identity; not to replace the national puzzle but to supplement it and to provide legitimacy to pan-European political and economic institutions. While some regarded the symbols as essentially superfluous and ineffective examples of fluffy rhetoric and wanted, instead, to invest in more tangible, material, and social measures, there were many who, like Carlo Curti Gialdino, put their hopes in the role of symbolism in expressing and consolidating common values into a condensed form. The reference in the above quotation to the symbols' collective binding force suggests that this was, to a large extent, a matter of trust and confidence.

The motto can be taken as an example to illustrate this. There is nothing surprising in the fact that a union's motto refers to the benefits of unification. This message can, however, be expressed in many different ways, which says something about the basic values of each such union. The United States has had the motto "In God We Trust" since 1956, while the EU has opted for a more secular set of symbols. "United in diversity" makes a virtue of necessity and attempts to redefine the inner (linguistic, cultural, and political) fragmentation from representing an insurmountable obstacle for integration to its most valuable resource. "In Europe We Trust" can be seen as its hidden message: communicating trust in Europe's positive role in the world. The previous US motto, *e pluribus unum*, which is still found on the dollar coin, means "out of many, one," and refers to the melting pot metaphor in which differences blend into a homogenizing union. In contrast, the EU motto builds on what may be called the salad bowl metaphor, where the aim is to preserve the differences within the evolving unity. The principle of subsidiarity and the respect for internal differences were a necessary response to powerful anti-federalist forces, and were also a means of ensuring legitimacy and trust in the common institutions, by carefully ensuring that they would never threaten local, national, and regional features. This was, thus, again a measure to meet the particular demands posed by transnational identification across geographical as well as political, social, and cultural borders. Clearly, the motto has to do with common trust—the confidence that a collective community can achieve something good in the world and that such a community is, therefore, worth identifying with.

Currency's Stable Mobility

The fifth EU symbol is the monetary symbol: the euro. Currency is far from being only a means of circulating economic value; its design conveys a symbolic value as a medium for collective identification. Currency requires trust in its economic function, and as an official symbol, it is further meant to create confidence, loyalty, and legitimacy as regards the envisioned European community; a community with physical borders and institutions, to be sure, but, equally, a sociocultural and, in some sense, imaginary community, the continuity of which is fully dependent on its citizens and its surroundings recognizing its rightful existence (Anderson 1983/1991, on the concept of imagined community).

In his large work on the philosophy of money, sociologist Georg Simmel stressed the way in which currency's mobility, symbolized by the round form of the coins, requires, at the same time, substantial stability. The liquidity of this most fleeting of things, presupposes a constant value content, guaranteed by banking systems and by other confidence-inspiring social institutions, in which the economic market system and the political state system converge (Simmel 1900/1989, 708, 714–716). Currency is the hub in a complex dialectic involving at least three dimensions: balancing not only the mobility and stability of values, but also the abstraction of the monetary systems and the concreteness of the individual denominations, as well as the collective social networks and the individual owner's own interests. In this context, the American sociologist Suzanne Shanahan has highlighted a number of parallels between identities and currencies, making the latter particularly effective in the consolidation of the former: "Currencies are the daily, ritualistic expression of the popular trust in the political regime. To use money is to pay homage to community" (Shanahan 2003, 166–167; cf. Kaelberer 2004, 162, 171). At the same time, both currency and identity have different meanings for different individuals, which may be said to correspond to the motto's union of collective unity and individualizing diversity. Currency has a peculiar power in that it performs the trick that Marx called "real abstraction": a mechanism that, regardless of the conscious thoughts of those concerned, in practice abstracts from the distinct characteristics of a phenomenon's use values to the benefit of societal exchange value (Marx [1858]1939/1993; Fornäs 2013). This provides currency with the ability to socially consolidate the same collective identities that it symbolizes on the basis of its use and its design.

Coins and banknotes are handled, on a daily basis, by virtually every citizen. They link together their collective communities without themselves needing to be the focus of anyone's active interest. Therefore, coins and banknotes constitute a shining example of what the British social psychologist Michael Billig has called "banal nationalism," which is supported by the everyday, discreet use of symbols (Billig 1995). The Danish media researcher Klaus Bruhn Jensen has drawn a distinction between "time-out" and "time-in" culture, that is, practices or symbols that are either lifted out of the daily flow in order to form the core of exceptional rituals, in the way that Europe Day and the anthem are often employed, or, in contrast, are deeply ingrained in the same everyday routines—and here currency is the best example, while the flag as a visual symbol can act as both (Jensen 2002, 5).

A Currency for Europe

Currency is, thus, not only a social, but also a cultural practice. Gold as a material certainly has some importance, but as regards today's coins and banknotes, the design is of much greater importance. The design of the euro banknotes and coins demonstrates an attempt to associate Europe with common values and notions: to provide meaning to a common iden- tification. This invites a contextualizing interpretation that positions these minimal media texts and communicative artifacts in relation to both the European project's overall direction and a number of other symbolic expressions, including currencies from other eras and geopolitical actors. What does the euro, then, tell us about Europe and its self-image?

Euro was introduced as the name of the currency in 1995 as a replace- ment for *ecu* (the European Currency Unit), which to the Germans sounded ridiculously similar to "a cow" ("ein Kuh"). The name is as short and catchy as "pound" or "dollar" and has the additional advantage of obviously belonging to Europe. The "€" symbol is based on the Greek letter epsilon (ε), and was meant to represent both the word "Europe" and ancient Greece as the cradle of this civilization; the two horizon- tal lines were intended to symbolize the currency's stability (Brion and Moreau 2001, 117, 120). This, alone, makes it clear that confidence is a key concept. The authenticity of the banknotes is guaranteed by various metallic threads and watermarks, and it is, in fact, only in these hidden codes that the "€" sign appears on the actual currency, even if it is used more frequently in other contexts.[6]

The European Central Bank, ECB, in cooperation with the mem- ber states' central banks, organized the printing and minting of the banknotes and coins in several stages and with the help of both compe- titions and experts (art historians, designers, and marketing profession- als). The decision was made early on that the banknotes, in addition to the seven denominations and certain technical codes, would include the circle of stars of the European flag in order to symbolize the "dynamics and harmony among the European nations." It was also decided that the motifs would be based on various eras in European cultural history: classical antiquity, Roman and Gothic architecture, the Renaissance, Baroque and Rococo, iron and steel architecture, and finally, modern architecture from the twentieth century. The obverses of the banknotes depict windows and portals from these eras, suggesting "the European spirit of openness and cooperation" among member states, while the reverse sides show bridge constructions from the corresponding peri- ods, symbolizing the "close co-operation and communication between Europe and the rest of the world." It was also agreed to avoid depicting individuals and specific, identifiable architectural structures, in order to prevent an imbalance between genders or between different countries and regions. A map of Europe was also printed on each note, where the overseas territories of France, Portugal, and Spain (in which the euro is also used) were shown, indicating the way in which Europe's boundaries and, thereby, its identity, are problematized by its colonial networks.

The obverse of each of the eight denominations of the coins displays the denomination, the name "EURO," and different versions of European maps, as well as, along half the rim, 12 stars linked by parallel lines. The first issue of the coins included three different map designs, in which the lowest denominations represented "Europe's place in the world" (a globe with Europe in the center), the middle denominations represented "Europe as a group of individual nations" (in which each country was separate from the others), and the highest a "unified Europe without borders." As a result of the successive EU enlargement, a revised series was launched in 2007 in which the motifs for the mid-level denominations had been reworked to be more similar to the highest denominations. At the same time, Norway was added and the European continent was extended to the east; all this to make the design easier to understand and prevent the coins from becoming outdated when the euro zone expanded. The reverse side of the coins is another story, to which I shall return shortly.

The Meaning of the Euro

The euro has been designed to create and radiate the credibility of the European project in a number of ways. The technical security features account for only one aspect. The visual and tactile design of the banknotes and coins has been deliberately constructed in order to express central values, with the intention of making the citizens feel at home in the world symbolically represented by the currency.

Maps of Europe are presented both on the reverse of the banknotes and the obverse of the coins. While national borders are distinguishable, Europe's protective external outline is emphasized, thus expressing the EU's desire to unite, while maintaining respect for internal differences. This type of map signals a sense of control and provides an overview; it provides substance, defines something that is otherwise difficult to envisage in its entirety, and presents a bird's eye view of its territory.

The circle of stars, borrowed from the EU flag, contributes with radiance—like a heavenly halo crowning Europe's understanding of itself as a chosen spearhead continent embodying the highest of cultural credentials. On the obverse of the coins, the stars have been realigned into two arcs, each with six stars, with parallel lines connecting them in pairs. This can be viewed as an expression of the way in which currency and the economy intertwine communities by weaving networks of dual relationships between individuals. The stars are used frequently, and are also found on the reverse of the coins and on the outer edges of some of them, which fits well with the notion of the round form as a common denominator.

The banknotes have also been designed in a deliberately clear-cut and abstract style, partly to avoid criticism for favoring specific nations or regions, ethnic groups, or genders. The design can be regarded as typical of the monetary system's integral tendency toward abstraction and dematerialization, with the transition to e-money as the most recent step (Kaelberer 2004, 168). However, this has also been criticized as a symptom of the excessively vague nature of the EU project, suggested by some to have a void core in its middle, much like the empty circle of the EU flag (e.g., see Delanty 1995). The stars are part of what is, in fact, an extremely general and nonspecific image, and the architectural elements have, indeed, also been made anonymous so as to not link them to a specific region. On the one hand, this can be perceived as a lack of concreteness and anchoring within citizens' lifeworlds, and thus as evidence of the failure of European integration. On the other hand, this image may have a point in terms of identification. As classical studies of everything from romantic novels to soap operas have shown, stereotypes of popular cultural genres do not necessarily create distance but can, in fact, open up to input from different groups of people and are, therefore, in line with the diversity motto. Every successful symbol must be sufficiently abstract and multilayered so as to enable various interpretations in different contexts and by a range of actors (Wintle 2009, 442). Whether the core of Europe is empty or open is, therefore, an open question.

The architectural motifs of the banknotes are interesting in several respects. From the very beginning, it was determined that the banknotes would portray different architectural styles from classical antiquity to the modernism of the twentieth century. If the motifs are viewed in the order of denomination, from the lowest, €5, to the highest, €500, they build a "money-story," which is not quite as obvious as it first appears.[7] The portrayed steady, progressive continuity in itself solidly anchors the EU in a cultural line of historical tradition. By skipping centuries of chaos and decline, this portrayal provides an image of Europe under continuous development and improvement but which, at the same time, treasures and conserves its traditions and bequeaths its rich heritage to the future. Having the present epoch on the notes with the highest denominations adds a typically modern "progressivistic" interpretation of history, where progress is seen in terms of accumulating value. This is the same view of history as that expressed in the Schuman Declaration's decisive steps out of the darkness toward an ever-brightening future—a view of history with ancient messianic roots but in a typically modern version of continuous movement toward perfection.[8] Matthias Kaelberer has highlighted the ideological force of such storytelling:

> The imagery on the euro banknotes attempts to establish links to a common European tradition. It refers back to the classical ancestry of Europe and deliberately constructs a common European historical memory... The chronological ascent in artistic styles also reads history in conventional European teleological fashion as the story of progress. While German banknotes visibly emphasized historical discontinuities, the euro can conveniently "forget" uncomfortable aspects of European history—such as war and imperialism—in the name of an optimistic and progressive vision of Europe. It "romanticizes" history as easily as national currencies do. (Kaelberer 2004, 170)

The way in which history is delineated and divided into epochs and eras is also very telling. For any other continent (or individual nation outside Europe), the results would have been different. It is only in Europe that, for example, the last two millennia are understood as an obvious historical totality and with the highlights of development located in just those periods selected for the seven euro denominations. The fact that ancient Rome, rather than ancient Greece, is the starting point—as the €5 banknotes show windows, doors, and bridges in the classical Roman style—also has a number of consequences. In geographical terms, the beginning of European history is thus placed in a more central position on the continent: in Rome rather than in Athens. This prevents the decentering effect that would otherwise have blurred the border between Europe and the Orient, given that Athens and the Greek cultural sphere had much stronger links to the East. The fact that the "€" symbol is inspired by Greece actually strengthens this interpretation, in that this symbol, and consequently the idea of Greece as the starting point, is thereby placed outside the actual European flow of history, as illustrated on the banknotes' motifs. This ties in, not least, with the notion of European culture as "eccentric"—in other words, with its imagined center outside itself, in Jerusalem and the Middle East—which is prevalent in Christianity, the Renaissance, and Classicism. Europe is continuously aware of its own inadequacies: it is always incomplete and on its way toward something else, which has been noted by Rémi Brague and Zygmunt Bauman, among others (Brague 1992/2002; cf. Bauman 2004). Furthermore, today's EU is more similar to the land-based territory of the Roman Empire than the sea-based island world of the Greeks.

Starting the monetary narrative in Rome also has a temporal aspect, which is far from unimportant as it positions Europe's stylistic birth to the time around year "0," the starting point for Western chronology.

This is a way of indirectly including Europe in a Christian sphere or, at least, such an interpretation is not threatened by referring back to the pagan Athens of a few centuries earlier.

Roman culture, with its blend of engineering skills and empire building, is, in fact, a more suitable representative of what the EU has, thus far, devoted itself to and which the motifs of the banknotes praise: the development of material and technological infrastructures. The decision to depict works of architecture (rather than natural phenomena, works of art, or people) ties in with politics' architectural metaphors of "building" a union, which depicts this process of building in terms of well-planned construction rather than, for example, organic growth, revolutionary leaps, or free market forces (cf. Shore 2000, 112). The solid, heavy, and stable building structures further prioritize the accumulable (rather than transitory) aspects of human culture: fixed rather than fluid capital, cultural heritage rather than the transient present, products rather than processes, collective rather than individual work, and combinations of harmonious aesthetics with practical utilizable engineering technology rather than other types of artifacts or skills. The construction metaphor invokes gradual reforms and the possibilities of constantly rebuilding and extending. The same notion is emphasized in an introductory CVCE text on "The Currency of the European Union"; these monumental motifs symbolize the stability of the currency and "pays tribute to the capacity of human labor to create great works and to improve them over time." The stability of the architectural works depicted on the banknotes is intended to create confidence in the expected stability of the euro and the EU, which can certainly be improved but which, at the same time, stands for the "desire to construct a solid and lasting whole of stone and iron, which is not dependent on economic and political contingencies but which mirrors the eternity linked to the motifs of classical culture." Even the absence of people and geographical references is, here, interpreted as a sign of an economy based upon "universality and intertemporality."[9] In this way, the motifs on the banknotes inspire confidence, not only in the currency, but also in the European project as a whole.

There is, however, much more to be said about these motifs, as this is, in fact, not a question of an arbitrary piece of architecture but specifically of doors, windows, and bridges. As was mentioned earlier, the intention was to express the willingness for cooperation and communication between the member states on the one hand, and openness and dialogue with the rest of the world on the other. An interesting tension can be identified here. What has been brought to the fore is the infrastructural framework for communicative action, rather than the content of the buildings or other forms of activity. The effect would have been completely different had residential or government buildings from different eras been depicted. Instead of ships and ports, airplanes and airports, or modern media technologies, archetypical windows and doors for people to see and move through, and bridges for people and vehicles to cross are depicted. This is clearly not only about a primarily land-based civilization, but also concerns the difference between the stability of the buildings and the mobility they are built to facilitate. Thus, Europe's fondness for geographical mobility and communication with others is underlined; an intercultural interaction that differentiates it from, for example, the older river-based high cultures around the Nile, Euphrates, Tigris, Ganges, or Huang He. Europe has always been relatively more dynamic: historically unstable and continuously traversed by groups of people on the move. The desire to mediate, link, and communicate can, in this perspective, be seen as key features of the collective, contemporary European identity as it is taking shape in our time. In this way, the motifs on the notes are also consistent with the motto "United in diversity," presenting architectural works that connect over distances while at the same time embodying respect for those differences.

A stable and safe communications infrastructure should, of course, increase rather than reduce openness and mobility. The individual who has trust in the bridges' stability will dare to be mobile, perhaps even nomadic. Windows, doors, and bridges are classic symbols for the dialectics between similarity and difference, closure and openness, and boundary and transgression. In his analysis of bridges and doors as metaphors for communication, Georg Simmel described people as "the connecting creature who must always separate and cannot connect without separating" and "the bordering creature who has no border"; and Gaston Bachelard referred to man as a "half-open" being (Simmel 1909/1994, 10, see also 5; Bachelard 1958/1994, 222–224). This is, admittedly, a universal and global condition of life, but in Europe it has been developed to perfection—or, indeed, to a mania, for better or worse. On the one hand, this condition can be seen in Habermasian terms as a capability for communicative action; on the other hand, in Foucauldian terms, as a compulsion to open oneself to the watchful eyes of others. European history is also full of communicative endeavors with ambivalent undertones: the Viking voyages, the Crusades, voyages of exploration, and colonial ambitions all not only had highly destructive dimensions but also included elements of a form of desire to communicate with others who are different. Tzvetan Todorov has written a fascinating description of the way in which this desire was articulated during the Spanish conquest of America. He pointed out that the aspiration to interact with new people and to have something to narrate was an important driving force, alongside economic, military, and religious motives (Todorov 1982/1992).

The bridges linking Europe to the surrounding world can also be interpreted in a number of ways, implying both a free openness and an expansionary desire for power. All communication channels facilitate not only unexpected meetings and influences, from migrants and tourists to new ideas and cultural patterns, but also new ways of controlling the surrounding. In the same way as the mass media are neither consistently authoritative nor emancipatory, so the ways in which communicative infrastructures are used are not determined in advance. The battle between opposing interests is far from over. Isolation does not appear to be a reasonable alternative—least of all for late modern Europeans.

The banknotes appear to narrate the story of a Europe that, over its continuously progressive course of two millennia, has combined aesthetics and technology in order to establish boundaries for the good of the population, only to then eagerly cross these boundaries. This illustrates the same basic idea as the motto: that community presupposes diversity and is, in fact, based on curiosity in those who are different: a desire to communicate with others.

United in Diversity

The banknotes certainly display various types of resources for communication, but they provide little fuel to support any notion of concrete difference in content. Their level of abstraction evokes, rather, a picture of universal uniformity, in line with the flag's indistinguishable stars. The obverses of the coins also do not do anything to change this picture. It is up to the users of the symbols to imagine the way in which communication can take a tangible form—or, through real actions, to populate the anonymous communication resources with meaningful content. The reverse of the coins provides an example of how this can be done.

Each euro country is allowed to create its own series of motifs on the reverse, although all of the coins can still be used throughout the euro zone. This means that small depictions are circulated of the plurality that is unified by the EU, moving in and out through its symbolic doors and windows. According to Romano Prodi and other leading representatives, the two sides of the coins are designed to give expression to the spirit of the EU motto: the fronts represent the unity of the European

Commission while the national reverse sides stand for the diversity of the European Parliament. It is, therefore, telling that it is the fronts that guarantee, by specifying the denomination, the financial value of the coin, while the reverse sides manifest the diversified symbolic and cultural aspects of identity. On each reverse side, the circle of stars is displayed on the periphery together with the year of issue, but apart from this, the individual countries have been given quite a free hand.

In the majority of monarchies, the ruler is represented on the basis of an old numismatic tradition, according to which the face of the king or queen confirms the legitimacy of the coin in a hierarchical and authoritarian state. In addition to depicting King Juan Carlos I, Spain, however, also has coins displaying Cervantes and the Cathedral of Santiago de Compostela, forming a triad of politics, culture, and religion. In addition, it is possible to discover a communicatively transnational aspect, as the cathedral is the destination of pilgrims coming long distances to this holy place, and is a symbol of the wide network of the Catholic Church. The various royal houses also represent a rather strange combination of the national and transnational institutions as they function as heads of state, yet at the same time are often tightly linked to other European monarchies through marriage.

A number of countries have chosen to present their national symbols, such as the Portuguese national seal, or coats of arms and heraldic animals that Finland, among others, has on its lowest denomination coins. In certain cases, there is also a built-in ambivalence. The Celtic harp that Ireland depicts on all its coins is certainly a respected national treasure; however, for the uninitiated, it might lead thoughts to Israel's old king Solomon, or more generally to music's communicative force to connect people across linguistic and political borders. And how should France's "Marianne" and the catchwords freedom, equality, and brotherhood be interpreted? These are certainly highly national; at the same time, however, they clearly have a universal appeal and effect, considering their global influence on history.

Historical events of a political or cultural nature are displayed on many coins through, for example, Greece's ships (typical of the country's marine character which, at the same time, forms a transnational bridge to the surrounding world) and heroes (who once sought support in Central Europe in the struggle for freedom against the Turks), the Austrian pacifist Bertha von Suttner and the composer Wolfgang Amadeus Mozart, Italy's suite of eight famous works of art or some historically significant landmarks. Berlin's Brandenburg Gate, which was built in 1791 during the reign of Frederick the Great to be a "Peace Gate" and which was, after the Napoleonic war, renamed "Victory Gate" and became a symbol for Prussia, belongs to this latter category. Throughout history, the gate has frequently been used to celebrate victories over France. During the Cold War, it became, as part of the Berlin Wall, a powerful symbol for a continent divided by the Iron Curtain; however, since reunification, the gate has been turned into a symbol of reunified Europe and is portrayed on the German euro coin as visibly open for passage, something that clearly ties in with the door motif of the banknotes.

Natural phenomena in the form of animals or plants are also used on various coins. It is true that these often carry national symbolic values; almost always, however, they can also be associated with transnational movement. This applies not least to Finland's two swans, as migratory birds are, indeed, excellent symbols for nomadic networks across the continent.

Mythical motifs can be found on French coins, and also on the highest Greek denominations, with the wise owl of Athens and Europa with the bull. The idea here is, perhaps, to embrace the wisdom of the European project, as well as, of course, to link it to the classical myth that is since antiquity associated with the name "Europe." In Greek mythology, Zeus becomes attracted to the Phoenician princess Europa, transforms himself into a virile white bull and, by means of seduction, carries her on his back over the water to Crete where she bears him three sons, one of whom, Minos, founds a new dynasty. This myth contains numerous fascinating details that support the interpretation that Europe sees itself as chosen and elevated as a result of its contact with the divine, while the movement from the east and south to the west and north, forced by the game of desire, corresponds to the actual migrations of peoples that once populated and developed the European continent. The meeting between a woman and a god-animal leads to both hybridity and eccentricity, in line with late modern ideals of mobility, and, again, ties in with the desire for communication, suggested by the banknotes.

Currency requires trust, and together with other official symbols, it is also intended to create loyalty toward, confidence in and legitimacy for a collective community. The currency crisis that centered on Greece in 2010 is proof of just how fragile the monetary system can be. Yet money plays a role not only on the global markets but also in our everyday life. There—in the interface between our personal lifeworlds and the institutional systems of markets and states—money serves as a multilevel symbolic glue, connecting individuals to collectives while, in this case, offering an interpretation of the European project.

Thus, both united and uniting through diversity, the euro contributes to balancing between the risks of federalism and fragmentation:

to avoid both the homogenized isolation within a "Fortress Europe," which threatens to alienate its own citizens, and the tattering of the community into mutually incompatible national entities. The coins create trust by subtly connecting the European obverses of the coins with the well-known national markers of identity portrayed on the reverse sides, thereby redefining them as European.

The issue remains open: Europe must demonstrate its trustworthiness by balancing the need to comprise an identifiable entity with respect for particular interests. The size of the European continent, the complexity of its patchwork of nation-states and the political as well as cultural divides crisscrossing its territory pose extraordinary demands on such unifying symbols. This is a circle which is not necessarily vicious, but which, like the hermeneutical circle, can be stretched and opened into a spiral where the symbols of the European project form steps in a movement in which local, regional, and national interests are woven together with a sense of shared transnational responsibility. Various dialectics are at stake here: between the local, regional, national, and transnational; between the cultural expressions of the symbols and the more or less institutionalized everyday practices; between the individual and the collective; between the concrete and the abstract; and between the economic, political, social, and cultural dimensions. It is in this fascinating borderland that trust is expressed and created.

Notes

1. The chapter is based on a pilot study on the euro (Fornäs 2007) and a more extensive book that analyzes and interprets a number of different symbols for Europe, with the intention of detecting and interpreting central but often conflicting ways in which European identity has been thematized (Fornäs 2012).

2. There is plenty of literature on European identity, for example, Delanty (1995), Heffernan (1998), Uricchio (2008), and Wintle (2009). See also Stråth (2000/2010) on Europe's relation to other communities.

3. European Convention (2004): *Draft Treaty Establishing a Constitution for Europe*, Brussels: The European Convention.

4. *Final Act, Official Journal of the European Union*, 2007 C 306–267.

5. Carlo Curti Gialdino: "The Symbols of the European Union," CVCE, http://www.cvce.eu/obj/the_symbols_of_the_european_union_full_text-en-e135ba77–1bae-43d8-bcb7-e416be6bc590.html; see also Curti Gialdino (2005).

6. All facts on the euro can be found in numerous primary and secondary sources; for further references, see Fornäs (2012).

7. The expression "money-story" has been coined by Vida Zei (1995, 337–338).

8. According to Cris Shore (2000, 115), the notes express "transition, mediation, movement and the promise of a brighter future."
9. "The Currency of the European Union," CVCE, www.cvce.eu/obj/the_currency_of_the_european_union-en-de0d4ede-f55d-4610-b666–8ac20a-f880ab.html.

References

Anderson, Benedict. 1983/1991. *Imagined Communities: Reflections on the Origin and Spread of Nationalism*, 2nd ed. London: Verso.

Bachelard, Gaston. 1958/1994. *The Poetics of Space*. Boston, MA: Beacon Press.

Bauman, Zygmunt. 2004. *Europe: An Unfinished Adventure*. Cambridge, UK: Polity Press.

Billig, Michael. 1995. *Banal Nationalism*. London: Sage.

Brague, Rémi. 1992/2002. *Eccentric Culture: A Theory of Western Civilization*. South Bend, IN: St. Augustine's Press.

Brion, René, and Jean–Louis Moreau. 2001. *A Flutter of Banknotes: From the First European Paper Money to the Euro*. Antwerp: Mercatorfonds.

Curti Gialdino, Carlo. 2005. *I Simboli dell'Unione Europea, Bandiera—Inno—Motto—Moneta—Giornata*, Rome: Istituto Poligrafico e Zecca dello Stato S.p.A. (parts of which are translated to English on the website European Navigator, www.ena.lu).

Delanty, Gerard. 1995. *Inventing Europe: Idea, Identity, Reality*. Basingstoke; London: Palgrave Macmillan.

Fornäs, Johan. 2007. *Reading the €uro: Money as a Medium of Transnational Identification*. Norrköping: Tema Q (also Linköping University Electronic Press, www.ep.liu.se/ea/temaq/2007/001).

———. 2012. *Signifying Europe*. Bristol: Intellect Press.

———. 2013. *Capitalism: A Companion to Marx's Economy Critique*. London; New York: Routledge.

Heffernan, Michael. 1998. *The Meaning of Europe: Geography and Geopolitics*. London: Arnold.

Jensen, Klaus Bruhn. Ed. 2002. *A Handbook of Media and Communication Research: Qualitative and Quantitative Methodologies*. London; New York: Routledge.

Kaelberer, Matthias. 2004. "The Euro and European Identity: Symbols, Power and the Politics of European Monetary Union." *Review of International Studies* 30:161–178.

Marx, Karl. [1858] 1939/1993. *Grundrisse*. London: Penguin Books; New Left Review.

Shanahan, Suzanne. 2003. "Currency and Community: European Identity and the Euro." In *Figures d'Europe / Images and Myths of Europe*, edited by Luisa Passerini, 159–179. Bruxelles: P. I. E.–Peter Lang.

Shore, Cris. 2000. *Building Europe: The Cultural Politics of European Integration*. London; New York: Routledge.

Simmel, Georg. 1900/1989. *Philosophie des Geldes*. Frankfurt am Main: Suhrkamp.

———. 1909/1994. "Bridge and Door." *Theory, Culture & Society* 11 (1): 5–10.

Stråth, Bo. Ed. 2000/2010. *Europe and the Other and Europe as the Other*, 4th printing with changes. Bruxelles: P. I. E.–Peter Lang.

Todorov, Tzvetan. 1982/1992. *The Conquest of America: The Question of the Other*. New York: HarperCollins.

Uricchio, William. Ed. 2008. *We Europeans? Media, Representations, Identities*. Bristol: Intellect.

Wintle, Michael. 2009. *The Image of Europe: Visualizing Europe in Cartography and Iconography throughout the Ages*, Cambridge, UK: Cambridge University Press.

Zei, Vida. 1995. *Symbolic Spaces of the Nation State: The Case of Slovenia*. Iowa, IA: Communication Studies, University of Iowa.

CHAPTER 3

Can Auditing Generate Trust? The Organization of Auditing and the Quality of Government

Maria Gustavson and Bo Rothstein

The democratic model of society may be said to be based on a contract between the people and the authorities. The people grant to the authorities—for simplicity's sake, we will use the term "the state" here, but it could just as well be regional or local authorities—the administration of a number of public goods. In modern societies, this not only applies to defense and the legal system, but also to other duties, such as health care, social insurance, education, and infrastructure. In order for this to be achieved, significant financial resources (taxes) are also transferred from the people to the state. Even if there is a continual political and ideological discussion in terms of the exact proportion of these tasks to be managed within the public sphere, and as regards how much the citizens should be expected to pay for this, in the majority of societies there exists a relative consensus that such tasks are of major importance to the citizens and that the resources to be reserved must be significant. Consequently, the social contract needs to be based on a huge dose of trust. Citizens must be able to be confident that the public goods the state is committed to provide will be executed, and executed in a legitimate manner. On the day when a citizen needs, for example, health care, pension, or elderly care, then these services are to be available and are to be delivered in an acceptable and effective manner. Representative democracy implies that citizens are able to exercise control to ensure that this is the case by voting in general elections.

Politicians wishing to be reelected then, according to this model, have a strong interest in appearing to be reliable in terms of having fulfilled the terms of the social contract.

So far so good, at least in theory. One problem with this model is, however, that the individuals who are to actually execute these activities, that is, the various groups of publicly employed officials, cannot be removed through election. Not only police officers, social insurance officials, and judges, but also public employees such as teachers and doctors, often exercise significant power over the welfare of citizens when it comes to the performance of common functions. As trust in these individuals cannot be assured by the mechanism of having them "removed through election," if it is found that they do not fulfill the conditions of the social contract, other measures need to be incorporated into the system to ensure this trust. Such a measure can be *auditing*, and this is the subject of our discussion in this chapter.

Having some form of organized audit of the public officials and the organizations executing political decisions is a concept that is deeply anchored in our view of the democratic social contract. By having special officials executing audits to ensure that public administrative units are managing their commitments in accordance with the relevant legislation and political goals, we have an increased expectation that the public sector will work more appropriately. At the same time, the execution of audits themselves contributes to the legitimacy of public authorities and to the sense of trust that they will provide the public goods as they are intended to. In addition, politicians need a special audit organization, as they usually do not have the opportunity to keep themselves sufficiently informed in terms of what is taking place within the public administration.

Hence, the necessity of auditing crosses institutional boundaries of trust and points toward an interesting interplay between trust and mistrust at the societal level where the latter, we argue, comprises the actual foundation of how modern societies are organized. On the one hand, auditing can be seen as an institutionalization of mistrust in the system. If all public officials could be relied upon to act as they should then, of course, no audit would be required. On the other hand, as we will further develop in the following text, auditing may also be regarded as a means to create trust in the public administration.

Thus, the aim of this chapter is to reflect on the phenomenon of auditing from this perspective of trust. We begin with an overall discussion of the starting points of auditing and provide a historical perspective as to the reasoning applied at various time periods throughout history in determining the necessity of auditing. We then focus more specifically on the relationship between auditing and the public's trust in the public sector. How can we understand auditing as a trust-building mechanism in society? And how is trust in auditing in itself generated? What are the features that have developed in order to create trust in this institution?

The concluding section of this chapter begins with a reflection on different forms of trust and the foundations for trust in public authorities that can be distinguished in various types of societies. Does auditing operate differently depending on the context in which it has developed? If so, what then happens to how trust is generated if these geographical boundaries are crossed? Is it possible to talk about different "trust regimes"? If so, how is trust generated within one regime then affected by the crossing of institutional boundaries to another kind of trust regime?

The discussion in this part of the text has its empirical point of departure in a thesis on how the National Audit Offices in sub-Saharan Africa handle international audit standards (Gustavson 2012).

Audit and Societal Trust: A Historical Overview

The fundamental idea of establishing a public authority assigned to review other public authorities, such as auditing, is based on the assumption that it cannot be taken for granted that all publicly employed officials will execute their duties and administer the public resources in a completely efficient and correct manner. As it is usually difficult for citizens and politicians to obtain insights into administrative operations, requirements have been made to have external actors, auditors, to review the organizations.

There are many researchers who claim that audit of public sector activities has increased dramatically during recent decades as a result of deregulation and decentralization, even the to the degree that the term "audit explosion" might apply, or that we live in an "Audit Society" (cf. Power 1999, 2005). However, reviewing and auditing are not new phenomena. As long as resources have been handled by people who are not the original owners of those resources, control functions have existed, both within private business activities and within states (Flint 1988). In the same manner as medieval kings and queens had officials who collected taxes, they also appointed special officials to check that the tax-collecting officials administered the funds in a correct manner. In the United Kingdom during this era, these processes were legal and individual officials could be held accountable directly to the queen or king if they had mishandled their assignments (Normanton 1966). The United Kingdom is also regarded as the predecessor of modern audit institutions, especially in Scotland, where auditing developed as a profession at an early stage. As early as 1734, there were a number of established independent auditors, and in 1853 the auditors in Scotland founded their own professional organization (Cassel 1996). Systems similar to the British, where individual officials could be held responsible to some form of judicial committee, also existed in European countries and their existence played a significant role in the state administrations (Normanton 1966). It was not only kingdoms that had the equivalent of today's auditing profession, but also in early Athenian democracy there were special officials appointed to review how other officials handled the public funds. Even Aristotle emphasized the necessity of this function within the democratic state:

> But since some, not to say all, of these offices handle the public money, there must of necessity be another office that examines and audits them, and has no other functions. Such officials are called by various names— Scrutineers, Auditors, Accountants, Controllers. (Aristotle, *The Politics*, Book VI, 1322b5–15)

In addition to the financial audit, early Athenian democracy also had a form of performance audit. Officials were required to regularly inform the elected assembly regarding the manner in which they managed public activities. If the accounts of such management were insufficient, the elected assembly had the power to hold individual officials accountable through legal processes (Day and Klein 1987). Audit of the public administration, as part of democratic accountability, is thus a very early idea of how democratic systems should be organized.

The importance of auditing the public administration within the framework of democratic systems was also proposed at an early stage by the liberal philosopher John Stuart Mill (1861/2001). Mill was of the opinion that it is difficult for citizens to obtain insight into the public administration; therefore, there is a need for specially appointed officials to examine their activities. This should be done to constrain the power of the public administration:

> But political checks will no more act of themselves than a bridle will direct a horse without a rider. If the checking functionaries are as corrupt or as negligent as those whom they ought to check... little benefit will be derived from the best administrative apparatus. (Mill 1861/2001, 24)

As Mill claims in the above passage, the regulations and procedures put in place to check that the public sector fulfills its objective are not particularly important if there is no entity to ensure that such regulations and procedures are complied with. It should also be noted that he assigns importance to the significance of the fact that the entity executing the audit should have the competence and ethical stance to ensure that they are less corrupt and less negligent than the officials they audit. As will be discussed further on in this chapter, the development of auditing as a profession, and the regulations surrounding it, can be seen to comprise the profession's own expression of the principles emphasized by Mill. Through regulating entry into the profession, a high level of competence can be guaranteed as regards the auditors, and by creating a professional identity, specific, professional, and ethical values can be promoted. The fact that the audit profession has established this type of mechanisms can also be understood as a means whereby they can create trust in their assignment, among the public as well as among politicians and other stakeholders.

Auditing and Trust: Two Dimensions

As seen in the introductory discussion, two distinct dimensions in the relationship between auditing and trust can be discerned. The first dimension concerns auditing as a public authority whose role is to contribute, through its examination, to an effective and correct functioning public administration. Our contemporary society is today so complex that institutional spheres are intertwined and the trust in individual institutions is depending on the trust in other institutions. In this context, auditing as institution in particular serves as an institutional boundary-crossing mechanism of trust, as trust in auditing is likely to affect trust in the institutions under their scrutiny. At least indirectly, auditing contributes to generation of trust in the public administration and in society in general. Are we then able to verify this relationship between the efficiency and effectiveness of the public administration and the degree of trust found in society?

In a large number of studies, trust between people has been shown to constitute a particularly important asset for society, not only as regards people's economic welfare but also as regards the quality of democracy in society (Uslaner 2002; Rothstein 2005). Furthermore, there is a clear relationship between such trust between people and various measurements of human well being, both concerning people's health as well as more subjective measurements of well being (Putnam 2000). The differences in levels of trust between people in various countries are surprisingly large, however. According to the extensive surveys executed by *World Value Study*, approximately 60 percent of the population in the Nordic countries believes that they can, in general, rely on other people. In Continental European countries, this figure, rounded off, is 40 percent, in southern Europe around 25 percent, and in countries such as Brazil, Romania, and Turkey, around 10 percent (Medrano 2009). One central issue in research on trust and social capital is how to explain these considerable differences. Is the explanation to be found in the character of certain cultures, which inherently implies that people trust, or do not trust their fellow citizens? Or are these differences in the level of trust in others related to the issue of trust in political institutions?

There are two central theories as to how these variations can be explained. One points toward the importance of involvement in voluntary associations (Putnam 2000) and the other to the importance of reliable, noncorrupt, and fair public institutions (Rothstein 2005). Surprisingly, empirical research has for once here provided a clear answer, that is, that social trust can primarily be explained by the existence of trust in the organizations assigned to implement public policy. According to a large number of research reports using data from various countries, trustworthy, noncorrupt, neutral, and nondiscriminating authorities appear to have a positive effect on the degree of social trust in a society (Herreros 2004; Delhey and Newton 2005; Freitag and Buhlmann 2005; Herreros and Criado 2008; Widmalm 2008; Freitag and Traunmüller 2009; Dinesen 2011; Robbins 2011; Rothstein 2011). The reason may be that if people perceive the police, health care personnel, judges, and teachers in society as not being trustworthy (because they discriminate, accept bribes, or undertake other dishonest activities) then neither can people in general be trusted. In addition, the likely correct assessment is that other people in societies with dysfunctional authorities are more or less forced to become involved in corrupt or other dishonest activities in order to have their needs fulfilled (healthcare, education for their children, police protection, and protection by the courts). A corrupt public administration quite simply makes people act dishonestly, whether they want to or not and thereby, per definition, they cannot be trusted (Rothstein 2005).

This is an argument in favor of the view that an effective and efficient audit institution, which has as its purpose to review public officials' actions, crosses institutional boundaries and is of central importance for social trust in society. Of course, officials who know that they will be audited by a competent auditor have a major reason to refrain from all sorts of inappropriate activities and instead try to execute their, often delicate, duties in a correct, effective, and professional manner. Consequently, in such a society, citizens themselves have any reason neither to resort to any dishonest methods in their interaction with the administration, nor to suspect others of doing so. In other words, the degree of interhuman trust should be positively impacted by the execution of audits.

Nevertheless, the relationship between trust and auditing is more complex than this. How can citizens rely on the auditors being unimpeachable and that their work will be executed in an honest and competent manner? This question is relevant not only to the auditing field. As the chapter by Gustafsson and Tamm Hallström in this book illustrates, the growth of control and review authorities tends, in turn, to generate a need to control and review those authorities' own operations. As is shown in our own as well as in the contribution by Gustafsson and Tamm Hallström, this dilemma is solved in a variety of ways within different fields. However, the common point is the partly paradoxical coexistence of both trust and mistrust, which any attempt to institutionalize audit and control mechanisms appears to give rise to, irrespective of the context. On the one hand, auditing is naturally based on mistrust—if it could be assumed that all public officials behaved correctly, no audits would be required. On the other hand, auditing generates trust as it increases the probability of the majority of public officials refraining from taking part in all sorts of dishonest activities. Corruption, to take one example of such an activity, is shown to be very dependent on frequency of occurrence. If the majority of public officials believe that the majority of other officials demand bribes, then the probability of these officials demanding bribes also increases. But the opposite also applies; if the majority of the officials believes that bribery seldom takes place, for example, due to the existence of an effective audit institution, then the probability of them demanding bribes decreases (Persson, Rothstein, and Teorell 2013).

The other dimension in the relationship between auditing and trust pertains, in other words, to how the auditing itself should be organized in order to promote public trust in its operations. Auditing is dependent on us relying on the auditor fulfilling his or her role as a reviewer. If the public or politicians cannot rely on the audit authority, there is an overhanging risk that it eventually will lose legitimacy and may come to be seen as an organization hiding abuses, instead of calling attention to them. In order to increase trust in the profession and in its work, the auditing profession has established various mechanisms to better guarantee, for the public and the politicians, that they fulfill their role as reviewers. This refers to the importance of being independent, professional, and the fact that auditors follow the norms established for auditing. In the next section, these mechanisms will be examined in greater detail.

Independence and Professionalism: Key Questions for Trust in Auditing

If auditing, as a public authority, were historically based on the concept that we cannot ensure that all officials administer the public goods properly, auditing, itself is also dependent on society believing that the profession properly executes its task as reviewers. As discussed above, this form of review can be traced back in history. For an equally long period of time, it was also claimed that a special type of officials should be assigned for this task and preferably be kept separate from the other officials. In the same manner as Aristotle emphasizes in the quotation given previously in the chapter, that the officials executing the audit are separate from those working with managing the state's resources, the quotation from Mill shows that there should be special "checking functionaries" who are to control the officials. This premise of auditing, that it is separate from and independent of the authorities being audited, is a reoccurring concept in terms of how auditing is to be structured. For example, a number of researchers believe that the entire idea of auditing is based on the premise that it should be executed by an external entity that is independent of the audited organization. If the audit is not independent, then the organization in question could undertake a self-estimation of its performance with the imminent risk that they would overvalue their own performance in order to try to appear to be as successful as possible (see, e.g., Mautz and Sharaf 1961; Ahlbäck 1999; Power 1999, 2005). As auditing is an institution intended to bridge a lack of trust in the entities administering resources, it is a basic precondition that it is independent from the operations it reviews.

Nonetheless, independence has several dimensions. As regards the auditing of the public administration, it is usually noted that the National Audit Office is to be independent of the government, whose activities they review, and instead is to report to Parliament. Ahlbäck (1999) points out that the degree to which the national audit authorities have the capability of executing an independent audit also depends on how they are organized. In order to study this, she chooses three aspects in her comparative study of the degree to which the previous Swedish national auditing authorities (*Riksrevisionsverket* and *Riksdagens revisorer*) lived up to the ideal of independence. The aspects address the prerequisites for independently choosing review areas and audit methods, and how independent the authorities were in the presentation of their conclusions (Ahlbäck 1999, 94). In addition, one can discuss the degree of independence in terms of how the audit authorities are financed: if they receive sufficient resources, how the senior management is appointed and what protection they have from dismissal.

The importance for the auditors to be independent may also be illustrated by the fact that the professional organization established for National Audit Offices, The International Organization of Supreme Audit Institutions (INTOSAI), has pursued this requirement for several decades. Their joint declaration, the Lima Declaration, in 1977 was a call for independent governmental audits and that such independence should be guaranteed in the countries' constitutions (INTOSAI 1998, 2007). This also illustrates another important characteristic of auditing, namely that it is, to a considerable degree, a self-regulating profession (Öhman 2007). Not just anyone may call themselves an auditor; there is a need for certain skills and qualifications to be able to enter the profession. Such requirements are likely followed by the effect that we trust in the auditors' competence to a greater degree. We rely on the fact that the auditors make correct assessments and that they have a high level of knowledge making it possible for them to identify irregularities that political leaders may not have identified, as they are laymen in this context. Similar to what Mill (1861/2001) emphasizes we also trust that the auditors are not as negligent or corrupt as the officials they are auditing. If there is any doubt as to whether the auditors are sufficiently competent, this impacts the trust in their assessments and reports (Flint 1988).

The fact that auditors' competence is controlled and guaranteed through a profession is considered to constitute a prerequisite for creating reliability in their work and through this reliability, trust in the entire profession (Cassel 1996). Consequently, it is important for the profession that it regulates its members, for example, through certification of their competence, norms for the execution of work processes, and through self-governing institutions, such as the Swedish Supervisory Board of Public Accountants, which assesses any possible carelessness or negligence in Swedish auditors' work. A part of the trust in auditors' competence is based on whether the auditors follow the norms that the profession has established for their work, that is, the professional auditing standards (Power 2003; Jonnergård and Erlingsdottir 2008). This is particularly important when assessments are made to determine whether the auditor has failed to properly execute her or his assignment. Byington, Sutton, and Munter (1990) illustrate this principle by reviewing a number of legal cases in which the courts have tested whether auditors had been careless. In their assessments, the courts applied the auditors' professional standards and assessed the degree to which the auditors had complied with these in their work, as a measure of the quality of the work.

The Significance of Audit "Output" for Social Trust

As discussed above, a number of mechanisms have been created in order to maintain trust in auditing as an institution for reviewing the public administration. However, these mechanisms are generally focused on the "input" side of auditing, that is, how the auditors' competence and working procedures are regulated and controlled, the organizational and financial relationships with the audited entities and whether the audit is independent. However, what has received less attention is the output side of auditing and whether the audits actually lead to the desired effects, which is far from obvious. As we have previously mentioned, it is true that research demonstrates a relationship between reliable and effective public authorities and the degree of social trust. But does the examination undertaken in audits actually lead to higher levels of effective and reliable public administrations?

There is no simple answer to this question. In fact, several researchers within this area emphasize the negative consequences of audits (e.g., Smith 1995; Power 1999; Pentland 2000). Audits are claimed to lead to increased administration and to transfer focus from doing the "right things" to instead "do things right," which means a move from quality in the work to a focus on what is measurable and gives positive results in the reviews. Yet, if audits do not contribute to any of the desired effects, but rather contribute to a negative development of the administration, perhaps the question should be asked whether auditing should exist in its present form? Regardless of whether auditing, through its very existence, creates legitimacy and generates trust in the belief that the public sector organizations work as desired, there is clearly an overhanging risk that this trust is eroded in the long term, if the reviews by the auditors do not provide any positive effects on the output side.

In order to obtain some order in this matter, we should first clarify that the measuring of effects of an activity as auditing can be complicated. A part of the mechanism of auditing can be seen to be one of anticipation and, consequently, self-regulation. As public officials know that they can be audited at any time, the effect arises that they become less likely to embezzle or waste the state's resources. Naturally, if and how such results arise is something which is impossible to measure, but if this anticipatory effect were completely reliable, we would today have public administrations that would work optimally, where the citizens would receive the best possible services and where misuse, corruption, and embezzlement of public resources would be unknown phenomena. This would be due to the fact that, in principle, all organizations within the public sector are liable to audit. Through rather simple, empirical observations of reality, we know that public sector organizations do not work really quite that well.

As this self-regulating mechanism inherent in auditing cannot always be presumed to result in a major impact on the administration, it is required, when deficiencies are identified, that the audit information is used by someone with the objective of undertaking change. Who can then be seen to be the recipient of the information that the auditors have generated regarding the public authorities, and who is responsible for ensuring compliance with the recommendations provided in the audit? An international comparison demonstrates that state audits can be structured in a variety of ways. In some countries (e.g., France) the national audit authority operates as a court through which the authority has the opportunity of imposing sanctions and fining the audited authority if irregularities are identified. In other countries, such as in the United Kingdom and Sweden, the audit is based on recommendations that are provided to political and administrative leaders (Pollitt and Summa 1997). In the latter model, it is primarily the political and administrative leaders' responsibility to take action on the basis of the auditors' reports.

It has been shown that the importance management assigns to the audits may have decisive consequences as regards the possibility to take measures to correct malfunctions in the administration. In a comparative study between two similar Swedish regions, where one had experienced problems with corruption, researchers found that management's actions played an important role. In the region with the problems, the management had been less interested in using existing opportunities for control and for holding officials accountable, the audits were weak, and the audit reports were not given any attention by the management (Andersson and Bergman 2009).

In addition to administrative and political management, media and citizens can also be regarded as stakeholders in the auditors' reviews, as the audit reports are published and recognized. The fact that citizens have access to information regarding the performance of various authorities may contribute to the democratic control of the public administration. In particular, information that is produced by an independent oversight authority, such as auditing, can create trust in public administration (James 2010). For example, audit reports have been shown to be able to exert a major influence on how citizens demand political accountability through elections. As a stage in efforts against corruption, in 2003, the Brazilian government initiated an expanded audit of randomly selected municipalities. The results from the audit were published on the Internet and were provided to local media. These audit reports verifying the existence of corruption in certain municipalities proved to have major significance in terms of the reelection of leading politicians in municipal elections. Corrupt politicians reported upon in the audit were reelected to a lesser degree. And the reverse, the probability of reelection increased significantly in cases when the audit reported that politicians were not involved in any form of corruption (Ferraz and Finan 2008). Similar to this study, other studies have shown that citizens are considerably impacted by the audit information they receive regarding the performance of the public authorities. Their expectations and degree of satisfaction increase with audit information demonstrating that a public authority performs well and vice versa; in cases where the audit information produced negative opinions regarding the performance, the citizens' degree of satisfaction with that public authority decreases (James 2010).

Nonetheless, the degree to which the information generated by an audit is accessible and actually used by citizens may be questioned. In the Ferraz and Finan (2008) study described above, the audit reports were used extensively by the local media, which the authors argue was of decisive importance in the behavior of the voters. Hanberger (2009) argues, however, that direct contact between the authority executing the audit and citizens seldom works, few citizens have sufficient knowledge concerning audit reports and they experience that the reports are difficult to understand, languagewise. At the same time, Hanberger finds in his study that political decision makers ascribe major significance to audits, in spite of the fact that the auditors, themselves, claim that their recommendations are not followed to any large degree (Hanberger 2009, 12–13). Hanberger's study was undertaken in Sweden, but similar results are found in Gustavson's (2012) study of the National Audit Offices of Namibia and Botswana. Some auditors in the study point out that in pace with the professionalization of the offices, the audit reports have become more technical. Consequently, it had become more difficult for parliamentarians to understand what the reports actually said as well as becoming more difficult for them to build up any real view of the situation in the public sector organizations.

This technical and professional distance may be due to the fact that the opinions of the actual aim of audit appear to differ between stakeholders and the auditing profession. For example, Larsson (2005) demonstrates in his study that the majority of corporate leaders believed that auditors had an obligation to identify and report tax crimes, embezzlement, and corruption. However, the auditors' own professional organization claimed that this was not at all part of their assignment. Instead, they saw the assignment as focusing on providing a statement as to whether the annual accounts provided a true and fair view of the company's financial situation (cf. Power 1999). Similar conclusions are drawn by Öhman et al. (2006) in their study of the auditors' own understanding of their assignment and role. The authors argue that auditors generally lack sensitivity to the interests of the general public or other stakeholders. They also conclude that this circumstance will probably not change, as auditing, to a considerable degree, is a self-regulating institution. This situation where the general public and other stakeholders, such as corporate leaders, have an understanding of the audit's role and responsibility other than the one held by the audit profession is a well-known phenomenon and is usually discussed in literature as "the expectation gap" (Larsson 2005).

Even if the state through legislation regulates some of the auditors' role and responsibility, it is probable that the growth of a strong auditing profession is the reason for the occurrence of such an "expectation gap." This gap between expectations illustrates how the auditing profession has created institutional boundaries of what *they* consider their responsibility, which primarily focuses on trust in their profession generated through the input side of auditing. As discussed, considering the reason for establishing auditing in society, politicians, the general public, and other stakeholders are likely to still have an interest in auditing as a mechanism creating trust across institutional boundaries, that is, to generate trust also through the output side of auditing.

With the above reflections as a point of departure, one can conclude that the two dimensions in the relationship between trust and auditing are actually linked and are closely interwoven with each other in an intricate interaction. Auditing is an institution aimed at creating trust in public authorities and that they provide public goods in accordance with the political goals and regulations established by society. However, auditing is, in turn, dependent on trust from society in their auditing institution. This second dimension of the relationship between auditing and social trust can be understood from two perspectives. The auditing profession's procedures in creating trust in its operations and reviews have primarily focused on creating guarantees for the input side of audit. On the output side, auditing appears more ambiguous as it is unclear if the audits actually result in the public sector working more appropriately, and as the auditors sometimes have another understanding of their assignment than that of the general public, politicians, and other stakeholders. As we mentioned in the introduction to this section, there is a risk that if the output side of auditing does not meet expectations, the trust in auditing as a review mechanism may decrease in the long term. In the remaining part of this chapter, we address the issue of the universal nature of these relationships and discuss what happens when geographical and institutional boundaries of trust regimes are crossed. Can it be said that the role of auditing in the creation of trust—and trust's significance for auditing and its activities—looks the same, regardless of the context and circumstances?

Auditing and Trust Regimes

For the necessity of auditing to emerge as a review mechanism in the public sector, an established administration in society must first exist, which is based on the separation of private and public spheres and in which formal regulations in general are followed. In addition, universalism as a principle for decision making, meaning that similar cases and circumstances are treated similarly, must be an established norm in the administration.

This form of bureaucracy is usually referred to as the Weberian bureaucracy. Nevertheless, from a historical and international perspective, the Weberian bureaucracy is an exception. Rather, it is an administrative principle that has spread in the West during the latter part of the nineteenth century. Papakostas (2009) claims that the spread of this formalized manner of organizing the public administration, as implied by the Weberian model, is based on a general mistrust between people and between groups in society. By establishing formal regulations that are to be applied according to a universal principle, the degree of predictability of the decisions increases, regardless of which official makes the decisions. This also implies that the risk of decisions being based on arbitrary judgments or impacted by the individual making the decision being a family member or someone from the same, or another, ethnic group, decreases. Papakostas (2009) argues that the formalized organization of the administration has channeled general mistrust and has neutralized special interests existing in society in form of, for example, class, ethnicity, religion, or political party affiliation. Nonetheless, this theory comes into conflict with the empirical research results reported above, namely that there is a clear relationship between a high degree of social trust in a country and the existence of reliable, noncorrupt, nonpartial, and nondiscriminating authorities, that is a Weberian administration.

As discussed, the Weberian bureaucracy, and the fact that this form of administration has been perceived as trustworthy to a fairly large extent in several societies, is an exception both historically and geographically (see, e.g., Fukuyama 2011). Perhaps, the reason for this trust is based on the fact that we also know that different forms of power distribution principles and various review authorities, such as auditing, exist in parallel, which implies that the officials' discretion is limited. However, from a historical perspective, the most common form is that the administration is based on satisfying various particularistic interests. Instead of trusting that individual interests are treated impartially and are accommodated by the public, regardless of which officials are handling the case, particularistic interests are expected to be assured by individuals coming from their own groups. Especially, if individuals have access to power and resources as publicly employed officials, they are expected to share this power and these resources with their relatives, tribal members, or other particularistic networks.

Particularly in Africa, public institutions are often described as primarily based on such informal particularistic networks, which determine how operations are to take place at the expense of compliance with formal regulations and procedures (see, e.g., Ake 1996; Bratton and Van de Walle 1997; Hyden 2006). This form of trust in informal particularistic networks is described by some researchers as a part of the culture in African societies, which has a long history and which has continued to function, in spite of the African societies being forced to adopt new administrative structures during colonialism (Ekeh 1975; LeVine 1980). Other researchers, however, claim that the major importance of the informal, particularistic networks, in terms of how African public institutions operate, is a consequence of colonialism. The Europeans destroyed the traditional systems of governance that existed in African societies when they colonized the continent. The traditional systems of the African societies were often complex governing systems with built-in procedures to limit the power of kings and chiefs, but were destroyed when the colonial powers established their own structures. The Europeans appointed their own administrative chiefs who were allocated important positions of power and were given the possibility to create their own patronage networks. These networks, which rather are based on trust and loyalty than blood relations, have remained intact since that time and today they constitute the basis of how the African states operate (Mamdani 1996).

In other words, the manner in which trust in public institutions is shaped is described to be very different in African states compared to the West. African citizens' trust in their officials is said not to be based on whether they follow regulations and procedures in managing public resources but rather on whether the officials are part of the same networks or not (Bayart 2009). If they belong to the same networks, it is expected that the officials share the public resources in order to make the network, and the individuals belonging to the network, richer and more influential. By understanding that the African context is different to West, in terms of how trust regimes have developed, it may be asked whether auditing in Africa, consequently, functions differently in comparison with auditing as we recognize it from countries in Europe, for example.

Special Conditions of Auditing Outside the West

Although there have been varying forms of mechanisms and procedures aimed at limiting the power of those governing societies throughout history in Africa, contemporary audit institutions were established in conjunction with the colonial powers forcing other administrative structures onto the countries. When these structures were established, both geographical and institutional boundaries for how trust in public institutions ought to be generated were crossed, and the different historical and cultural context in which auditing exists in Africa could be assumed to imply that auditors have an understanding of their role and assignment that differs from the norms in the West.

Gustavson's (2012) study of National Audit Offices in southern Africa shows something else, however. As we could expect, audit institutions in this context have far fewer resources than in the West, in terms of auditors with the right competence, technical equipment, and so on. Additionally, these organizations are often characterized by a high level of staff turnover, as salaries are low in comparison with the private sector. Yet, a high level of staff turnover is not something that is limited to National Audit Offices, but a well-known problem within the public sector in many developing countries. Similarly, lack of resources is not specific to only auditing but also impacts the public authorities that are audited. For instance, the study illustrates that it is common that auditors point out various shortcomings in routines for resource management, such as the person who makes purchases should not also sign the invoices. In spite of comments from auditors, it can still be difficult for the organizations to address the problems as they possibly lack the resources to hire additional people.

While the study illustrates that the infrastructural and material conditions for auditing in the African context are distinctly different, the results also demonstrate that African auditors' norms for the role of auditing and its execution do not differ from the norms existing for auditing in the West. The original Western, professional norms for auditing, which today are found in the international standards for auditing, also characterize the African National Audit Offices' work. The African National Audit Offices work continuously with reforming their own organization, with the aim of better compliance with the requirements in the international standards.

The study points toward the importance of caution when it comes to drawing conclusions on the basis of cultural explanations. When the National Audit Offices in Namibia and Botswana tried to undertake changes in order to better comply with the standards, there was a certain resistance to such reforms among some auditors and sometimes there were difficulties in implementing new work procedures in accordance with the standards. At first sight, this resistance and implementation difficulties could be interpreted as the standards failing to function in this culturally and historically different context. But the answers provided by the auditors in the study do not have much to do with culture. One reason for resisting the changes appears rather to have been the constant increases in the auditors' workloads, caused by the introduction of the standards. Through using the standards, requirements for more careful planning and documenting of work arose. Sometimes a routine had just been established when the auditors were expected to change their methods due to the fact that the standard had changed, and the support needed was not always available. For instance, one of the organizations had introduced a new computer system; however, there was no support accessible for the auditors when they had problems. One auditor in the study made the following statement about this situation: "If you get stuck, you cannot work. You ask your boss and he is also stuck. The facilitators were available on e-mail, but if you get stuck and then you e-mail, maybe you will get a response the week after" (Gustavson 2012, 176). As this quotation illustrates, the difficulty in implementing work processes may be a consequence of the lack of resources, infrastructure, and technical competence, rather than cultural differences as such.

The study also brings to light another reason for resistance to stricter standards among certain auditors. Some of the auditors in management positions in the organizations studied had been employed 15 to 20 years ago, when educational levels were significantly lower in these countries. They had eventually worked their way up to a managerial position without needing to live up to the level of competence required for auditors employed by the offices today. The introductions of transparent work processes, together with increased documentation, consequently risked exposing their possible lack of competence, as well as reducing their opportunities to exercise power and influence, which is why there were several reasons for these individuals to oppose such changes. Accordingly, resistance in this case was also less about any exotic African culture clashing with a Western approach but rather about people's fear of losing their positions and becoming redundant. Despite certain resistance from individuals, the clearest result of the study is a strong professional identity among the auditors. This professional identity crosses geographical boundaries and implies that the auditors see compliance with international auditing standards as something that is self-evident. The auditors argue that it is unnecessary that they "invent the wheel" as it has already been invented. If there are well-established practices for auditing representing what they believe is "the best practice" of auditing, there is no reason for them not to comply with these practices.

The African auditors argue that there are advantages when audits are conducted in a similar manner all over the world. This creates opportunities for individual auditors to work in other countries and in international organizations that contract auditors. The fact that countries apply the same auditing system also creates opportunities for National Audit Offices all over the world to work together and support each other. Such cooperation takes place between European and African countries in more traditional development cooperation. However, the auditors in the study do, above all, emphasize cooperation opportunities within the region, which follows from having common auditing practices. For example, the auditors have utilized occasions when they meet at regional courses or conferences to develop their networks with other National Audit Offices in the region. Such meetings have sometimes been developed into practical cooperation, for example, regarding computer programs or auditors being seconded from one organization to work at and support another, on a temporary basis. This more practical dimension of cooperation between countries in the region, that the use of the same auditing standards has made possible, probably has greater importance for countries in sub-Saharan Africa than for a country in Europe. This is because African auditors' access to the right competence as regards, for example, a computer program, is in all probability more limited, while their need for such competence is greater (Gustavson 2012). Hence, how geographical boundaries were crossed in the establishment of contemporary auditing norms appears to have little significance to the African auditors today, as they regard their profession as international and emphasize the advantages in using similar methodologies across the world. As will be discussed in the following section, these results may also impact the shape of institutional boundaries, in generating different regimes of trust in society.

Previously in the chapter, we have described a perhaps more classical manner of studying public officials. This approach presumes that in contexts where more particularistic forms of trust have developed, public officials are primarily considered to be loyal toward the local context, that is, vis-à-vis relatives, tribal members, and/or religious or financial networks. Nonetheless, this is an image that needs to be nuanced. As officials in many non-Western societies reach an increased degree of professionalism and now also become part of an international context, identities are reshaped and new loyalties are created—for example, toward their own profession. Such a changed collective identity among public officials, from local and particularistic to professional and international may eventually also impact how general trust in society is structured. As we discussed previously in this chapter, research has shown that impartial, nondiscriminatory authorities generate general interpersonal trust in societies. When auditors' loyalties change, in pace with professionalization and internationalization, and become focused on the execution of the professional assignment—which is based on universal principles and a separation of private and public—this may contribute to a change of the public authorities, the audit authority as well as the audited administrations, to become more impartial and neutral in relation to local interests. Long term, this may reshape institutional boundaries of trust, and impact society in its entirety to progress in a direction from a regime based on particularistic trust to a regime based on universalism, where a higher degree of general trust in society is generated.

Concluding Reflections: Auditing and the Paradox of Trust

Overall, we can describe the relationship between trust and auditing as a paradox. In the social contract that forms the basis of modern societies, extensive trust issues arise. How can citizens trust that what is promised in the contract, in the form of important, very extensive, and complex public services, will also be executed and provided as the contract stipulates? Although elections are a fairly blunt instrument, politicians who abuse citizens' confidence in democracy can be voted out of their position and replaced by other politicians who are, hopefully, more reliable. However, there is no equivalent mechanism as regards the large groups of public officials needed to execute the public tasks. Hence, the need for an auditing body. Ultimately, this aims at creating trust in public authorities and, consequently the all-important trust between citizens.

At the same time, the actual establishment of a public auditing authority should be regarded as an expression of general mistrust in those executing public power in society. We cannot simply assume that public officials would not abuse their positions. The organization of our societies is generally based on such skepticism, where various forms of reviewing agencies, power distribution systems, and regulated procedures are examples of how such distrust is kept in check. Accordingly, auditing as a public authority may be regarded as a mechanism in which the tensions between trust and distrust are woven together into an intricate interaction. This may be expressed as a paradox: auditing is an institutionalized form of distrust that is intended to generate trust.

References

Ahlbäck, Shirin. 1999. *Att kontrollera staten. Den statliga revisionens roll i den parlamentariska demokratin.* Uppsala: University Publications from Uppsala.

Ake, Claude. 1996. *Democracy and Development in Africa.* Washington, DC: Brookings Institution.

Andersson, Staffan, and Torsten Bergman. 2009. "Controlling Corruption in the Public Sector." *Scandinavian Political Studies* 32:45–70.

Aristotle. 1996. *The Politics and the Constitution of Athens,* edited by Steven Everson. Cambridge, UK: Cambridge University Press.

Bayart, Jean-François. 2009. *The State in Africa. The Politics of the Belly,* 2nd ed. Cambridge, UK: Polity Press.

Bratton, Michael, and Nicholas Van de Walle. 1997. *Democratic Experiments in Africa.* Cambridge, UK: Cambridge University Press.

Byington, Ralph J., Steve Sutton, and Paul Munter. 1990. "A Professional Monopoly's Response: Internal and External Threats to Self-Regulation." *Journal of Corporate Accounting and Finance* 1:307–316.

Cassel, Filip. 1996. *Den reviderade revisorsrollen: en oren berättelse.* Stockholm: Nerenius & Santérus.

Day, Patricia, and Rudolf Klein. 1987. *Accountabilities. Five Public Services.* London: Tavistock.

Delhey, Jan, and Kenneth Newton. 2005. "Predicting Cross-National Levels of Social Trust: Global Pattern or Nordic Exceptionalism?" *European Sociological Review* 21:311–327.

Dinesen, Peter Thisted. 2011. *When in Rome, Do as the Romans Do. An Analysis of the Acculturation of Generalised Trust of Non-Western Immigrants in Western Europe* (Diss.). Aarhus: Aarhus University.

Ekeh, Peter. 1975. "Colonialism and the Two Publics in Africa: A Theoretical Statement." *Comparative Studies in Society and History* 17:91–112.

Ferraz, Cladio, and Frederico Finan. 2008. "Exposing Corrupt Politicians: The Effects of Brazil's Publicly Released Audits on Electoral Outcomes." *The Quarterly Journal of Economics* 123:703–745.

Flint, David. 1988. *Philosophy and Principles of Auditing: An Introduction.* Basingstoke: Macmillan Education.

Freitag, Marcus, and Martin Buhlmann. 2005. "Political Institutions and the Formation of Social Trust. An International Comparison." *Politische Vierteljahresschrift* 46:575.

Freitag, Marcus, and Richard Traunmuller. 2009. "Spheres of Trust: An Empirical Analysis of the Foundations of Particularised and Generalised Trust." *European Journal of Political Research* 48:782–803.

Fukuyama, Francis. 2011. *The Origins of Political Order. From Prehuman Times to the French Revolution.* New York: Farrar, Straus and Giroux.

Gustavson, Maria. 2012. *Auditing the African State. International Standards and Local Adjustments.* Gothenburg: University of Gothenburg.

Hanberger, Anders. 2009. "Democratic Accountability in Decentralised Governance." *Scandinavian Political Science Studies* 32:1–22.

Herreros, Francisco. 2004. *The Problem of Forming Social Capital: Why Trust?* New York: Palgrave Macmillan.

Herreros, Francisco, and Henar Criado. H. 2008. "The State and the Development of Social Trust." *International Political Science Review* 29:53–71.

Hyden, Göran. 2006. *African Politics in Comparative Perspective.* New York: Cambridge University Press.

INTOSAI. 1998. *The Lima Declaration.* Originally adopted at the IX INCOSAI in Lima in October 1977. Vienna: INTOSAI General Secretariat.

———. 2007. *Mexico Declaration on SAI Independence.* Vienna: INTOSAI General Secretariat.

James, Oliver. 2010. "Performance Measures and Democracy: Information Effects on Citizens in Field and Laboratory Experiments." *Journal of Public Administration Research and Theory Advanced Access*, October 21, 2010, doi: 10.1093/jopart/muq057.

Jonnergård, Karin, and Gudbjörg Erlingsdottír. 2008. "Mellan autonomi och kontroll: Om professionella strategier, legitimitet och identitet vid införandet av nya kontrollformer." In *När den professionella autonomin blir ett problem,* edited by Karin Jonnergård, Elin K. Funck, and Maria Wolmesjö, 57–84. Växjö: Växjö University Press.

Larsson, Bengt. 2005. "Auditor Regulation and Economic Crime Policy in Sweden, 1965–2000." *Accounting, Organisation and Society* 30:127–144.

LeVine, Victor T. 1980. "African Patrimonial Regimes in Comparative Perspective." *Journal of Modern African Studies* 18:657–673.

Mamdani, Mahmood. 1996. *Citizen and Subject. Contemporary Africa and the Legacy of Late Colonialism.* Princeton, NJ: Princeton University Press.

Mautz, Robert Kuhn, and Hussein Amer Sharaf. 1961. *The Philosophy of Auditing.* Iowa City, IA: American Accounting Association.

Medrano, Jaime Diaz. 2009. *Interpersonal Trust.* JDS Data bank. World Value Study. http://www.jdsurvey.net/jds/jdsurveyActualidad.jsp?Idioma=I&Seccion Texto=0404&NOID=104.

Mill, John Stuart. 1861/2001. *Considerations on Representative Government.* Kitchener: Batoche Books.

Normanton, E. Leslie. 1966. *The Accountability and Audit of Governments: A Comparative Study.* Manchester: Manchester University Press.

Öhman, Peter. 2007. *Perspektiv på revision: tankemönster, förväntansgap och dilemman.* Sundsvall: Department of Social Sciences, Mid Sweden University.

Öhman, Peter, Einar Häckner, Anna-Maria Jansson, and Finn Tschudi. 2006. "Swedish Auditors' View of Auditing: Doing Things Right versus Doing the Right Things." *European Accounting Review* 15:89–114.

Papakostas, Apostolis. 2009. *Misstro, tillit, korruption—och det offentligas civilisering.* Lund: Studentlitteratur.

Pentland, Brian T. 2000. "Will Auditors Take over the World? Program, Technique and the Verification of Everything." *Accounting, Organisations and Society* 25:307–312.

Persson, Anna, Bo Rothstein, and Jan Teorell. 2013. "Why Anti-Corruption Reforms Fail: Systemic Corruption as a Collective Action Problem." *Governance: An International Journal of Policy, Administration and Institutions* 26:449–471.

Pollitt, Christopher, and Hilka Summa. 1997. "Reflexive Watchdogs? How Supreme Audit Institutions Account for Themselves." *Public Administration* 75:313–336.

Power, Michael. 1999. *The Audit Society. Rituals of Verification,* 2nd ed. Oxford, UK: Oxford University Press.

———. 2003. "Auditing and the Production of Legitimacy." *Accounting, Organisation and Society* 28:379–394.

———. 2005. "The Theory of the Audit Explosion." In *The Oxford Handbook of Public Management,* edited by E. Ferlie, L. E. Lynn, and C. Pollitt, 326–344. Oxford, UK: Oxford University Press.

Putnam, Robert D. 2000. *Bowling Alone: The Collapse and Revival of American Community.* New York: Simon & Schuster.

Robbins, Blaine G. 2011. "Neither Government nor Community Alone: A Test of State-Centred Models of Generalised Trust." *Rationality and Society* 23:304–346.

Rothstein, Bo. 2005. *Social Traps and the Problem of Trust.* Cambridge, UK: Cambridge University Press.

———. 2011. *The Quality of Government: Corruption, Social Trust and Inequality in a Comparative Perspective.* Chicago: University of Chicago Press.

Smith, Peter. 1995. "On the Unintended Consequences of Publishing Performance Data in the Public Sector." *International Journal of Public Administration* 18:277–310.

Uslaner, Eric M. 2002. *The Moral Foundation of Trust*. New York: Cambridge University Press.

Widmalm, Sten. 2008. *Decentralisation, Corruption and Social Capital: From India to the West*. Thousand Oaks, CA: SAGE Publications.

CHAPTER 4

From Global Consumer Power to Local Worker Power

Niklas Egels-Zandén

Prior to the London Olympics in 2012

In June 2011, a proud email circulates around the world. It reports that Indonesian trade unions have signed a contract regarding Freedom of Association, with both a number of retail chains selling sporting goods, apparel, and footwear—such as Nike, Adidas, and so on—and the largest Indonesian producers of garments and footwear. The signing of the contract was preceded by two years of negotiations leading to the local unions succeeding in establishing the contract. Seen from the outside, it was surprising that the Indonesian trade unions, fragmented and with limited resources, and which normally would find it difficult to initiate collective bargaining with the Indonesian factory executives, had now succeeded in negotiating a contract with both these factory executives and a number of large, multinational corporations. This chapter analyzes this development, showing how the ability to leverage trust as a political tool to span organizational, institutional, and geographic boundaries was central for ensuring local trade unions' place at the negotiating table and the signing of a contract.

The Indonesian case is an example of the manner in which we, as Western consumers, are linked together via different intermediaries with those workers in developing countries who manufacture the products for which we are the end consumer. Such a straightforward relationship is far from obvious in the global value chains characterizing the production of sporting goods, apparel, and footwear. From the picking of cotton up to the point at which the Nike T-shirt can be purchased in sports chain stores, these garments have been handled by a large number of suppliers. Even if we limit ourselves solely to the actual sewing of the Nike T-shirt, this activity is sometimes undertaken in two or three stages. This implies that Nike's suppliers, in turn, have subcontractors who also employ subcontractors. In order to enable the consumers to make an impact, in terms of improving working conditions on the shop floor, it is, thus, required that a certain form of intermediary create a relationship between relatively wealthy consumers in the West and the Indonesian workers.

The organization Playfair represents such an intermediary. Playfair works to convince the companies producing sporting goods, apparel, and footwear (such companies will be referred to hereinafter as "sporting goods companies") to take responsibility for the working conditions at their suppliers' factories. Playfair is comprises global nongovernmental organizations (NGOs) and trade unions and has built up its operations by recognizing that global sporting goods companies organize their market strategies around important events, such as the Olympic Games, Football World Cup, and NBA finals. During such events, large corporations are the most prone to "scandals" that undermine their trust among consumers with purchasing power and other interest groups in Europe and the United States. Since the Beijing Olympics in 2004, Playfair has consciously utilized trust as a political tool to put pressure on the sporting goods companies, and this chapter analyzes the manner in which this threat against consumer trust among the companies involved was used to span organizational, institutional, and geographic boundaries in order to connect consumers, organizations from the transnational civic society, and local trade unions in Indonesia prior to the Olympic Games in London in the summer of 2012.

In the next section, I briefly discuss how trust for many sporting goods companies has been negatively affected by scandals involving their subcontractors, and how these companies attempt, subsequently, to restore trust. I demonstrate, first, the manner in which various attempts to restore consumer trust has, to date, been built on the results-based logic that has marginalized local organizations and the workers who the companies claim to wish to help and, in this context, I point to an alternative process logic with a larger local participation. I follow this with a brief description of industrial relations in Indonesia, with a focus on the prevailing power imbalance and the insufficient trust between employer and worker. Thereafter, I present, in relative detail, the Playfair negotiations during the period 2009–2011, and, subsequently, discuss the manner in which we, through viewing trust as a political tool, can see that the consumer power has, partly, been transferred to worker power, through a solution based on a hybrid between results-based and process logics.

Restoring Trust through Result or Process

The Problem—Substandard Working Conditions at the Suppliers' Factories

Corporate Social Responsibility (CSR) is currently a hot topic. Corporate executives compete as to who contributes most to society, NGOs search for closer cooperation with the business world, consumers vote with their wallets, the media uncover and reveal "corporate scandals," and so on. The goal for companies' involvement in CSR is to restore and maintain trust in the business world. This goal is packaged with phrases such as "strengthening the brand" and "minimizing the risks."

However, the problem faced by companies wanting to demonstrate that they take a social responsibility is related to the fact that working conditions at their subcontractors are often substandard. This is, in turn, a result of the fact that those companies have, for a long time, been moving their operations out of Europe and the United States to, mainly, Asia, where working conditions are significantly worse—and thus, both salaries and, ultimately, also the purchase price are lower—and where the employment regulations are not followed (Frenkel 2001; Cooke 2004; Taylor 2005). Consequently, corporate executives of many large international companies, since the beginning of the 1990s, have continuously been forced to explain, in the media or in other contexts, why they use child and forced labor in their production, why they work with illegally low salaries or report problems with both health and safety of the workers, and so on (Bartley 2007; Ählström and Egels-Zandén 2008). These media scandals are often created by NGOs and trade unions in the Western world that, in different ways, reveal the discrepancy between the companies' glossy communication and the actual working conditions prevalent in those factories in the developing countries where the companies' products are manufactured.

In order to protect and restore the trust of consumers and other interest groups, companies have—after a certain opposition—accepted a moral responsibility for the working conditions at their suppliers' factories (Bartley 2007; Ählström and Egels-Zandén 2008). Many companies have, thus, employed entire departments whose sole goal is to ensure that their subcontractors have acceptable working conditions and, consequently, an industry comprising external consultants and experts has emerged offering assistance for companies in their trust work. The trust problem has, as a result, led to comprehensive corporate investments and has contributed to the growth of a new professional group: "CSR specialists."

The Dominant Solution—Private Regulation of Working Conditions at Suppliers' Factories

It has been easier for large corporations to note that substandard working conditions in places where products are manufactured affect the company's trust than it has been to actually find solutions for these problems. Simply accepting the responsibility for working conditions does not satisfy consumers and other interest groups, and the companies, as the next step, have, also, been required to introduce systems aiming to actually improve working conditions at the suppliers' factories. The companies have been forced to introduce corporate-run, private regulation of working conditions, which, for example, has meant that the companies have adopted so-called codes of conduct and have threatened to cease business relations with suppliers if the codes are not followed in practice. Moreover, the companies have employed either their own, or external, controllers to ensure that the codes are actually complied with (Bartley 2007).

This private regulation has grown in parallel with the existing national regulations regarding working conditions in countries such as China, India, and Indonesia (Egels-Zandén 2009). In practice, the actual working conditions are regulated in combination with a well-established—but poorly functioning—national framework of regulations and growing global private regulation (Locke, Amengual, and Mangla 2009; Amengual 2010). In spite of this double system, we are continuously faced in the media with new scandals where it is revealed that subcontractors act in contravention of both the adopted codes of conduct and the applicable local national legislation. It does not seem, therefore, that the attempts made by global companies—often on a serious scale—to improve working conditions for the employed necessarily lead to actual improvements on the shop floor at the suppliers' factories.

The limited research undertaken concerning the extent to which codes of conduct and private regulation function seems to support this picture. Chan and Siu (2010, 167) demonstrate, for example, that "academic articles published on the impact of corporate social responsibility (CSR) initiatives are in basic agreement, that the efforts to implement corporate codes of conducts are often ineffective." Wells (2007, 53) further claims that "there has been little progress in improving labor standards through such [private] regulation" and Locke et al. (2007, 21) are, in turn, of the opinion that codes of conduct do not result in "the large and sustained improvements in working conditions that many had hoped they would." In their study of 800 of Nike's suppliers in 51 countries, Locke et al. (2007) demonstrate that working conditions at almost half of the suppliers had not improved over time and that, in fact, a greater number of suppliers had demonstrated deterioration in working conditions (36%) compared with the number of suppliers showing improved working conditions (20%).

It has, thus, proved difficult for the companies to improve working conditions at their suppliers' factories with the help of this form of private regulation, despite major investments and ambitious attempts.

Results or Processes as the Key to Trust?

There is an important difference between the underlying logics in private regulation via code of conducts on one hand, and traditional national regulation of working conditions on the other. While traditional national regulations are based on local negotiations between employers and workers (with a varying degree of state involvement and legislation), codes of conduct are based on global standardized norms included in, for example, UN and International Labour Organization (ILO) conventions. The degree of participation of local worker representatives, including trade unions, differs significantly between these regulatory systems. In private regulatory systems based on codes of conduct, workers and trade unions are rarely consulted or are ignored (Anner 2012) because the working conditions deemed to be in need of improvement are already predetermined in the code of conduct, that is, focus is on results in terms of improvements in line with predetermined standards. This differs from traditional national regulations, in which trade unions have a central role in continuous negotiations for the improvement of working conditions, that is, focus is on establishing standards in addition to implementing them.

This difference can be described as a conflict between two different institutional logics (Marquis and Lounsbury 2007).[1] On one hand, we have a "results-based logic" that dominates codes of conduct and private regulation and stresses that trust is created by fulfilling preestablished principles. This can be executed by demonstrating that, as a supplier, one does not use child labor, does not discriminate against women, and does pay the statutory minimum wage, and so on. In this way, one can expect to be able to create trust for the company. On the other hand, we can relate to a "process logic" that is primarily based on national regulations and, instead, stresses that trust is created through local negotiations. By showing that a subcontractor negotiates with trade unions, grants trade unions access to relevant information, engages the local population in the decision-making process regarding the operations, and so on, the company is expected to also be able to build trust in other parts of the world. Through these constantly ongoing negotiations, definitions of workers' rights are expected to change continuously and thus a focus is put on the local negotiation processes rather than on various forms of global conventions (Northrup and Rowan 1979; Huzzard, Gregory, and Scott 2004). Results-based and process logics, respectively, represent, thus, two different models of the manner in which the companies' trust shall be secured or restored.

As I intend to show in this chapter, the role of trust also differs between the results-based and process logics in the sense that fewer organizational and geographic boundaries have to be spanned in the results-based logic in order to connect Western consumers with local workers. This is so because the input of local (non-Western) organizations and actors is toned down in the results-based logic, implying that connections only have to be created between Western organizations. This is in sharp contrast to the process logics that require close connections between Western and non-Western organizations. In other words, to leverage trust as a political tool is more complex in the process logic, since it requires the spanning of more organizational and geographic boundaries.

How Did I Measure This?

In order to study the manner in which trust is leveraged as a political tool to span organizational, institutional, and geographic boundaries, I have followed a series of negotiations in Indonesia between a number of global companies, their suppliers, international trade unions, and NGOs, as well as trade unions and NGOs at local level. These are the so-called Playfair negotiations. My study of the Playfair negotiations is a part of a larger study of private regulation of worker rights in Indonesia. In this larger project, 130 interviews were conducted during the period 2008–2011, not only with representatives of Indonesian trade unions, NGOs, and governmental authorities, but also with factory managers, workers, and various international operators who are active in Indonesia (including actors in the business world, auditors, NGOs, and global trade unions).

The interviews took, on average, an hour and were conducted either in English or with the help of an interpreter. The majority of the interviews were taped and transcribed, and supplemented with visits to a number of factories producing for international companies. During the collection of empirical material for the larger project, the Playfair negotiations in Indonesia were initiated and, from the first negotiation meeting at the end of 2009 to the signing of the contract in summer 2011, I had the opportunity to continuously compile empirical data on those negotiations. Interviews were conducted with all the main participants, with the exception of representatives for the suppliers who all, unfortunately, chose not to make themselves available for interview. Certain meetings and negotiations were also observed in order to be able to follow negotiations in real time, and a large number of different documents were translated and analyzed.

Industrial Relations and Codes of Conduct in Indonesia

In order to understand why the Playfair negotiations were needed to strengthen the Indonesian trade union movement and improve local working conditions, a brief background information on industrial relations is required, as well as a review of the insufficient achievements that codes of conduct have historically resulted in, in Indonesia. The country has the world's fourth largest population (with over 240 million inhabitants) and the largest working population in South East Asia (almost 100 million workers). The large proportion of low-skilled workers in the labor force has been the base for foreign and domestic investor's interest in establishing labor-intensive manufacturing companies in the country. Many international brands in industries such as furniture, electronics, garments, and footwear are today using Indonesian manufacturers as subcontractors. In 2008, the garment and textile industry constituted around 10 percent of the Indonesian manufacturing industry and the total export of the textile sector amounted to US$10,399 million, of which the export of textiles and garments to the United States amounted to US$4,241 million. Exports to companies within the European Union (EU) amounted to €1,579 million.

Indonesia has a history of organized workers dating back to the early twentieth century, but the trade union movement experienced great setbacks during the dictatorship of Soharto between 1967 and 1998 (Caraway 2006). During the Soharto era, a nationalist-industrial relationships system was founded, which, in 1985, led to the establishment of a state-backed national trade union Serikat Pekerja Seluruh Indonesia

(SPSI) and the suppression of independent unions (Ford 2000). The official goal was to create a system with a balanced relationship between labor and capital, but, in practice, SPSI controlled and excluded the workers it claimed to represent (Caraway 2006). Nevertheless, some underground workers' groups were able to organize workers in different ways, arrange illegal strikes and provide worker education. These underground groups then formed the foundation of the fragmented labor movement that developed after the transition to democracy in 1998.

Democratization, but without Much Improvement

After the collapse of the Suharto regime in 1998, the labor law was changed as to allow for Freedom of Association (FoA) in accordance with the core ILO conventions. Within less than a year, 17 of the now over 90 union federations had registered and the number of independent local and national unions increased drastically from 1998 onward. However, these federations have low representation rates and are highly fragmented (Ford 2009). For example, less than 2 percent of the total labor force in the industries under analysis is unionized (Caraway 2004).

Despite the ratification of ILO conventions, changes to labor laws and an emerging union movement, reports of workers' rights problems in Indonesia are commonplace. For example, according to the British organization, Oxfam, there are frequent reports of FoA violations, including employers refusing to recognize factory-level unions, and threatening and dismissing suspected union members. Similarly, national restrictions on contract workers are frequently not followed, with certain factories employing 60–70 percent of workers through temporary contracts. Other severe problems include salaries well below the estimated living wage.

There are several reasons for the current situation. A common perception is that the Indonesian government is to blame, as it has, continually, undermined workers' rights, protected employers, and not enforced its labor laws (LO-TCO 2009). Another perception is that the Indonesian government has been subject to pressures from lenders, such as the International Monetary Fund (IMF) and the World Bank, to make Indonesia more attractive to foreign investors by increasing flexibility on the labor market (AMRC 2003). This increased flexibility on the labor market has, according to local trade union representatives, led to both difficulties in the organization of workers and an increasing exploitation of the labor force (Tjandraningsih and Nugroho 2008). The problems for workers are further exacerbated by widespread corruption, with employers often having the choice of paying their way out of legal cases or simply not appearing in court. The state has, thus, done relatively little to balance the employers' influence and their position of power.

The Significance of Codes of Conduct in Indonesia

In Indonesia, codes of conduct have received a high amount of attention due to the weak position of the trade unions compared with employers, the limited support for trade unions and other organizations from the state as well as the recurring violations of worker rights. The implementation of codes of conduct has been perceived as a way of creating better working conditions for workers in the Indonesian export industry. As in most countries (Locke et al. 2007), codes of conduct have been extremely common in the Indonesian sporting goods industry. Within this industry, representatives for Indonesian trade unions and various other NGOs have been involved in discussions over codes of conduct from as early as the mid-1990s onward.[2]

In spite of the fact that the Indonesian trade unions, and other labor organizations in place to improve the conditions within these industries, have extensive experience of codes of conduct, both in general and in relation to specific international campaigns in which codes have been applied, many of their representatives are skeptical of the improvements that may be achieved through codes of conduct. My own analysis of the Indonesian cases in which codes of conduct have been applied reinforces this skeptical view, as the codes are rarely considered to have resulted in long-term structural improvements in Indonesia. Prior to the initiation of the Playfair negotiations, both the local trade unions and NGOs were, thus, well informed on codes of conduct and the companies' private regulation; however, they were skeptical to such a high degree that they, more or less, stopped applying, and showing interest in, codes of conduct.

The Playfair Negotiations

Playfair: The Route to Indonesia (2003–2009)

The Playfair campaign was initiated prior to the 2004 Olympic Games in Athens, and the engaged organizations included global and national trade unions (such as the International Textile, Garment and Leather Workers Federation [ITGLWF], the International Trade Union Confederation, and the Trade Union Congress), and a number of NGOs (such as the Clean Clothes Campaign and Oxfam). In the six-month run-up to the Athens Olympic Games 2004, the campaign organizers estimated that it had generated approximately 500 local events (i.e., demonstrations, protest actions, picket lines, etc.) in 35 countries.

The basis for the Playfair campaign is that sporting goods companies, in conjunction with major sports events, are especially sensitive to information, which may damage their trust in the eyes of, above all, the end consumers. On a temporary basis, this provides the organizations in the Playfair campaign with increased influence over the companies, which is a strategic necessity for these organizations, as they would otherwise have a relatively weak position against the companies. For example, on the one hand, global union federations have been described as underfinanced, with limited resources and low capacity (Fairbrother and Hammer 2005), and the low representation rates in the sporting goods industry makes this particularly evident in this industry. Many NGOs—such as Oxfam and Clean Clothes Campaign—are depicted, on the other hand, as influential (Frooman 1999; Hendry 2006) and, in many contexts have successfully forced brands to assume responsibility for workers' rights in their supply chains (Egels-Zandén and Hyllman 2006; Bartley 2007). However, compared with the major multinational companies' resources, NGOs clearly have less funding and, thus, the opportunities for setting aside the resources needed for more long-term projects are limited. Hence, sporting events provide unions and NGOs with an opportunity to partially level the playing field against the brands.

After extensive and seemingly successful campaigns in conjunction with the Olympic Games in Athens and Beijing, in 2004 and 2008, respectively, the representatives for the Playfair campaign and some of the major sporting goods companies resolved to initiate a collaboration and create a pilot project, in order to proceed beyond the abstract and more campaign-focused discussions that had, up to then, characterized their relationships. The parties also agreed on the fact that Indonesia was a country with a large potential to carry out such a project, largely owing to the active Indonesian trade union movement.

A Coalition of Local Trade Unions and NGOs

When the pilot project was to be initiated in Indonesia, the international trade unions and a number NGOs (mainly Oxfam, the Clean Clothes Campaign, and ITGLWF) decided to adopt a passive approach and, instead, create space for the local actors to negotiate. This was an unusual strategy compared with previous international campaigns where local organizations, generally, have had a limited role (Bartley 2007; Ählström and Egels-Zandén 2008). The strategy also required the Playfair representatives to succeed in uniting the fragmented Indonesian labor movement in order to assist the local actors to collectively negotiate with the companies and suppliers. After a certain amount of fieldwork, a coalition of five local trade unions (SPN, GSBI, KASBI, SPTSK, and Garteks SBSI), as well as a NGO within legal consultancy, was established. One SPN representative provided a good description of the challenge of working together:

> We had problems making our five unions collaborate, since we rarely meet and come from different backgrounds. SPN has huge number of members; KASBI is a progressive union and so on. There were many discussions between us over more than three months before we could agree on a draft protocol. (Interview with SPN union leader, Jakarta, September 2010)

All these Indonesian organizations had previously applied codes of conduct, participated in international campaigns, and were, as previously stated, skeptical of such codes. Thanks to the fact that the Playfair negotiations differed, on four points, from the way in which local actors viewed codes of conduct, the organizations decided to participate in the negotiations. First, the Playfair negotiations were considered to imply a more continual and proactive type of communication between the labor organizations and the global companies, compared with the previous communication, which, essentially, dealt with managing the existing disputes on working conditions in various factories. Second, the Playfair agreement is legally binding, whereas codes of conduct are voluntary guidelines from the companies (the complicated process for making an agreement legally binding is described below). Having a legally binding agreement was pivotal for the Indonesian actors as they had negative experiences of self-regulating codes of conduct.

Third, trade unions became central to the assurance of compliance with the Playfair agreement, which is rarely the case with codes of conduct. This was attractive for the trade unions, as it would provide them with more power in the implementation process, compared with codes of conduct in which the controllers are, instead, employed directly by, and also report directly to, large international companies. Finally, the opportunity of taking part in the negotiations in terms of both the content and the implementation of the Playfair agreement was also regarded as an important difference in terms of the manner in which codes of conduct are usually produced. This difference would, again, strengthen the role, which the local actors had in the development and implementation of the CSR policy.

Retail Companies and Suppliers

The differences between codes of conduct and Playfair, which made Playfair attractive for Indonesian trade unions and NGOs, also posed a threat against the positions of both sporting goods companies and suppliers. Playfair altered both the previous one-sidedness of the codes (which were entirely controlled by the companies) and the balance of power between the suppliers and trade unions. The alterations would, thus, possibly, provide the trade unions with a stronger position. Through the negotiations regarding Playfair, the companies were also made part of the local negotiations, and their CSR policies changed from voluntary to legally binding. The companies claimed, initially, that the negotiations revolving around working conditions would be the responsibility of the trade unions and the factory executives. The role of the global sporting goods companies was—according to themselves—to act as mediators who would assist in balancing the requirements of the trade unions and the profit focus of the factory executives. However, in order for the Playfair negotiations to be different from the codes of conduct, the Indonesian unions and NGOs found it necessary to include the global companies in the local negotiations as a way of gaining an advantage over suppliers and, in such a way, to improve the distorted local balance of power.

After a number of discussions had taken place, the companies (Adidas and Nike in particular, which had representatives on location in Indonesia) were also made part of the negotiations, which is illustrated, for example, by the fact that the representative of Adidas acted as a spokesperson for both the sporting goods companies and the suppliers in the negotiations. Even though the Playfair agreement was to be implemented at suppliers' factories, the suppliers did not have their own spokesperson in the negotiations. In this way, a clear link was established between the coalition of local Indonesian trade unions and the NGOs on the one side, and the international sporting goods companies on the other, in a manner, which could not be found in either the codes of conduct or on the Indonesian labor market. The fact that the sporting goods companies, in the end, accepted—albeit unwillingly—this more extensive role was based on their endeavor to protect their trust and they hoped, as expressed by their representative, that as long as negotiations carried on, at least negative campaigns damaging their trust would be avoided.

While the multinational large companies hesitated to assume a more active role in the negotiations, the Indonesian subcontractors were hesitant to participate in the negotiations in the first place. Their hesitation was based on the lack of trust between the factory executives and the trade unions, with its origins in the previous confrontational relationships at the factory level with strikes from the workers' side and attempts to reduce the influence of the trade unions from the employers' side. Thus, it fell on the large sporting goods companies to persuade, or require, their most important subcontractors to participate in the negotiations, which they eventually did.

Freedom of Association as the First Area of Negotiations

With all actors in place, the first Playfair meeting was held in November 2009, with representatives for all parties involved. Prior to the meeting, the Indonesian trade unions had identified three key issues, which were to form the agenda for the meeting: salaries, temporary workers, and freedom of association. The fact that local trade unions were allowed to define the agenda was considered unfair by the representatives of some of the large global companies who, themselves, wished for a greater role at this stage of the negotiations. The companies did, however, accept the agenda, and the first stage in the negotiations, thus, became determining the topic, which would become the starting point for the continuing negotiations. The parties, however, had differing views on the issues with which to start the discussion. Most of the representatives for trade unions wished to initiate the negotiations with the topic of salaries, while certain representatives for trade unions and most of the companies wished to start with the topic of freedom of association. In the end, the companies were able to put freedom of association on top of the agenda by, for example, arguing that it would be difficult to calculate a living wage, it being more simple to define freedom of association and that an agreement on freedom of association is of more use as a tool in solving local conflicts.

There were various reasons for the Indonesian actors' acceptance of the companies' suggestion to start with freedom of association. All of the trade unions had been involved or were involved in cases in which they considered the factory executives to have failed to fairly respect freedom of association. According to the unions, freedom of association was a right that opened new doors for them and which, in the long term, would provide them with a stronger position vis-á-vis the factory executives. In addition, freedom of association had been, compared to salary details, ambiguously defined in the current regulations. This latter point is particularly interesting, as freedom of association is regulated both in Indonesian labor law and in ILO conventions. The Indonesian trade unions and NGOs, however, were of the opinion that freedom of association had been vaguely defined in these texts. There was plenty of room for interpretation of what freedom of association, in fact, means in practice, which made it difficult to determine whether the factory executives violated freedom of association or not. For example, did the cooperation between the factory executives and the pragmatic trade unions, and the fact that they actively opposed more radical trade unions in the same factory, violate freedom of association? On the basis of the lack of balance of power between the trade unions and the executives, this ambiguity also implied that the interpretation of freedom of association held by factory executives often prevailed.

Consequently, starting with freedom of association as the first topic became an acceptable compromise for all parties, as it enabled businesses and suppliers to postpone the potentially expensive negotiations on salaries; however, this provided the local trade unions and NGOs a definition of freedom of association, which would be more practical and applicable in the future.

A Draft of the Agreement and Opening Negotiations

When the decision to start with freedom of association had been taken, the local trade unions and NGOs presented a first draft of the agreement on freedom of association. This took place in the beginning of 2010. When the first draft had been submitted to the sporting goods companies and suppliers, it became evident that the parties stood far apart from each other and had differing views, particularly in terms of the number of members who were to get time off from work in order to engage in trade union activities. According to the proposal by the trade unions and NGOs, 13 to 15 members of the trade union (depending on the size of the factory) would be released from duty; however, they realized that such a requirement might be unreasonable. As expected, the opposing party did not agree with this proposal and countered, instead, that, at most, the club chairman of the trade union could be released from duty.

After these negotiations, the trade unions revised their first draft, altered some minor parts of the text and lowered, in particular, the number of trade union members who could be released from duty. The large sporting goods companies and their subcontractors did not, however, accept the new figures and their second draft was, in principle, identical to their first draft.

Although the issue of the number of trade union members who could be released from duty represented the most problematic area, similar deadlocks arose in various other matters. These deadlocks concerned areas such as whether the agreement would apply to suppliers at all tiers of the supply chain, or only to first-tier suppliers, whether the trade unions would have the right to use the company's Internet access in their work, where the notice board of the trade union could be placed in the company, the size and location of the office and notice boards of the trade union, the production-related information to which the trade union could have access, and that the draft of the trade union included detailed specifications of the manner in which the potential monitoring of the workforce would be undertaken, while the draft of the sporting goods companies and suppliers did not include any such information. With regard to all these matters, the second draft of the parties was, in principle, identical to their first draft; thus, as regards the contents of the agreement, the negotiations had reached a deadlock in which the representatives of the business world were unwilling to alter their first drafts and the trade unions were unwilling to make any further changes to their second draft.

A Breakdown in the Negotiations and Demonstrations

The deadlock in the discussions continued until the spring of 2010, at which point the trade unions, in the end, chose to leave the negotiations and organize a demonstration with approximately 150 workers in Jakarta, in June of the same year. The purpose of the demonstration was to exert pressure on the companies and suppliers, and the demonstration received some attention in the local media in Indonesia. While the local Indonesian trade unions organized the demonstration, the international Playfair organizations attempted to persuade the large sporting goods companies to resume the negotiations. For example, the Playfair organizations held regular discussions with the companies (primarily representatives for Adidas). In such a manner, the international trade unions and NGOs could, together, solve certain misunderstandings and discreetly exert pressure on the businesses by indicating that a breakdown in the Indonesian negotiations could, in the following stage, result in international campaigns damaging the sporting goods companies' trust.

Resumption of Negotiations

As a result of the international pressure, an international representative for Adidas visited Jakarta in order to demonstrate the company's willingness to resume negotiations. The visit was regarded as a positive development by the Indonesian labor organizations, as they considered the global companies to be more compliant in terms of accepting their requirements than the local subcontractors had been. Thus, in the autumn of 2010, the parties reunited and agreed on various important paragraphs in the agreement, including the number of trade union members who would be released from duty. The final agreement regarding the case of members released from duty became a compromise between the trade unions' second draft and the sporting goods companies and suppliers' initial position, that is, the trade unions were forced to lower their demands again in order to reach an agreement.

The negotiations were, then, continued in the autumn of 2010 and the spring of 2011, with various attempts to solve the remaining issues. For example, the trade unions argued strongly for the agreement to apply to all suppliers who produced the various brands, regardless of the level of the supply chain in which they operated, while the large multinational companies loudly argued for the agreement to only apply to first-tier suppliers, with whom they had a direct relationship. As first-tier suppliers subcontract a major portion of their production to subcontractors and the working conditions are often worse for second-tier and third-tier suppliers, the sporting goods companies' proposal would leave many of the workers (and trade union members) involved in the production of apparel and footwear outside the scope of the agreement. The trade union representatives regarded this as unacceptable, and many of them emphasized the ambition of including the entire supply chain as one of the major differences between the Playfair agreement and the codes of conduct. After heated discussions, the companies' position of restricting the scope only to first-tier suppliers was, however, approved; the trade unions were, nevertheless, able to include a reservation that these suppliers would, in turn, encourage their subcontractors to implement the agreement as well.

The trade unions and NGOs were similarly forced to lower their demands in terms of the size of the offices of the trade unions and the number of notice boards to be used by the trade unions. The unions and NGOs though achieved a major victory in terms of the legal status of the agreement. Up until the spring of 2011, the legal status of the negotiations had been unclear. During the spring negotiations, however, the unions and NGOs required that the agreement be made legally binding, as they perceived a need of a last resort for resolving disputes. As a representative for SPTSK stated, "If the agreement is only an ethical responsibility, then where is the sanction?" The trade union representatives' previous experience of the restricted impact of the codes of conduct was an important reason behind their assertion that legal sanctions were necessary as a last resort.

The sporting goods companies and suppliers wished, however, to ensure that potential conflicts would be solved through the committees, at factory and national level, which would be established after the agreement had been signed. One reason for this was that it was time consuming to take a conflict to court, and another reason was that they presumably wanted to maintain the voluntary character of the agreement. In the end, however, the trade unions were able to include, in the agreement, a paragraph stating that a violation of the agreement constitutes an action violating freedom of association, and that any conflicts would, as a last resort, be resolved in court.

Implementation and Continued Negotiations

The next step after the parties had signed the final version of the agreement was to begin to implement it. Two different committees were established for the implementation—one at the factory level with only representatives of subcontractors and trade unions, and one at the national level with representatives from all parties. In addition to resolving conflicts regarding freedom of association, the committees would formalize the ongoing dialogue between the sporting goods companies, suppliers, and trade unions. The large multinational companies hoped that the committees at factory level would ensure that the local actors (trade unions and suppliers), would, through joint negotiations on location, both identify and resolve potential conflicts regarding freedom of association. This would not only improve working conditions but also reduce the need for the companies' controllers to ensure compliance with the code of conduct and freedom of association, as well as minimizing the trade unions' demands on the companies' engagement in "more simple" conflicts. As the committees were established in 2012, it remains to be seen whether they will actually work. In late 2012, the parties also carried on their discussions and started to negotiate a contract about temporary workers at factories.

From Global Consumer Power to Local Worker Power

Global Mobilization Creates a Hovering Hand

Although the negotiations in Indonesia were formally initiated at the end of 2009, the actual negotiations started as early as 2003–2004, when the international trade unions and NGOs created Playfair and began to launch extensive international campaigns damaging sporting goods companies' trust. Economists are happy to discuss the way in which the "invisible hand" creates desirable effects; however, in the Playfair case, it is more reasonable to state that the international trade unions and NGOs, through campaigns, managed to create a "hovering hand," which acted as a driving force. The hovering hand comprised a credible threat of international campaigns, in conjunction with, for example, the Olympic Games, that could considerably damage trust in companies that did not live up to the demands of the Playfair campaign (cf. Frooman 1999). This hovering hand was a strong contributor to the willingness of the multinational sporting goods companies (and their subcontractors) to take part in negotiations with the local Indonesian actors. Without it, the negotiations would have been neither initiated nor resumed after they had been broken down.

The establishment of a hovering hand was dependent on the cooperation between international trade unions and NGOs (cf. O'Rourke 2003; Braun and Gearhart 2004; Ford 2006). Such cooperation has, however, in other situations, proven to be problematic, as trade unions and NGOs often, for various reasons, come into conflict (Egels-Zandén and Hyllman 2006, 2007, 2011). A potential reason for the ability to cooperate in the Playfair case was that, in Playfair, focus was placed on overall requirements and negotiations-specific details were managed by local Indonesian actors. Thus, the international trade unions and NGOs did not have to agree on concrete requirements, which in other cases have proved to be problematic.

Building trust through a process logic, rather than results-based logic, thus, has the advantage that potential conflicts between trade unions and NGOs are, at least partially, transferred from the global to the local arena. In other words, using trust to span geographic boundaries has the advantage of making it easier to span organizational boundaries among international unions and NGOs. In the Playfair case, the conflicts between the trade unions and NGOs were managed, in the local Indonesian arena, through the resolution to allow only local trade union representatives to take part in the negotiations, which meant that the other organizations served solely as support functions and, as a result, only one of the NGOs actively took part in the local negotiations.

The Limits of Consumer Power and a Results-Based Logic

After the international trade unions and NGOs, through the mobilization of primarily Western stakeholders, had created a hovering hand, they took a pivotal decision in the Playfair negotiations held in Indonesia. They chose to, in many respects, abandon the results-based logic that had governed the manner in which private regulation and codes of conduct had functioned since the beginning of the 1990s. Up until the Playfair negotiations in Indonesia, focus in the international campaigns had, nearly entirely, been placed on international media campaigns, with requirements for the companies to follow the ILO and UN conventions and/or to address and solve specific problems in specific factories. The requirements had either been previously predefined in the current conventions or had been of a reactive nature, with a focus on attempting to redress the situation (dismissed leaders of local trade unions, nonexistent salary payments, or the closing down of factories).

The pressure of labor organizations, founded on the results-based logic, had successfully made companies adopt codes of conduct based on the ILO and UN conventions, and employ auditors. The pressures had also led to an increased engagement, by consumers and other Western stakeholders, in the working conditions in developing countries. However, as shown in the empirical part of this chapter, these successes had been hard to translate into improvements on the factory floor with workers and their representatives being unable to acquire an improved negotiating position thanks to codes of conduct. In other words, codes had not succeeded in delivering within the area that is regarded by the local trade unions to be the most important—that is, the improved organizing of factory workers.

In addition to limited improvements, the focus on codes of conduct, founded on the results-based logic, had also made Indonesian actors to regard themselves as marginalized within private regulation of worker rights. This marginalization of local actors is not unique for Indonesia (Egels-Zandén and Hyllman 2006; Khan, Munir, and Willmott 2007). After having studied the manner in which Western businesses addressed child labor in the Pakistani supply chains, Khan, Munir, and Willmott (2007), for example, stated that it was the Western consumers' notions and the trust of the companies' products that mattered, while the local workers' notions on solutions for the "problem" were of little interest to international companies and international unions and NGOs.

As a result, codes of conduct, founded on the results-based logic, have been accused of representing a classical attempt to impose Western values on the developing countries (Blowfield and Dolan 2008). Thus, workers and trade unions become production factors in need of help rather than people with rights (Barrientos and Smith 2007). As a result of this other side of the coin of the results-based logic, trade unions and NGOs in Indonesia had lost interest in codes, forcing the

Playfair organizers to use trust as a political tool in a new innovative way in order to persuade local trade unions and NGOs to participate in negotiations.

From Consumer Power to Worker Power

However, deficiencies are not limited to codes of conduct and the results-based logic, but similarly exist in the traditional process-based national regulation of worker rights. Fragmented local trade unions with insufficient resources and low membership levels imply that, although local actors participate in the negotiation processes, they are rarely able to achieve improvements in terms of, for example, freedom of association. A traditional process logic, thus, addresses the exclusion of local actors; however, the same problems persist as with codes of conduct, that is, insufficient long-term and structural improvements for workers and their representatives.

That which makes the Playfair negotiations in Indonesia so interesting is that, in these negotiations, a hybrid of the results-based and process logics has been created, which potentially addresses the shortcomings found in both logics (cf. Glynn and Lounsbury 2005). The pressure from international trade unions and NGOs, according to results-based logic, created a hovering hand as a result of their ability to mobilize consumer power and damage the trust of sporting goods companies. This work based on the results-based logic forced sporting goods companies and their suppliers to the negotiation table. The difference compared with the traditional international campaigns was, however, that, instead of requiring that the companies meet requirements X, Y, or Z, the international trade unions and NGOs required that they negotiated with the Indonesian trade unions and NGOs. Thus, international trade unions and NGOs required that the sporting goods companies participate in a certain *negotiation process*, instead of guaranteeing a certain *result*. The required result was, thus, that a process be initiated.

Thus, the global actors transferred their power to the local Indonesian trade unions and NGOs, due to their ability to damage the trust for sporting goods companies. In other words, the Indonesian trade unions and NGOs did not obtain their place in the negotiations on the basis of their ability to organize their workers but, instead, on the basis of their newly acquired ability to—via their global allies—threaten the trust in sporting goods companies. Through this innovative use of trust as a political tool to span organizational and geographic boundaries,

Indonesian trade unions and NGOs were, thus, able to negotiate on freedom of association in a manner that would not have been possible in the past. The international trade unions and NGOs' feat was, in this manner, through the mechanism of trust, to translate global consumer power to local worker power. The influential, yet short-term, character of Western consumer power could, thus, through this trust mechanism, be translated into local worker power and potentially more long-term improvements for Indonesian trade unions and NGOs.

The creation of a hybrid between the results-based and process institutional logic of how to leverage trust as a political tool and the establishment of a mechanism that translates consumer power into worker power was, however, not enough. The international trade unions and NGOs also had to unify the fragmented Indonesian trade union movement in order to create a platform of organization that could act as a legitimate opposing party to the global companies and their subcontractors, that is, a platform of organizations that could act as the recipient of the trust transferred by the international actors. In spite of an increased influence through both the creation of a platform of local organizations and the translation of consumer power, the Indonesian trade unions though still remained relatively weak in the negotiations. This is most clearly illustrated by the manner in which they were initially not able to address the wage issue—their primarily goal—in the negotiations, and the manner in which they repeatedly had to lower their requirements on the number of trade union members who were to be released from duty to participate in the activities of their trade union. The position of the trade unions was, thus, strengthened to a sufficient degree to sign a contract that would not have been possible previously; however, in certain respects, the contract was relatively diluted.

A Hybrid Logic to Span Organizational and Geographic Boundaries

In one respect, however, the Indonesian trade unions and NGOs were highly successful. They were able to make the freedom of association contract legally binding and, in such a manner, establish a link between the companies' private regulation and national legislation. They were, thus, able to translate the companies' requirement of trust globally to worker rights legislation locally. The companies CSR work was in this way translated into traditional regulation of workers' rights, with the twist that, before taking the matter into the legal system, the disputes must pass through committees at the factory and national level, involving the Western sporting goods companies.

Thus, the Playfair negotiations illustrate the manner in which a hybrid institutional logic is created through a process whereby global consumer power and international campaigns (results-based logic) are combined with local negotiations on workers' rights (process logic). This hybrid logic is promising as it leverages the political tool of trust as a way to span organizational boundaries (both between international unions and NGOs, and between international and local actors) and geographic boundaries. The hybrid logic thus mobilizes, connects, and provides local trade unions and NGOs with a stronger role in negotiation and implementation of worker rights. It also shows signs of providing outcomes (provided that the freedom of association contract is implemented in practice) that improve the long-term negotiation position of Indonesian trade unions and NGOs, that is, it could potentially achieve what neither the results-based private regulation nor the process-based traditional regulation have been able to achieve.

The hybrid logic of Playfair, therefore, carries the potential to create the critical link between global trust processes and local negotiation processes, which is required in order to address the deficiencies that have previously been identified in both the results-based and process logics. Even if the Playfair negotiations are only a drop in the ocean of activities that are based on either the results-based or process logics, it is a drop worth acknowledging. It may, conceptually, constitute a part of the solution to the way in which local workers' rights in developing countries may be strengthened in the long term, and show the potential of using trust as a political tool to span organizational, institutional, and geographic boundaries.

Notes

1. Institutional logics can best be simplified as cultural notions and rules that structure how we see the world (Marquis and Lounsbury 2007). At an organizational level, institutional logics lead, therefore, to a situation in which decision makers understand, and propose, a limited number of problems and solutions (Thornton 2002; Greenwood et al. 2010).
2. For example, a trade union representative, when interviewed, remembered having held speeches on codes of conduct in various European countries in 1996. By means of comparison, in the same year, discussions of codes of conduct were initiated in Sweden, and in 1997, H&M adopted its code of conduct.

References

Ählström, Jenny, and Niklas Egels-Zandén. 2008. "The Processes of Defining Corporate Responsibility: A Study of Swedish Garment Retailers' Responsibility." *Business Strategy and the Environment* 17 (4): 230–244.

Amengual, Matthew. 2010. "Complementary Labor Regulation: The Uncoordinated Combination of State and Private Regulators in the Dominican Republic." *World Development* 38 (3): 405–414.

AMRC. 2003. *Workers' Rights for the New Century*. Hong Kong: AMRC.

Anner, Mark. 2012. "Corporate Social Responsibility and Freedom of Association Rights: The Precarious Quest for Legitimacy and Control in Global Supply Chains." *Politics & Society* 40 (4): 609–644.

Barrientos, Stephanie, and Sally Smith. 2007. "Do Workers Benefit from Ethical Trade? Assessing Codes of Labour Practice in Global Production Systems." *Third World Quarterly* 28 (4): 713–729.

Bartley, Tim. 2007. "Institutional Emergence in an Era of Globalization: The Rise of Transnational Private Regulation of Labor and Environmental Conditions." *American Journal of Sociology* 113 (2): 297–351.

Blowfield, Michael E., and Catherine S. Dolan. 2008. "Stewards of Virtue? The Ethical Dilemma of CSR in African Horticulture." *Development and Change* 39 (1): 1–23.

Braun, Rainer, and Judy Gearhart. 2004. "Who Should Code Your Conduct? Trade Union and NGO Differences in the Fight for Workers' Rights." *Development in Practice* 14 (1–2): 183–196.

Caraway, Teri L. 2004. "Protective Repression, International Pressure, and Institutional Design: Explaining Labor Reform in Indonesia." *Studies in Comparative International Development* 39 (3): 28–49.

———. 2006. "Freedom of Association: Battering Ram or Trojan Horse?" *Review of International Political Economy* 13 (2): 210–232.

Chan, Anita, and Kaxton Siu. 2010. "Analyzing Exploitation: The Mechanisms Underpinning Low Wages and Excessive Overtime in Chinese Export Factories." *Critical Asian Studies* 42 (2): 167–190.

Cooke, Fang L. 2004. "Foreign Firms in China: Modeling HRM in a Chinese Toy Manufacturing Corporation." *Human Resource Management Journal* 14 (3): 31–52.

Egels-Zandén, Niklas. 2009. "Transnational Governance of Workers' Rights: Outlining a Research Agenda." *Journal of Business Ethics* 87 (2): 169–188.

Egels-Zandén, Niklas, and Peter Hyllman. 2006. "Exploring the Effects of Union-NGO Relationships on Corporate Responsibility: The Case of the Swedish Clean Clothes Campaign." *Journal of Business Ethics* 64 (3): 303–316.

———. 2007. "Evaluating Strategies for Negotiating Workers' Rights in Transnational Corporations: The Effects of Codes of Conduct and Global Agreements on Workplace Democracy." *Journal of Business Ethics* 76 (2): 207–223.

———. 2011. "Differences in Organizing between Unions and NGOs: Conflict and Cooperation among Swedish Unions and NGOs." *Journal of Business Ethics* 101 (2): 249–261.

Fairbrother, Peter, and Nikolaus Hammer. 2005. "Global Unions: Past Efforts and Future Prospects." *Relations Industrielles/Industrial Relations* 60 (3): 405–429.

Ford, Michele. 2000. "Research Note: Indonesian Trade Union Developments since the Fall of Suharto." *Labour and Management in Development* 1 (3): 1–10.

———. 2006. "Migrant Labor NGOs and Trade Unions: A Partnership in Progress?" *Asian and Pacific Migration Journal* 15 (3): 299–318.

———. 2009. *Workers and Intellectuals: NGOs, Trade Unions and the Indonesian Labour Movement.* Singapore: Singapore University Press; Hawaii University Press; KITLV.

Frenkel, Stephen. 2001. "Globalization, Athletic Footwear Commodity Chains and Employment Relations in China." *Organization Studies* 22 (4): 531–562.

Frooman, Jeff. 1999. "Stakeholder Influence Strategies." *Academy of Management Review* 24 (2): 191–205.

Glynn, Mary A., and Michael Lounsbury. 2005. "From the Critic's Corner: Logic Blending, Discursive Change and Authenticity in a Cultural Production System." *Journal of Management Studies* 42 (5): 1031–1055.

Greenwood, Royston, Amalia M. Díaz, Stan X. Li, and José C. Lorente 2010. "The Multiplicity of Institutional Logics and the Heterogeneity of Organizational Responses." *Organization Science* 21 (2): 521–539.

Hendry, Jamie R. 2006. "Taking Aim at Business: What Factors Lead Environmental Non-Governmental Organizations to Target Particular Firms?" *Business & Society* 45 (1): 47–86.

Huzzard, Tony, Denis Gregory, and Regan Scott. Eds. 2004. *Strategic Unionism and Partnership: Boxing or Dancing?* Basingstoke: Palgrave Macmillan.

Khan, Farzad R., Kamal A. Munir, and Hugh Willmott. 2007. "A Dark Side of Institutional Entrepreneurship: Soccer Balls, Child Labour and Postcolonial Impoverishment." *Organization Studies* 28 (7): 1055–1077.

Locke, Richard, Matthew Amengual, and Akshay Mangla. 2009 "Virtue out of Necessity? Compliance, Commitment, and the Improvement of Labor Conditions in Global Supply Chains." *Politics & Society* 37 (3): 319–351.

Locke, Richard, Thomas Kochan, Monica Romis, and Fei Qin. 2007. "Beyond Corporate Codes of Conduct: Work Organization and Labour Standards at Nike's Suppliers." *International Labour Review* 146 (1–2): 21–40.

LO-TCO Biståndsnämnd. 2009. *Kränkningar av Fackliga Rättigheter 2009: Indonesien.*

Marquis, Christopher, and Michael Lounsbury. 2007. "Vive le Résistance: Competing Logics and the Consolidation of U.S. Community Banking." *Academy of Management Journal* 50 (4): 799–820.

Northrup, Herbert R., and Richard L. Rowan. 1979. *Multinational Collective Bargaining Attempts.* Philadelphia, PA: University of Philadelphia Press.

O'Rourke, Dara. 2003. "Outsourcing Regulation: Analyzing Nongovernmental Systems of Labor Standards and Monitoring." *The Policy Study Journal* 31 (1): 1–29.

Taylor, Timothy. 2005. "In Defence of Outsourcing." *CATO Journal* 25 (2): 367–377.

Thornton, Patricia H. 2002. "The Rise of the Corporation in a Craft Industry: Conflict and Conformity in Institutional Logics." *Academy of Management Journal* 45:81–101.

Tjandraningsih, Indrasari, and Hari Nugroho. 2008. "The Flexibility Regime and Organised Labour in Indonesia." *Labour and Management in Development* 9:1–14.

Wells, Don. 2007. "Too Weak for the Job: Corporate Codes of Conduct." *Global Social Policy* 7:51–74.

CHAPTER 5

The Certification Paradox: Monitoring as a Solution and a Problem

Ingrid Gustafsson and Kristina Tamm Hallström

Trust and Mistrust—the Double Nature of the Market

In Egels-Zandén's chapter we could see how multinational shoe companies work in order to create trust in their brands by using a process logic framework in their Corporate Social Responsibility (CSR) efforts. In other words, the companies and their suppliers undertake a dialogue and negotiate with the actors within civil society as to a reasonable interpretation of the freedom of association. This example indicates that confidence has become all the more important in today's market exchange. It is no longer sufficient to offer products and services of high quality at a reasonable price but, instead, it has also become important to, as a producer, be transparent and open for dialogue. One must be able to demonstrate that the production process has been conducted in an acceptable manner, in terms of specific values, such as sustainability, the work environment, and human rights. If consumers, civil society actors, and journalists discover that a company has used child labor, harmful chemicals, or has denied its employees acceptable working conditions, there is a high risk that the company will be criticized in the media, which, in turn, can seriously damage its reputation and the possibility of market survival.

It can, however, be difficult to gain insight into production conditions, especially if the production activity or the purchasing in question is executed in countries located far away from the markets in which the consumers are located, and if there are no reviewing civil society actors geographically close to the producing entity.

Transnationally valid standards and certification systems have come to play a central role in this context. During recent years, the choices as regards the possible standards embodying an emphasis on values such as sustainability, quality of the working environment, and human rights have increased dramatically (Brunsson and Jacobsson 2000; Bernstein and Cashore 2007; Bartley and Smith 2010; Bartley 2011; Marx 2011; Reinecke, Manning, and von Hagen 2012). So-called management system standards have seen a particular breakthrough, the idea being that organizations create management systems for their operations, documenting measurable objectives and the organizational processes and routines that should be used to reach goal fulfillment, which they, subsequently, follow in their daily work. ISO 9001 for quality management, ISO 14001 for environmental management, and standards from the Forest Stewardship Council (FSC) regarding sustainable forestry are examples of management system standards used for certification where the control refers above all to the auditor reviewing the documents of the management system in order to determine if the processes and work procedures are analyzed and well formulated. In these cases, the written documentation of the business's management system constitutes the sample serving as the basis of certification. Certain standards require that field trips should also be conducted in accordance with certification in order to further control the manner in which the standards are complied with in practice. Certification refers primarily to a so-called office audit, involving the review of the documents, manuals, and the procedures that are in focus.

Standards are developed by many different types of actors, for example, not only environmental organizations, professional organizations, intergovernmental organizations, and formal standardization organizations, such as the International Organization for Standardization (ISO), but also by companies and business associations, or by various combinations of such organizations (Abbott and Snidal 2009). By adjusting to the standards considered to be relevant in terms of organizing and managing business operations, and with regard to appropriate values, different market actors can be seen as legitimate and trustworthy (Powell and DiMaggio 1991; Brunsson and Jacobsson 2000; Bartley 2007). For companies to be able to demonstrate that they actually follow the standards and, consequently, deserve trust, a special tool is applied: third-party certification. This phenomenon will be the focus of the discussion presented in our chapter.

In line with Egels-Zandén, our interest lies in how trust issues found in markets are managed, but we focus, in particular, on third-party certification as a specific trust tool. With the help of third-party certification, companies can appear to be trustworthy—this is a method to manage the downsides of the market. However, certification is also a service offered by certification firms competing in a market. We show here that these auditing companies struggle with their own trust issues and that the market for certification, where the products sold are trust techniques as well (see Lindeberg 2007), also has its downsides. In other words, this chapter will focus on the trust issues on the market for trust.

Our discussion will revolve around how systems for certification are structured and legitimized. We will paint a picture of a complex network of interest groups contributing to the creation of certification as a trust tool. Our studies show that the certification systems comprise entities ranging from the companies choosing to be certified for various reasons: certification companies and industry-related groups of certification companies to so-called accreditation bodies that are sometimes managed as national authorities or as associations of authorities, but can also be managed as companies.[1] There are, consequently, more actors involved in this system than merely the certified entities and the certifying entities. As a result, we see a number of different driving forces and logics impacting the manner in which these controls are organized. In this chapter, we focus mainly on the system's organization: *Why is the system organized in this particular way? How is it argued that this particular organization of the system contributes to trust in markets?* We emphasize two characteristics of the certification system that we find central and distinctive: certification as a commercial service and certification through chains of control. We also discuss how certification is not limited to individual countries but, rather, has grown to be a part of a transnational system. As will become evident, certification as a tool for trust thus transcends organizational, institutional, and geographic borders, making it an especially interesting case in the study of confidence-building systems.

Method and Material

The empirical discussion in this chapter is based on studies carried out by the authors during the period 2009–2012. Overall, we have conducted approximately 50 interviews with certification auditors, industry organizations representing certification companies, and accreditation organizations in Sweden, the United Kingdom, and the Netherlands, as well as with accreditation managers in Sweden and the United Kingdom at ministerial level. We have spoken to representatives of the international membership organization for accreditation bodies in the European Union (EU)—European Cooperation for Accreditation (EA)—and we have interviewed market actors on the newly established Swedish market for motor vehicle inspection. We have also interviewed the certified companies while, at the same time, making observations of the certification processes, during both the so-called office audits and during visits to the companies that have been audited.[2] During these observations, the main focus has been on investigating how certification as a trust tool is constructed and organized, as well as how it is legitimized (alternatively opposed) by the various involved interest groups.

In addition, we have analyzed a number of websites and documents, which, in different ways, form and depict the certification system. These documents vary in character; some are formal, political documents, functioning as appropriation direction for authorities or government bills, others are internal policy documents aimed at forming the behavior of the studied organization. We have continuously asked the interviewees and searched the documents for understanding of how they work to create trust and to prevent mistrust. We have also selected our data to reflect what we find to be a coherent, transnational monitoring system. This system, which has its basis in commercial logic, is characterized by monitorings conducted in a number of steps, similar to a monitoring chain. To distinguish the various "levels" in this system, we have researched how these levels are created, justified, and maintained.

In the following section, we explain, roughly, what certification is-who performs certifications and how they are performed. Furthermore, we place the current form of certification, a service exchanged on the market, in the larger context of market reforms. This is followed by a section related to the paradox of certification, where we discuss the problems arising due to the commercial dimension of certification, as well as the monitoring chains—these "chains" or "layers" of monitoring are presented as "solutions" to problems of trust in our data. As a conclusion, we return to our initial discussion about the market's double-sided nature and present some suggestions for further research.

Certification as a Trust Tool

What Is Certification?

Third-party certification (shortened below to: certification) implies that an external third party—a party that is independent of both the seller and the buyer—is hired by the seller to monitor if the seller's operations

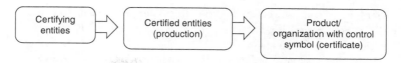

Figure 5.1 Ideal types of connections between auditors.

or product follow a specific standard. This can refer to transitional CSR standards or other standards stressing different types of values. The analysis below comprises both compulsory inspections (e.g., previous statutory vehicle inspections) and voluntary certifications (conducted in the private sectors during many years, such as management system certifications). Regardless of whether certification or inspection is voluntary, the relationship (in ideal-typical terms) is as illustrated in figure 5.1. Our analysis will be devoted to the section to the far left, namely what happens among those who carry out the certifications (the certifying entities).

Even though certification has expanded in line with increased globalization, certification is not only used for transnational market exchange, but the method is also used locally in many countries, for example, by dentist practitioners, in relation to their clients, suppliers, and other interest groups to show that they are certified in accordance with quality assurance and environmental management systems. Certification may also be a requirement stated in government regulation. For example, according to Swedish law, suppliers participating in public procurements must be certified under the quality system standard ISO 9001.

Certification as a monitoring tool is proliferating not only in Sweden but also in Europe and globally as well. Used both globally and locally, certification as a trust tool crosses geographic boundaries, the idea being that a producer in Europe should be able to trust its manufacturer in China. In recent decades, certification has developed into a conventional method as a monitoring mechanism to show compliance with international standards. ISO 9001 certification constitutes a visible example: according to the American organization, ANSI-ASQ National Accreditation Board (ANAB), over a million organizations in the world are certified in accordance with this quality system standard (ANAB 2012), which implies that over a million organizations receive annual visits from one or more certification auditors working for a certification company. We believe there is reason to see certification not only as a result of the increased spread of standards, but also as a sort of monitoring trend that is spreading to more and more areas. One could say that it has become "fashionable" to become certified. Deficiencies within different areas of society are constantly challenged on the debate pages of daily newspapers, and certification is often presented as a solution to a various set of problems.

As we have already indicated, the expansion of certification-related operations may also be interpreted as an answer to the lack of confidence in market exchanges. Complying with standards can be seen as an important tool in terms of creating confidence for a producer in the market but as noted in the introduction, in practice, it is not enough to only *say* one is complying with a standard. Third-party certification's role is to convince interest groups that standards have, indeed, been followed. The need for review and monitoring may also be attributable to the lack of belief that market actors in their striving to generate profits actually take into consideration all of the values regarded as important in society (that does not necessarily increase profit). Values are *regulated* via standards but the *monitoring* of their implementation is conducted via certification. Through certification, producers in the market can indicate that they follow standards regulating those values assessed as legitimate and, possibly, necessary. In other words, certification constitutes a communicative tool to create confidence and a good reputation for the producer's environment (Haufler 2001; Bartley 2007). The result is manifested through visible diplomas hanging on the walls of various organizations or through symbols on various product packaging. In contrast to creating confidence via process logic, where companies seeking to strengthen their trustworthiness open up for dialogue and negotiation with their environment (described in the previous chapter), certification refers more to a one-sided communication where confidence is thought to be associated with the presentation of a well-known symbol or diploma.

Marketization Trend in a Large Number of Areas

The average consumer often encounters certification in the form of these well-known symbols that appear on more and more types of products and indicate that the product is certified. At the same time, there may be confusion as to what certification really is for companies in the wholesale and retail sectors buying several products from countries located at a far distance, as well as for the consumers who see the symbols on products in the stores. Confusion refers to, for example, what the different symbols actually regulate, what is monitored in the certification process, and whose responsibility it is to make sure the correct aspects are being monitored.

In other words, consumers purchasing certified products—for example, food products labeled as organic—are faced with complex information in which various types of symbols are crowded and where it is often difficult to see what the symbols actually are meant to represent (Harbaugh, Maxwell, and Roussillon 2011). Certain food products, for example, coffee, tea, chocolate, and rice, may display four to five symbols on their packaging. Such symbols often focus on various aspects of production; while some (for example, the Swedish organic label KRAV), mean that the product is made without chemical pesticides, others, such as the Fairtrade symbol, emphasize social and ethical consideration in terms of the working and living conditions of farmers in developing countries.

Consumers may be unaware that this explosion of symbols is related to the fact that certification is, in itself, a market-based industry where certification services are offered to companies on a market with free competition between the certifiers. Certification can be compared to many other operations, which, over the last few decades, have shifted from being conducted and offered by state organizations to being sold on markets. The growth of the certification market can, in itself, be traced back to the deregulations of the 1980–1990s that aimed at introducing a market approach in many areas by replacing, or at least complementing, publicly run operations with private alternatives (Rose and Miller 1992; Haufler 2001). The deregulation of Televerket (the former Swedish government agency for telecommunications), the pharmacies, the school system, health care, and pensions system are a number of Swedish examples of this "marketization trend" in which markets are seen as a positive example of social coordination. The same rule applies to operations aimed at conducting various types of compulsory inspections, such as safety labeling of lifts, harmful products, bicycle helmets, and motor vehicle inspection—these operations have also, over the last two decades, undergone deregulation and opened up to a market logic.

In line with increased global economic exchange, various types of private governance tools, such as standards, have been developed for the purpose of transnational coordination (Djelic and Sahlin-Andersson 2006; Bernstein and Cashore 2007). Management system standards in particular have had a major breakthrough, with a shift from a focus mainly on quality and efficiency, to comprising more "political" values, such as the work environment, human rights, child labor, and food safety. In line with this development, the discussion on market downsides has intensified and less successful examples and misuse of these values within various industries have been raised in the public debate. Discussions in the Swedish media regarding scandals in privatized elderly care serve as a good example. In some cases, such criticism has resulted in reregulation of the newly (de)regulated markets, or to a stricter regulation in the markets that had already been established. This has, in turn, resulted in a significantly larger need to control and audit, which has led to an expansion of certification operations. Self-regulation within standards and certification has increased as a method used by individual actors or groups of actors to enhance their reputation and their trustworthiness. In some cases, government organizations participate in a, more or less, active manner in standardization work, or encourage and contribute to the increased use of standards (Elad 2001; Tamm Hallström 2004; McNichol 2006; Tamm Hallström and Boström 2010; Bartley 2011). At times, standards and certification are also assigned a mandatory status due to the fact that a certification requirement is stipulated in legislation. There are in other words no clear-cut boundaries between institutional spheres here; certification crosses over the private sphere and the public sphere.

Even if market solutions have received regular attention in the media, marketization reforms of monitoring (inspections and certifications), which were implemented when Sweden prepared to join the EU, and which adjusted the Swedish monitoring structure to the single market, have almost entirely escaped the public debate. In contrast to the marketization of health care or schools, there is no debate regarding marketization of monitoring. For some reason, the crossing of boundaries (the political and the private sphere) in this particular case does not appear to be as political as in other cases.

We demonstrate in this chapter that inspection and certification as a market-based control does not constitute an exception from "the downsides of markets." Certification can increase mistrust, as well as evoke the need to regulate and monitor these markets in various ways. However, what is different is that much of the regulation and monitoring has originated in the absence of public debate about the problems and deficiencies of the markets, which make them differ from, for example, elderly care and the free-school market, areas that are often highlighted by the media as being problematic.

The Paradox of Certification

Certification as a Commercial Service

The market is the overall ideal for the organization of certification of third parties. The idea is that certification companies, in both voluntary areas and mandatory inspection areas, are to compete with each other and be operated as a private, not public, operation. These are markets with an expanding demand; as previously mentioned, there are, for example, currently more than a million organizations having the ISO 9001 certification alone.

The commercial aspect of certification is shown at several levels. Each arrow in figure 5.1 symbolizes a commercial act—commercial in the sense that a payment is the basis of the transaction. A customer chooses a product that has been marked with a certificate—this may be a consumer buying detergent with the Nordic Ecolabel or chocolate with the KRAV or Fairtrade symbol. It may also comprise a purchasing department choosing a supplier with an ISO 9001 certificate for their operations. The commercial aspect also exists at the following level— the certified actor pays the certifier for their certification and the audit itself is, thus, a commercial service.

Certification and its commercial character have, in political contexts, been emphasized as a flexible and market-adjusted form of monitoring. In a government report from 2006, the investigators basically did not find any problems with a system of commercial monitoring against international standards. Certification was characterized as the commercial sister of governmental supervision—a modern and nonbureaucratic form of monitoring (SOU 2006, 113). This image could surely be problematized; however, we choose to set aside the potential ideological and political aspects of the commercial character of certification. Instead, we will highlight the consequences this marketization brings for the way in which the certification system, and its various levels, is organized. This also leads us to the issue we regard as particularly important from a trust perspective: the fact that commercial monitoring breeds a need for more monitoring (cf. Shapiro 1987).

As previously mentioned, certification can be understood as a tool aiming to create trust in markets. But when we further examine certification markets, we find that there is an interesting tension that, in turn, creates new trust issues and is the driving force behind the organization of the certification system. Certification is thought to function as a remedy against the perversions of the markets in vastly different business areas. It is, however, in itself a business area and as such, it is also organized according to a market logic. This logic may result in the type of perversions and trust issues that the certification operations are thought to prevent (cf. Bernstein and Cashore 2007; Bartley 2011). Perhaps the most important of these issues deal with trust in the independence and neutrality of the certification auditor. A company wishing to be monitored (certified and inspected) contracts a certification company and pays for certification services. Thus, there is an economic dependence between the certifier and those being certified. At the same time, a clear precondition in order for the monitoring to function is that the certification auditor should be neutral and independent in the auditing role. Here, the risk of mistrust in the market for certifications comes into play. How could we trust that the certification is neutral and independent when there is an economic dependence between the purchaser and seller of certification services? How do we know that a certification auditor is not biased and does not let things slide in the hope of attaining a satisfied, returning customer?

As certification is used to secure values such as safety, work environment, human rights, and issues relating to labor law, the tension between the requirement of neutrality and commercial logic becomes ever greater. There is a certain reporting in the media on companies that, despite mistrust and offences against the regulation of the standards, have been allowed to retain their certificates (Elad 2001; Courville 2003; Turcotte, de Bellefeuille, and den Hond 2007). This strengthens the image that there are certain downsides in the commercial logic of certification; however, the general impression is the absence of criticism of certification as a monitoring practice. Instead, we have discovered a comprehensive activity of *preventative organization* with the aim of building trust in commercial certification and inspection.

Certification through Chains of Monitoring

We argue that the commercial character of certification results in an increased demand for further levels of confidence-building practices. Certification aims to provide trust in a product, a service, or an organization; however, it also raises questions about the trustworthiness of the certifying entity. How is this dilemma solved within the certification industry?

One possible measure could have been that of certifying companies certifying each other, for example, on the basis of the ISO 9001 standard for quality assurance, in a similar way as producers in other markets address their confidence problems. But this is not the solution we find in the certification markets. Another alternative would have been for certification auditors to organize themselves professionally, just like auditors within financial auditing, in order to increase trustworthiness regarding their independence and professional conduct. Within accounting research, the way in which the commercial relationship between auditor and auditee impacts the trust of the auditing activity has been studied (Jeppesen 1998; Power 2003). A solution to trust problems between the auditor and the auditee has been that the auditor profession collectively creates stricter and clearer regulations for their members regarding professional conduct (Willmott and Sikka 1995; Wallerstedt 2009).

In the certification market, a completely different kind of solution has been created. We can observe a chain of organizational monitoring measures in the form of *accreditation*. Accreditation is a monitoring of the certifiers, conducted by an accreditor who can be understood as a metacertifier, a "monitoring of the monitoring," with the intention of securing the trustworthiness of certification as a form of monitoring. By being accredited, a certifier is able to appear as trustworthy and credible *despite* the fact that the certification service is sold commercially. Just like standards and certifications, accreditation as a phenomenon has expanded dramatically over the last few decades. Products and entire organizations are certified by a certifier who, in turn, is accredited by an accreditor. The system is characterized by a form of monitoring conducted at several levels. We wish to highlight this characteristic with the help of an empirical example: Swedish vehicle inspection.

On July 1, 2010, Swedish vehicle inspection was deregulated. Prior to this date, inspection of vehicles had been conducted in the form of a monopoly, through the (partially) state-owned company, Svensk Bilprovning AB. But as of 2010, the government allowed other inspection companies to enter the market and compete for the vehicle inspection services (which can, given the commercial feature of the monitoring, be regarded as a form of certification service).

Calling this "deregulation" is, however, a simplification. The government has maintained partial control of the market by making accreditation a mandatory requirement for all companies wishing to enter the inspection services market. Accreditation occurs at several levels, like a chain of monitoring. First, if an inspection company comprises several inspection sites, the headquarter must be accredited; this refers to a monitoring activity resembling the certification of management systems. Second, each inspection unit of the mother company must be accredited, and, third, each inspection technician working at the station must be certified—which, fourth, must be carried out by an accredited certification body.[3] This way of organizing is motivated by the fact that the state must be able to guarantee quality and security in the inspections conducted when a market with commercial actors is created. The reorganization of vehicle inspection as a result of the introduction of commercial monitoring, that is, a market for inspection, provides a clear example of how ensuring trust in one form of monitoring creates the need for more monitoring. We see a type of monitoring chain in which the monitoring that was previously at one level (vehicles inspected by the motor vehicle inspection), has now been replaced by a system comprising chains of control in four different steps.

Leaving the Swedish example, we see how the chains of monitoring continue at the regional and international levels. At a European level, national accreditation organizations within the EU are peer reviewed by the EA, and at a global level, accreditation organizations both inside and outside of the EU are peer reviewed—an "accreditation of the accreditation" by the organization called the International Accreditation Forum (IAF). We find that certification is a transnational system that transcends the nation-state as the sole actor conducting monitoring. The purpose of certification, as we found in our data, is often formulated in terms of free trade. The transnational orders are primarily developed due to the fact that the standards against which the certifications are conducted are international and hence transcend national borders. A product or an organization certified in Sweden is to be viable/marketable in another EU country or another country with which an agreement has been established. It is no coincidence that the slogan of the IAF is, "*Certified Once—Accepted Everywhere.*"

However, for the proper functioning of these international systems, agreements between countries are required as regards whether to approve monitoring conducted in other countries. These agreements are established in international organizations, the members of which include national control actors. Within the EU, the organization, EA, has grown stronger in recent years. One of the aims of the EA is to ensure that all of the national accreditation organizations in EU member states maintain the same quality level and an equal status in relation to each other. The EU regulation EC 765/2008 also imply that accreditation within the EU may not be commercial or competitive; that only one accreditation organization in each EU country is allowed; and that this organization needs to have the same status as a public authority or (as in the Swedish case) is to comprise a public authority. In other words, from an international perspective, we find that there are different logics for controls: certification is a commercial service whereas accreditation is not. In order for the system to be trustworthy, there should be an international consensus regarding the way in which the system of these monitoring activities is organized.

For example, and in accordance with this complex multistep logic, Swedish companies and their products are monitored through accreditation conducted by the national authority, Swedac. Swedac is, in turn,

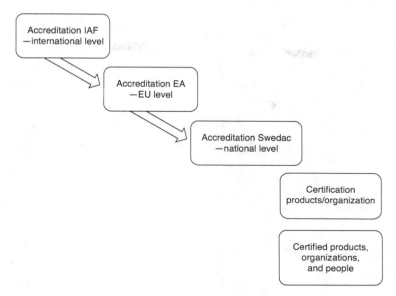

Figure 5.2 The control chain between products or operations.

approved by the EA, which is monitored at yet another level, interna-
tionally, through the IAF. We call these tendencies a type of *metafica-
tion* of monitoring and we argue that they are motivated by the attempt
to build trust. Paradoxically, the increased monitoring denotes mistrust
rather than trust. Why then is all this control necessary?

If we return to and develop figure 5.1 presented in the beginning, we
can now increase the number of links in the control chain and obtain
a wider view of this control system as in figure 5.2. Based on the idea
that commercially driven monitoring breeds more monitoring, similarly
to an expanding monitoring chain, this raises the question of where
this chain will end. Without a certain authoritative body, such as the
nation-state, special organizational prerequisites for the building of
trust emerge with a seemingly infinite need to create new monitoring
levels. These chains of monitoring result in a blurring of geographic,
organizational, and institutional boundaries that in itself illustrate the
complexity of the dilemmas created by conscious efforts at handling
problems of trust in contemporary markets. The geographic dimension
underlines the distance issue; both certification and accreditation are
argued for in terms of free trade or global relations, and one could say
that they constitute particular trust tools for organizations operating at
a distance from each other. The organizational dimension highlights

another kind of boundary crossing; the organizations involved in the monitoring chain are dependent on each other in an intricate manner. Certification is made on a business organization, accreditation is made on the certification organization, and "meta-accreditation" (made by the EA or IAF) is made on the accreditation body. The whole idea of monitoring through certification and accreditation crosses organizational borders, with one organization monitoring another in order to generate public confidence in the latter. Finally, the chains also blur institutional boundaries. We see how the public and private domains intertwine—certification was initially introduced as a private monitoring practice, the arguments being that public monitoring is too bureaucratic. But now we see that accreditation is gaining importance in securing trust for these systems; we may observe how the state is brought back in again. This makes the monitoring chain into a process where different institutional logics—the commercial and the public—meet and interact in the efforts to create and sustain public trust.

There are, of course, implications. These monitoring chains create an increased distance between the "end consumer," that is, the car owner or the consumer in a supermarket, and the monitoring activities performed to secure safety, health, or sustainability. Every link in the chain is one-step further away from the actual product or object of monitoring. A relevant question is of course: When does the distance become so great that trust in this complex monitoring system is itself put into danger? How much distance can trust accommodate?

Conclusions—Confidence or Mistrust?

At the beginning of this chapter, certification was framed as a tool for building trust on markets. Somewhat simplified, we described it as a three-way relationship—the consumer is to trust the products of the producer, and in order to strengthen trust in these products, the producer becomes certified. As argued in this chapter, it is not only about *one single* (product) market, but the certification services sold to the producer comprise a market too, a market that we refer to as a market for monitoring practices and that we have analyzed here as a market for trust. The fact that markets for monitoring are created is not surprising in itself; more and more areas of society are reorganized to follow market logic. However, what the monitoring market clearly exemplifies is that what is usually referred to as deregulation is often rather a matter of *reregulation* or, as our example of vehicle inspection shows, additional regulation (Ahrne and Brunsson 2004). In a similar manner, the certification market shows the limited extent to which market reforms actually deal with markets but, instead, rather with more organization. In this context, our analysis sheds light on an interesting phenomenon: a growing niche for organizations whose business idea is to build and sustain trust in other organizations. Interorganizational relations, and the crossing of organizational boundaries involved in them, here become an important site of confidence creation and/or manipulation.

In this chapter, we have put forward an argument that certification involves a paradox and that this paradox has generated the many layers of monitoring and the high degree of organization. The paradox consists of selling control as a commercial service, which aims at building trust in products and producers in other market exchanges. As we have shown, the commercial dilemma has been solved by adding more monitoring bodies monitoring each other so that the monitoring chain expands (cf. Shapiro 1987). Certification is to strengthen trust in products and services, and accreditation is to strengthen trust in certification. What we call meta-accreditation, which takes place through membership in various international organizations, forms further links in the chains. We have chosen to study these control chains as a cohesive system and have shown interest in the way in which this system is organized. However, this system of trust may just as well be studied as a system of mistrust (cf. Power 1994; Walgenbach 2001). If we choose to change the perspective, is it possible to question whether all of these organizations operate, in fact, on a market of mistrust? If we fully trusted each other, surely there would be no need for certification services. And if certification were not required, there would be no need for accreditation or meta-accreditation. As mistrust is built into the trust tool of certification, each attempt to build more trust also becomes a way of strengthening mistrust.

In this chapter, we have also sought to draw attention to the certification market; although the monitoring chains do indeed, grow, they do so without a greater societal debate. Certification appears to be politically unproblematic and is considered to compose a neutral and practical tool in an increasing number of areas. There seems to be no big scandals in the area of certification or accreditation (perhaps due to their "low key" nature), which means that we cannot explain the expanding monitoring chains as measures to reinstall trust after such scandals. Rather, the system of monitoring seems to be of a more preventative nature, and appears to be driven "from above." Through a number of interviews and by studying a large number of documents, we have gained the impression that this system is not driven by consumers in the end market but, instead, by the actors at other levels in the system.

Although referring to these orders as a system, we do not wish to claim that the order is completely stable. Representations of the system signal robustness and stability—that there is a coherent and unified system and that the system is organized in a well thought-out and self-evident manner. From our studies and the growing body of literature on transnational regulation referred to in this chapter, we find that there is not only *one* system for certification as a tool for trust. There are various alternative orders that in many ways resemble what we have described here in terms of commercial certification and monitoring chains. However, the systems also differ on certain key points, often because certain organizational solutions within an established system have been regarded, by some, as problematic, whereupon an alternative order, with somewhat different organizational solutions, has been established. For example, the certification system established for the FSC standard is also based on accredited commercial certification; however, accreditation is obligatory and it is not conducted by governmental actors but by a foundation wholly owned by FSC. Furthermore, FSC certification differs from other management system certifications by including more detailed requirements, some of which are performance based, as well as by including requirements on supplementing office audits with field visits. With this example, we wish to point out that there are alternative solutions—or competition, if one wishes to use that term—as regards certification as a trust tool. On the basis of our studies, we would argue that it is a dynamic world in which striving for trustworthiness on the certification market results in a continuous change in organization.

In this chapter, we have taken a first step in clarifying that certification is part of a greater "system" based on the principles of the monitoring of routines and written regulations. We have shown that there are various levels in these systems and various actors—private, civil society, and governmental—who contribute to forming and maintaining them. Moreover, we have argued that it is important to analyze each of them from an organizational perspective in order to enable an analysis of the actors involved and the significance of their institutional abode. We also note that there are several, competing systems and have pointed to the need for continued, comparative studies of the similarities and differences between the systems: for example, in terms of strategies employed by various actors in order to both stabilize and challenge the continued growth of these systems, which seem to be virtually unlimited, both geographically and in terms of the values and aspects appropriate for certification. For such studies, our discussion on the certification paradox proves a suitable point of departure.

Notes

1. For certain standards regarding the environment, sustainability, and fair working conditions, accreditation is also conducted by nongovernmental organizations (NGOs), as is the case for the certification made under standards such as FSC for sustainable forest management, the Marine Stewardship Council (MSC) for sustainable fisheries, and SA 8000 for fair working conditions. We do not, however, discuss this type of certification in the present chapter (see Tamm Hallström and Gustafsson 2013 for a discussion of the differences between accreditation forms).
2. As regards the management system certification, we would especially like to thank the Research Council Formas for financial support to one of the authors of this chapter within the framework of the project *Sökandet efter den 'goda' marknadsaktören* ("Searching for the 'Good' Market Actor") in 2009–2011, and as regards the organization behind the product labels, we would like to thank the Swedish Retail and Wholesale Development Council for financial support during 2012–2014 for the project *Kan vi lita på certifiering?* ("Can We Trust Certification?").
3. Accreditation is conducted only on *organizations*, which differs from certification, which can be conducted on organizations, as well as on products and individuals. The control of inspection technicians does not constitute accreditation but, instead, *certification of individuals*.

References

Abbott, Kenneth, and Duncan Snidal. 2009. "Strengthening International Regulation through Transnational New Governance: Overcoming the Orchestration Deficit." *Vanderbilt Journal of Transnational Law* 42:501–578.
Ahrne, Göran, and Nils Brunsson. 2011. "Regelexplosionen." In *Regelexplosionen*, edited by Göran Ahrne and Nils Brunsson. Stockholm: Ekonomiska Forskningsinstitutet (EFI) Stockholm School of Economics.
ANAB. 2012. ANSI-ASQ National Accreditation Board, http://www.anab.org/resources/fast-facts.aspx, accessed January 18, 2012.
Bartley, Tim. 2007. "Institutional Emergence in an Era of Globalization: The Rise of Transnational Private Regulation of Labor and Environmental Conditions." *American Journal of Sociology* 113 (2/September 2007): 297–351.
———. 2011. "Certification as a Mode of Social Regulation." In *Handbook on the Politics of Regulation*, edited by David Levi-Faur, 441–452. Cheltenham, UK; Northampton, MA: Edward Elgar.
Bartley, Tim, and Shawna Smith. 2010. "Communities of Practice as Cause and Consequence of Transnational Governance: The Evolution of Social and Environmental Certification." In *Transnational Communities. Shaping Global*

Economic Governance, edited by Marie-Laure Djelic and Sigrid Quack, 347–374. Cambridge, UK: Cambridge University Press.

Bernstein, Steven, and Benjamin Cashore. 2007. "Can Non-state Global Governance Be Legitimate? An Analytical Framework." *Regulation & Governance* 1:1–25.

Brunsson, Nils, and Bengt Jacobsson. 2000. *A World of Standards*. Oxford, UK: Oxford University Press.

Courville, Sasha. 2003. "Social Accountability Audits: Challenging or Defending Democratic Governance?" *Law & Policy* 25 (3): 269–297.

Djelic, Marie-Laure, and Kerstin Sahlin-Andersson. Eds. 2006. *Transnational Governance. Institutional Dynamics of Regulation*. Cambridge, UK: Cambridge University Press.

Elad, Charles. 2001. "Auditing and Governance in the Forestry Industry, between Protest and Professionalism." *Critical Perspectives on Accounting* 12:647–671.

Harbaugh, Rick, John Maxwell, and Beatrice Roussillon. 2011. "Label Confusion: The Groucho Effect of Uncertain Standards." *Management Science* 57 (9/September 2011): 1512–1527.

Haufler, Virginia. 2001. *A Public Role for the Private Sector: Industry Self-Regulation in a Global Economy*. Washington, DC: Carnegie Endowment for International Peace.

Jeppesen, Kim Klarskov. 1998. "Reinventing Auditing, Redefining Consulting and Independence." *The European Accounting Review* 7 (3): 517–539.

Lindeberg, Tobias. 2007. *Evaluative Technologies: Quality and the Multiplicity of Performance*. Copenhagen Business School. PhD Series 7.

Marx, Alex. 2011. "Global Governance and the Certification Revolution: Types, Trends and Challenges." In *Handbook on the Politics of Regulation*, edited by David Levi-Faur, 590–603. Cheltenham, UK; Northampton, MA: Edward Elgar.

McNichol, Jason. 2006. "Transnational NGO Certification Programs as New Regulatory Forms: Lessons from the Forestry Sector." In *Transnational Governance. Institutional Dynamics of Regulation*, edited by Marie-Laure Djelic and Kerstin Sahlin-Andersson, 349–374. Cambridge, UK: Cambridge University Press.

Powell, Walter W., and Paul J. DiMaggio. Eds. 1991. *The New Institutionalism in Organisational Analysis*. Chicago: University of Chicago Press.

Power, Michael. 1994. *The Audit Explosion*. London: Demos.

———. 2003. "Auditing and the Production of Legitimacy." *Accounting, Organisations and Society* 28 (4): 379–394.

Regulation (EC) No. 765/2008 of the European Parliament and of the Council.

Reinecke, Juliane, Stephan Manning, and Oliver von Hagen. 2012. "The Emergence of a Standards Market: Multiplicity of Sustainability Standards in the Global Coffee Industry." *Organisation Studies* 33 (May–June): 791–814.

Rose, Nikolas, and Peter Miller. 1992. "Political Power beyond the State: Problematics of Government." *British Journal of Sociology* 43 (2/June 1992): 172–205.

Shapiro, Susan. 1987. "The Social Control of Impersonal Trust." *American Journal of Sociology* 93 (3): 623–658.

SOU. 2006. *Öppna system för provning och kontroll*, SOU 2006:113, Statens offentliga utredningar, Stockholm: Fritzes.

Tamm Hallström, Kristina. 2004. *Organizing International Standardization: ISO and the IASC in Quest of Authority*. Cheltenham: Edward Elgar.

Tamm Hallström, Kristina, and Ingrid Gustafsson. 2013. "Neutralizing Markets— Legitimacy in the Making." In *Organizing Values and Value Conflicts in Markets* (preliminary title), edited by Tamm Hallström K. and S. Alexius. Cheltenham, UK; Northampton, MA: Edward Elgar.

Tamm Hallström, Kristina, and Magnus Boström. 2010. *Transnational Multi-Stakeholder Standardization: Organizing Fragile Non-State Authority*. Cheltenham, UK; Northampton, MA: Edward Elgar.

Turcotte, Marie-France, Stéphane de Bellefeuille, and Frank den Hond. 2007. "Gildan Inc: Influencing Corporate Governance in the Textile Sector." *Journal of Corporate Citizenship* 27 (Autumn 2007): 23–36. ABI/INFORM Global.

Walgenbach, Peter. 2001. "The Production of Distrust by Means of Producing Trust." *Organization Studies* 22 (4): 693–714.

Wallerstedt, Eva. 2009. *Revisorsbranschen i Sverige under hundra år*. Stockholm: SNS Förlag.

Willmott, Hugh, and Prem Sikka. 1995. "The Power of 'Independence': Defending and Extending the Jurisdiction of Accounting in the United Kingdom." *Accounting, Organisation and Society* 20: 547–581.

CHAPTER 6

The Triumph of Feelings: On the Power of Imagery in Business

Lars Strannegård

The Trust Dimension of Image

In recent years, images, brands, opinions, and attitudes have attracted an increasing amount of attention, both from representatives of organizations and from individuals. And as a result of this shift, researchers in business administration have begun to take an interest in matters concerning trust, images, and reputation. Searches for terms, such as "branding," "employer branding," "trust," "performance," and "reputation," produce a hugely larger number of hits in academic databases today, than even just a few years ago.

All of these terms refer to the same issues, that is, visibility, credibility, trust, and confidence. Among the great number of attempts to define "a brand," one of the most quoted is "a brand is a promise." In other words, a brand is closely associated with credibility, and reputation is a guarantee that whatever is promised, will, actually, be delivered.

This chapter takes as its point of departure the observation that while our societies are becoming increasingly preoccupied by the task of controlling, monitoring, and measuring performance as a way to build, safeguard, and manage reputation, simple production of numbers and figures (e.g., in form of rankings) does not seem to be enough to reach that end. Instead, the mass media have come to play an increasingly ubiquitous role as the key discursive intermediary between organizations and the general public, with power to "translate" such figures into stories and images that have direct impact on how an organization is perceived by the outside world. By possessing this power, the media increasingly influence the ways in which organizations act and activities are organized, acquiring a constitutive role in the organization of society.

In this chapter, I reflect upon the role played by the media in generating, transmitting, and shaping credibility, reputation, and the public image of societal actors, particularly companies. In particular, I want to draw attention to the ways in which the media logic increasingly permeates other institutional spheres, turning the media's creation of reputations and images—and thus production of trust—into an act of institutional border crossing.

In the immediately following section, I will attempt to demonstrate the manner in which rumors and reputation have assumed a key role in nearly every organized activity in society, and address the fact that the search for transparency has become more intense in society in general. In the wake of this search, various forms of monitoring systems have been developed. The subsequent sections address the media and its increasing influence and, more specifically, the increase of such influence on organizations and corporate activities and the way in which this has led to credibility, reputations, and rumors being shaped and determined in the open, public arena. The closing section addresses the increased importance of appearance, and the way in which organizations, people, and activities are perceived.

Increased Monitoring

Trust, credibility, and confidence are concepts that have spread very widely, indeed, in recent years. In historical terms, this may seem a bit odd as the modernity of the twentieth century can, in many instances, be described as the battle of knowledge against preconceptions. With the growth of industrialization, when factories began churning out products and the distribution network became more integrated and refined, the concept of scientifically based optimization took hold. Max Weber's ideas of ideal bureaucracies were a part of the spirit of that time: positions of power and power structures were to be allocated and established on the basis of competence and clearly defined rules. This was the era that saw the birth of modern business administration. Even though earlier philosophers had had an influence on the subject, Frederic Taylor's book, *Principles of Scientific Management*, published in 1911, can be regarded as the birth of the subject of business administration. This book included concepts, organized into a system, on how best to undertake industrial production in a scientific manner. The key was to search for the most efficient production methods, and the underlying theoretical models were based on ideas of mass production and cost control. The title of Taylor's book describes, literally, the ambition that this scientific approach would sweep away the previous arbitrary and non-systematic approaches. Management would become a science. Tradition and superstition were to be replaced by knowledge.

In modern times, with its base in the scientific approach, large systems were to be established with the help of systematic and rational decision-making processes, and well-oiled bureaucracies were to take care of administration in an optimal manner. Doing things arbitrarily and on a small scale, nepotism and vagueness were to be replaced by classification, professionalism, and clarity. Premodern selection methods, such as rumors and reputation, would be consigned to the scrap heap of history.

Some hundred years later, however, this is not the case. It is true, bureaucracies, systems, and a belief in common sense and rational decision-making processes are alive and well. However, at the same time, arbitrary, personal experiences and emotions have hardly been discarded in the modern, ideal world. Today, the power of rumors and reputation is definitively not obsolete.

A depiction with which many researchers of social sciences agree is that there is, today, an increased degree of lack of trust in Western society. Who is credible and who can be counted upon is something, which is far from being obvious. This state of affairs is sometimes referred to as post- or late modernism. In the twentieth century, systems and bureaucracies were created with the role of ensuring that loopholes, coincidences, nepotism, and the lack of continuity would be eliminated. Confidence in rational decision-making processes was great and systems were established so that everyone would be treated equally. Institutions, such as the Swedish National Board of Health and Welfare (*Socialstyrelsen*), the medical profession, and the universities enjoyed major legitimacy and a high degree of credibility.

In recent decades, increasing numbers of people have experienced that these systems appear to be eroding and, therefore, their faith in these institutions has also weakened. Authorities and experts who before enjoyed a large degree of legitimacy have lost a great deal of their former glory. In Sweden, physicians are monitored to a greater degree than was previously the case, teachers experience that their status has declined, and the state's capacity for maneuver has decreased as privatization and deregulation has increased.

Recent years have seen both private industry and the public sector swamped with initiatives, which, in various ways, aim to compare and control the way in which different operations are managed. In the corporate world, prizes, such as "Swedish Quality," are awarded, and organizations, such as Global Reporting Initiative, work with conferences, reports, and awards in order to ensure that companies become more transparent. Greenpeace and SwedWatch scrutinize companies' environmental and ethical responsibilities and alert the media if they find any irregularities. Commissioners specialized in trust issues are appointed, universities are accredited, the WHO publishes rankings over various countries' health care systems, cultural projects are appraised, and new means of enforcing the assumption of responsibility are tested. In other words, there is a striving toward increased transparency in society, in general. The objective is to make it easier for various types of stakeholders to control and obtain an insight into operations.

When the demand for transparency increases, reputation is seen as a valuable resource. Almost all organizations, regardless of their form of ownership, are currently investing in their departments working with the management of their reputations. Companies employ "branding experts" and are expanding their information departments. Business schools have personnel whose main task is to work with ranking issues. Today, public authorities and agencies have communication experts and managers to a far greater degree than was previously the case. The Swedish Institute works intensively with *nation branding* in a type of world championship to attract attention, respect, and trust, which the institute apparently believes is taking place. Hospitals work with "strategic communication" and universities have begun to employ bibliometrics experts in order to be better at describing their operations in a more positive light. And, at the same time that organizations invest more and more resources in reputation management, the number of public relations (PR) and communication consultants incorporating image management of both organizations and individuals in their service offerings, only increases.

Figures as Images

How does this increased focus on reputation relate to the increased requirements for quantitative-based information? To put it simply, one could claim that reputation could be said to be soft and numbers hard. The reputation of an organization can be managed, negotiated, and changed, while a ranking of seven in a survey can be experienced as comprising a nonnegotiable "fact." A ranking, expressed in numerical terms, is factual and cannot be altered until the next version of that particular ranking is produced and presented. For example, in attempting to describe a certain university's ability to get its research known and appreciated, the emphasis is put on expressing presumed success in numerical terms: "The researchers at our university have produced a larger number of publications than those (researchers) working at the university located at the other end of the country." Rankings, figures, and other quantifiable data appear to be objective, clear, and universally describable.

The purpose of the increased importance assigned to figures, objectivity, and measurability is the creation of reliable and nonnegotiable descriptions and comparisons. The objective is that figures should speak for themselves. A seventh rank is better than an eleventh. But if figures actually spoke for themselves, there would be no need to employ marketing experts, communication managers, or ranking specialists. This suggests that figures do not, in fact, speak for themselves. They need allies—professional communicators who control and channel them and who put them into context. Herein lies the magical rope trick of reputation: figures and measurability are neither objective nor independent, and definitely do not speak for themselves. Figures have been transformed into images. Consequently, in spite of being "hard," they are a part of the entity's image creating reputation. Figures are the base on which communication managers create images. Reputation is, in other words, a result of the production of images, and this is obvious when one places reputation and confidence in the light of what political scientists, media, and communication experts call mediatization.

A Mediatized World of Images

The term "mediatization" has been used during many years to characterize the change processes in the political agenda. A generally accepted definition is that expressed by Strömbäck (2004), that is, that mediatization is at hand when events and processes are adapted to the logic and practices of mass media. A major issue on which researchers within political and communication studies have focused is the role media plays in shaping the political agenda (Asp 1986). This issue can be summarized as the media's power over political content and its power over the public. Media comprises not only a powerful player by actualizing certain issues, but also functions as an arena within which the interests and desires of other parties can influence the political agenda.

During recent years, mediatization has shown to be an epithet, which is applicable far outside the political sphere. Today, almost all aspects of our lives are impacted by the media's constant presence. Descriptions of the economy, cultural life, or sport are difficult to imagine, at all, without the media's continual monitoring and reporting. Mediatization impacts the manner in which various bodies in society function, as these entities are forced to take into consideration generally accepted beliefs regarding the media's working methods, the so-called media logic (Altheide and Snow 1979). This media logic can be described as a type of a translation chain in which one, in order to get peoples' attention, first needs to capture the attention of the media representatives. In turn, in order to do this, there is a requirement that the communication is presented in accordance with the logic applied by the media. A formulation from Petrelius Karlberg (2007, 19) states, "In other words, the media adapts the world to its logic and the world adapts itself to the media logic."

As different players in society act according to media logic, their operations also change, as does the manner in which they can be described and understood. When media becomes a central means of communication, then, such activities as political labor negotiations or organizations' internal communication become the subject of public transparency. This leads to consultants and interest groups increasingly participating in the interpretation and formulation of social reality. If we consider these effects, mediatization comes to represent a constituting activity, which—similar to other institutions, such as politics and religion—impacts the manner in which society, its players, and their interests are organized and depicted. In this manner, the discussion about mediatization also shifts from focusing on its impact on other societal institutions to it being considered to, itself, comprise an institution. Mediatization is, consequently, not only a process leading to a number of societal changes but is also, itself, a form of societal change.

Stig Hjarvard (2008, 113) summarizes this double nature of mediatization (*mediatiseringen*) in the following manner:

> By the mediatization of society, we understand the process whereby society to an increasing degree is submitted to, or becomes dependent on, the media and their logic. This process is characterized by a duality in that the media have become integrated into the operations of other social institutions, while they also have acquired the status of social institutions in their own right.

If mediatization is seen as an autonomous institution, a number of features impacting societal development appear. Included in these are the media's impact on the transfer of information and knowledge between players, the creation and diffusion of societal norms and regulations, and the communication activities that are increasingly packaged and turned into products. Mass media products are ever more important to the creation of symbolic and economic value, both for specific individuals and for countries, companies, and other organizations.

Mats Furberg (1997, 169) emphasizes the media's role as an active interpreter and depicter of reality. In turn, the media's interpretations are used by the public, to produce their own images and, thereby, a sort of chain of constructions and translations is created. Furberg's depiction is not dissimilar to the processes that Lars Engwall and Kerstin Sahlin (2007) assign to media when they talk about "edited companies." Engwall and Sahlin describe how the media comprises the basis for the manner in which knowledge and images of business operations and individual organizations are created and disseminated. They point out that it is the media's combined impact that creates the premises for how social reality is to be presented and understood. Furthermore, they show that mediatization is not a one-way process but, rather, a multidimensional exchange in which different interests meet and are transformed in an ongoing, dynamic process. In the corporate economic context, one can discern four perspectives forming the basis on which the media's input in actual, work-related terms can be described, that is, determination of the agenda, legitimizing of the companies' activities and their structures, image, and brand creation, and creation and dissemination of knowledge (Engwall and Sahlin 2007). All of these perspectives not only have direct implications for companies and their activities—for example, when a company establishes special units whose function is to present "positive" images of the operations, or when a company is forced by the media to undertake real changes in how their activities are organized and operated. But, these perspectives are also central to the construction of the social environments in which these activities are organized and assigned meaning.

Mediatized Business Operations

That business operations are mediatized is seen in the increased monitoring of their activities, and is also reflected in how companies are organized. Companies have developed specialized departments for handling media contacts (Engwall 2010; Grünberg and Pallas 2009. Through the development of a market for company information, the relationships between companies and the media have also been assigned new prerequisites. Popular news monitoring with a person-focused reporting leads to the company being individualized and to the media, as well as the companies, tending to use company management members as tools to explain and understand its actions and development (Petrelius Karlberg 2007). The media's increased influence can also impact a company's long-term survival and can stretch to other companies and other industries. An example is how the media's reporting of scandals regarding a certain insurance company not only impacted the company, but also other life insurance and pension companies, and even companies undertaking entirely different operations (Jonsson, Greve, and Fujiwara-Greve 2007).

That the media has become increasingly important is also seen in the fact that a greater and greater space is occupied by the media: business and economic journalism started to expand during the end of the last century (Hadenius and Weibull 1999). Between 1976 and 1990, the space taken by economic news in Swedish morning newspapers doubled (Hvitfelt and Malmström 1990) and, soon, every morning newspaper, with any self-respect, monitored the business world, as well as events pertaining to business. During the 1980s, public service Swedish Television (SvT) began to report share prices and, after 2000, economic news programs, both on TV and in the radio, increased their broadcasting time (Lindqvist 2001; Petrelius Karlberg 2007). In other words, one cannot underestimate the manner in which business and economic news has, during recent decades, become a part of the media landscape. Depictions of corporate activities failing to take into consideration the predominant importance of media are seen, therefore, to be inherently deficient. Nonetheless, the description of corporate activities as being dominated by the media is not, of course, in itself, anything new or original. Renowned theoreticians, such as Giddens (1984), Baudrillard (1994), and Bourdieu (1998), have all described how we as citizens and consumers experience and handle a mediatized reality, that is, a reality that is mediated via various forms of mass media. Mass media is entirely central to the manner in which knowledge is produced, which media theoreticians, such as Mcluhan (1964), purported already at least 50 years ago.

Against such a background, one can argue that the media's reporting on companies and company management is central to the manner in which people create images of and understand organizations and the activities of businesses. Within new institutional theory, organizations are seen in relation to rules, norms, and beliefs, which are developed and diffused by other organizations within the organizational field (DiMaggio and Powell 1983). A mediatized understanding of business operations is not created only outside the organizations and companies, but also from within. The media are, from a new institutional point of view, inasmuch bearers of norms and beliefs as regards what a business leader is and should do (Engwall and Sahlin 2007). Leading a company can, in this context, be seen as a process in which a large number of interested parties—such as communication experts, media-consuming corporate management, and the reporting media—jointly create the image of the business and of its management.

Accordingly, the images of business activities can be considered to be institutionally formed. Images of business operations and company management are mediatized and created within organizational fields. One example of institutional design in mediatized business life is the communications consulting industry, which has expanded notably. Many players in this industry have previous experience of opinion building, journalism, or media economics (Tyllström 2010). The informal network stretching over the formal, organizational boundaries is central to success in the industry and there are indications that the industry is experiencing an increased scrutiny and increasing requirement of transparency. It is, therefore, probable that there is an institutional format exerting normative pressure toward professionalization (DiMaggio and Powell 1983; Abbott 1988).

Pallas (2007) has shown that companies and media have developed a working method incorporating rules and norms as regards the manner in which they are to treat each other and interact. Companies and media have absorbed each other's working methods, routines, and valuations and preferences when it comes to what is to be published, in which form, and when. This common working method, which has developed, determines the manner in which companies and the media are to work together and how the final reporting is to be formulated. For the media's part, this implies that they can adapt the form of monitoring of important and sensitive issues, such as financial information or the companies' involvement in society. Here, close and personal relationships between the companies' communicators and the primary media play an important role in terms of how the news is to be interpreted and formulated. The companies' media activities are not focused only on the handling of various interests, that is, the companies' and media's different understandings of given events or issues. These activities are also characterized by a close and well-organized cooperation and are focused on the continual production of news, rather than the content of specific news.

Obviously, the companies and media are not differentiated but rather extraordinarily integrated in terms of working methods and the preparation of the daily agenda. The definitions of media, such as "the third state power," with an obvious role as an investigative function, can, therefore, be questioned. This definition can be further questioned, as mass media is, itself, most often a product produced within a corporate form (Czarniawska 2009). Media are not only "media," but also corporations exposed to all of the requirements, which other corporations must meet. Increasing and decreasing editions, viewers, and readers who cancel their subscriptions or take on new ones, personnel costs, and advertisement revenues—all of these are the components that, in the end, determine the profitability of a media company and its sustainability. The fact that media companies are, just that, companies, is obvious but, still, this has been neglected in studies regarding mediatization.

As mentioned above, political scientists and communication researchers have been interested in how mediatization impacts democratic processes and policy performance (Asp 1986; Strömbäck 2004). However, leaders of organizations must, just as politicians, create a level of confidence reaching far beyond the organization, which they, themselves, represent, something that interested party models and stakeholder theories have taken into consideration (for an overview, see Freeman 1984).

Mediatization of business operations can be said to imply that a company is in constant need of building confidence (Fredriksson 2008). Organizations have to win legitimacy in a variety of areas and mass media is one of the most important ones, as they are *mediating*, that is, they function as bearers of messages between various spheres and create attention regarding the company's operations and projects. This attention is not only something that can potentially create major advantages for the companies, but is also something that can cause them major damage. The increasing offering of media training programs is evidence of this (Petrelius Karlberg 2007). The term "management of visibility," which Thompson (1995) applied, indicates that mediatization has impacted how company management is undertaken and how activities are organized.

Mediatization and Reputation

Against this background, one could say that mediatization drives developments toward an increased importance of reputation. One could also say that reputation and confidence go hand in hand in the postmodern era. To have confidence in someone or something implies a belief in, or reliance on, that person or entity being capable of acting in a desired manner, and that they will also, actually, do so. To have confidence in someone implies having trust in him or her. And confidence becomes, in the mediatized society, a result of the reputation someone or something enjoys.

Visibility, image creation, and confidence have, in other words, come to fore as an entirely central phenomenon in current-day business activities. As a result of this development, issues regarding credibility have increased in importance. Michael Power (2007) of the London School of Economics has, during a long period of time, been interested in the reactions resulting from this striving after credibility, and in his book *Organized Uncertainty: Designing a World of Risk Management*, he addresses how reputation has become an increasingly topical issue for leaders. One of his points is that the so-called *risk management* tools that many organizations apply are deficient in handling reputation issues. Risks can be estimated and calculated but uncertainties cannot be quantified to the same degree. Reputation is uncertain by its nature. Power's major point is that reputation is becoming an organization's most important resource and that the handling of reputation is, then, the major duty of managers and leaders. A director's legitimacy and attractiveness is based on an aura of decision-making power and management characteristics. But neither an organization, nor an individual, can estimate the reputation risks to which they are subject. They have, in practice, limited control over the type of rumors that may be spread, or which "truths" are "made up." Nor do they have any idea as to where a reputation attack may have originated.

The frightening aspect in this development toward the importance of reputation has been pointed out by the legal researcher, Daniel Solove (2007), in his book *The Future of Reputation: Gossip, Rumour and Privacy on the Internet*. When typical social practices, such as gossip and guilt assignment, come out on the Internet, a snowball is set rolling downhill. Information that was previously very dispersed and not widely known, local, and undocumented is now, through blogs, digital commentary possibilities, and web forums, publicly available, easily accessible, permanent, and searchable. An opinion, a personal judgment, or a straightforward lie can flourish on the net and quickly grow in scope and "truthfulness." The negative side of this free flow of information, which by many parties is raised to the level of a virtue, is, in other words, that this flow can also undermine our possibility—now and in the future—of being experienced as credible.

Researchers within sociology, psychology, and marketing have, in various ways, shown that people are triggered by their emotions to a greater degree than what many sociological theorists have traditionally recognized and assumed (Frykman and Löfgren 2005). We purchase products and services from companies we rely upon, we work in organizations whose basic values we respect, and we recommend to others those products about which we, ourselves, are positive. The reputation of an organization or an individual is composed of attitudes, opinions, and feelings, and when these are to be controlled, brand makers and PR consultants give vent to new business opportunities. If people were less responsive to their emotions, the majority of the advertising agencies would have to close down and the majority of the PR consultants would have to look for jobs in other industries. But in the world described by authors such as Solove and Power, "emotive production" is central; associations, experiences, and relationships must be continually charged, and charged positively.

More and more actors are engaged in reputation building; at the same time, reputation attacks have become more common. Current conditions are, in other words, characterized by the creation of images and contraimages evoking the sought-after feelings and reactions. Power and Solove point directly at the rumor-dominated current state of affairs, but reputation issues will, with great probability, take more and more place in public debate. Communication consultants, directors, brand builders, artists, researchers, opinion makers, journalists, and media-consuming "grass rooters"—everyone is drawn into the reputation carousel, sometimes on the basis of unclear principals or anonymous financiers, but often with very obvious winners and losers.

This is to say that reputation in the content of a more open and broader flow of information has become such an important resource that the handling of media is on the daily agenda of decision makers. The collapse of respect for authority, and an increasing demand for transparency and visibility, has led to the images of organizations and individuals being entirely too important a feature of their existence to be handled in an arbitrary and unsystematic manner.

A Future Fixated on Appearance

The discussion in this chapter has so far focused primarily on the importance of reputation for (corporate) organizations, and thus the growing power of mass media over them. However, the trend toward the growing preoccupation with reputation and image is also something that to a very high extent affects individuals. I would like to illustrate this aspect with a short anecdote.

Some time ago, after finishing a lecture, a 20-year-old management student came forward and asked me for advice. The question concerned his forthcoming year at university and he faced three, according to him, equally viable, alternatives. The first was to continue his studies in Sweden in economics with a specialization in finance, at double pace. The second was to go abroad in order to improve his language skills. And the third was to spend the entire forthcoming winter season in the Alps. His justification for the third alternative was that skiing was the thing he loved the most in the entire world, and that it could be good for him in the future to show prospective employers that he was interested in more than just work. Which of these alternatives did I think *would look like the best alternative to have been chosen*? I was speechless. In the end, I managed to say that it was a difficult question for me to answer, that I believed he should do what he really want to do, and that he had to make his own decisions. Somewhat brusquely, and clearly dissatisfied with what was presumably experienced as a lack of precision in my response, he nodded his thanks and left.

This young student obviously took his curriculum vitae (CV) very seriously. It would appear that he was allowing his choices to be determined by the image they would produce in the future. It was not, necessarily, what he was actually most interested in or what would provide him with the knowledge to make a career that was most important; instead, he was more concerned with what would *look best*.

A 20-year-old management student works with his self-image in order to ensure that his future develops as he wants it to. He creates this through his CV, but he is not the only image maker creating his image. He can be seen in social media, such as Facebook, LinkedIn, or Twitter, in blogs, photo sites, or in articles. A Google search can result in a very varying image of a given individual within the space of one minute. Neither are the images of him created on the Internet, perhaps, exactly what he wants to see. He has the possibility of trying, with the help of information technology, to ensure that any negative aspects are less likely to appear in a search, while the more attractive images are prioritized. In this way, images are created and reconstructed constantly in the new media landscape, and reputation, credibility, rumors, appearances/perceptions, and presentation are only more and more important.

Perhaps one could object to the claim that society is moving toward a superficial phase in which image and appearance are more important than content. Already in the 1800s, Oscar Wilde responded to people's bitter complaints about superficiality by stating that it is only superficial people who do *not* judge on the basis of appearance. In other words, an interest in how people behave and what is seen as being positive, results in our entire society *looking as if* it is more obsessed with appearances. One can be abhorred, but one can also, as Oscar Wilde, argue

that the world's mysteries are found in, just that, the visible, and not in
the invisible.

References

Abbott, Andrew. 1988. *The System of Professions: An Essay on the Division of Expert Labor*. Chicago: University of Chicago Press.

Altheide, David, and Robert Snow. 1979. *Media Logic*. Beverly Hills, CA: Sage.

Asp, Kent. 1986. *Mäktiga massmedier: Studier i politisk opinionsbildning*. Stockholm: Akademilitteratur.

Baudrillard, Jean. 1994. *Simulacra and Simulation*. Ann Arbor, MI: University of Michigan Press.

Bourdieu, Pierre. 1998. *Om televisionen: följd av journalistikens herravälde*. Stockholm: Brutus Östlings Symposium.

Czarniawska, Barbara. 2009. *Den Tysta Fabriken: Om Tillverkning av Nyheter på TT*. Stockholm: Liber.

DiMaggio, Paul J., and Walter W. Powell. 1983. "The Iron Cage Revisited: Institutional Isomorphism and Collective Rationality in Organization Fields." *American Sociological Review* 48 (2): 147–160.

Engwall, Lars. 2010. "Perspektiv på mediafältet." In *Företag och medier*, edited by Josef Pallas and Lars Strannegård, 284–297. Malmö: Liber.

Engwall, Lars, and Kerstin Sahlin. 2007. "Corporate Governance and the Media: From Agency Theory to Edited Corporations." In *Mediating Business: The Expansion of Business Journalism in the Nordic Countries*, edited by Peter Kjaer and Tore Slaatta, 265–284. Copenhagen: CBS Press.

Fredriksson, Magnus. 2008. *Företags ansvar—marknadens retorik: En analys av företags strategiska kommunikationsarbete*. Gothenburg: JMG, Department of Journalism, Media and Communication, University of Gothenburg.

Freeman, R. Edward. 1984. *Strategic Management: A Stakeholder Approach*. London: Pitman.

Frykman, Jonas, and Orvar Löfgren. 2005. "Kultur och känsla." *Sosiologi i dag* 35 (1): 7–34.

Furberg, Mats. 1997. "Medialiseringar." In *Medialiseringen av Sverige*, edited by Anders Björnsson and Peter Luthersson, 39–59. Stockholm: Carlssons förlag.

Giddens, Anthony. 1984. *The Construction of Society: Outline and Theory of Structuration*. Cambridge, UK: Polity Press.

Grünberg, Jaan, and Josef Pallas. 2009. "Barbarians at the Gates? Organizations Protecting Their (Non)technical Cores through Institutional Boundary Spanning." In *Exploring the Worlds of Mercury and Minerva: Essays for Lars Engwall*, edited by Linda Wedlin, Kerstin Sahlin, and Maria Grafström. Acta Universitatis Upsaliensis, Studia Oeconomiae Negotiorum 51. Uppsala: Uppsala University Press.

Hadenius, Stig, and Lennart Weibull. 1999. "The Swedish Newspaper System in the Late 1990s." *Nordicom Review*, no. 1, 129–152.

Hjarvard, Stig. 2008. "The Mediatization of Society: A Theory of the Media as Agents of Social and Cultural Change." *Nordicom review* 29 (2): 105–134.

Hvitfelt, Håkan, and Torsten Malmström. 1990. *Ekonomi och arbetsmarknad. Journalistik i förändring.* Stockholm: Svensk Informations Mediecenter.

Jonsson, Stefan, Henrich Greve, and Takako Fujiwara-Greve. 2007. "Lost without Deserving: On the Scope and Dynamics of Reputation Loss in Response to Press Reports." Unpublished Working Paper.

Lindqvist, Mats. 2001. *Is i magen: Om ekonomins kolonisering av vardagen.* Stockholm: Natur & Kultur.

McLuhan, Marshall. 1964. *Understanding Media: The Extensions of Man.* New York: McGraw-Hill.

Pallas, Josef. 2007. *Talking Organizations: Corporate Media Work and Negotiation of Institutions.* Uppsala: Department of Business Studies, Uppsala University.

Petrelius Karlberg, Pernilla. 2007. *Den medialiserade direktören.* Stockholm: EFI, Stockholm School of Economics.

Power, Michael. 2007. *Organized Uncertainty: Designing a World of Risk Management.* Oxford, UK: Oxford University Press.

Solove, J. Daniel. 2007. *The Future of Reputation: Gossip, Rumor, and Privacy on the Internet.* Yale: Yale University Press.

Strömbäck, Jesper. 2004. *Den medialiserade demokratin. Om journalistikens ideal, verklighet och makt.* Stockholm: SNS Förlag.

Thompson, John. 1995. *The Media and Modernity: A Social Theory of the Media.* Stanford, CA: Stanford University Press.

Tyllström, Anna. 2010. "PR-konsultbranschens framväxt i Sverige." In *Företag och medier,* edited by Josef Pallas and Lars Strannegård, 169–191. Malmö: Liber.

CHAPTER 7

The Creation of a Crisis of Confidence: A Study of the Mediatization of the Red Cross

Pernilla Petrelius Karlberg, Maria Grafström, and Karolina Windell

A Crisis in the Swedish Red Cross

A shadow is falling over the leadership of the Red Cross. (*Dagens Industri*, January 22, 2010)

The situation is rotten in the Red Cross. (*ETC*, January 22, 2010)

Deep crisis of confidence in the Red Cross. (*Expressen*, February 6, 2010)

Thousands of members leave the Red Cross. (*Aftonbladet*, May 27, 2010)

These were some of the Swedish newspaper headlines on articles concerning the Swedish Red Cross and its crisis in the spring of 2010. Breathless headers followed hot on each other's heels as the organization and its representatives were criticized in a sea of news articles, letters to editors, and editorials. In the media, the loss of confidence in the Red Cross, and especially in the chairman of its board, Bengt Westerberg, was discussed heatedly. Within the Red Cross itself, however, these reports were perceived as being unfair. The Red Cross believed that its organization was open, fair, and democratic. While the media maintained that the Red Cross was suffering from a crisis of confidence, the employees in the organization could neither understand how such a crisis could arise, nor why the media attention was so drawn out and persistent.

Media consumers are faced with the kind of sensational headlines described above on a daily basis. The headlines either praise or condemn organizations and their leaders. The media creates heroes and villains, and the rights and wrongs of their actions are discussed and debated by journalists. Reporting in the media, consequently, plays a central role in both establishing and destroying confidence in organizations.

The actual definition of confidence and of actions that increase confidence levels depends on the social context or logic dominating the organization in question. From an institutional perspective, an organization's practices must always be understood in contextual terms. Institutional logics offer a way of understanding how the behavior of individuals is regulated and guided (Friedland and Alford 1991). This can be regarded as comprising a system of interpretations, regulations, and institutionalized norms and notions founded in reference to a specific practice (Thornton and Ocasio 1999). We will demonstrate that the logic that currently dominates media reporting differs from the logic prevailing within the Red Cross. We will also shed light upon the manner in which these different types of logic affect the notion of how confidence should be built up.

Thus, the question is whether these various notions of confidence-building actions impact each other and, if so, how? Research shows that the media's account of events, organizations, and people does impact the manner in which the public forms its own perception of reality (McCombs 2004). In other words, it is known that the manner in which news reports are formulated in the media affects the manner in which the public views the subject of the reports, as well as affecting the public's confidence in institutions and those in power in society. However, we are less well informed about the way an organization's perception of its own behavior is impacted by the media circus. Do its views on what is legitimate and desirable, right or wrong, and the way in which confidence is built change?

This chapter deals with how a crisis of confidence can arise in an organization during a period of negative publicity and whether the media impacts organizations' approaches to what is considered to comprise legitimate action. This chapter analyzes various ways of interpreting the confidence-building activities represented by the different actors, and the way in which they relate to each other.

A Study of the Red Cross—Method and Choice of Empirical Data

In this section, the Swedish Red Cross is examined, from both an external and internal perspective, in relation to the spring of 2010, when the organization was exposed to negative publicity in the media. Media reporting is analyzed by regarding the media as a type of external party imposing requirements on the Red Cross organization. We also analyze the manner in which the organization managed the negative attention from the media. In doing so, we illustrate how different logics compete in building and establishing confidence.

The choice of the Red Cross can be attributed to the fact that the organization has experienced extensive, negative media exposure and because it operates in a very distinct environment, which has been termed the "confidence industry." The organization is wholly dependent on inspiring confidence in order to be able to conduct its operations, raise funds, and attract and retain members. In addition, the Red Cross is heavily characterized by the nonprofit organization's distinction type of logic, as well as its special character (Wijkström and af Malmborg 2005). It is also included in the category of organizations that, in historical terms, have not necessarily been subject to examination and reporting in the media, and that are, consequently, not accustomed to close media scrutiny.

The empirical narrative presented in this chapter is based on observations and interviews with managers and officials within the Swedish Red Cross during the period January to October 2010 (Petrelius Karlberg 2011) and on a content analysis of articles (a total of 65) on the subjects of the Red Cross and Bengt Westerberg's fees during the same period. Observations and interviews were limited to the headquarters of the Swedish Red Cross. This study does not include members or volunteers at the Red Cross. The empirical data also includes all of the articles on the Red Cross and Bengt Westerberg that have been published in the following newspapers: the tabloids *Aftonbladet* and *Expressen*, the business newspaper *Dagens Industri* (*DI*), and the dailies *Dagens Nyheter* (*DN*) and *Svenska Dagbladet* (*SvD*).

The chapter continues by briefly describing the Red Cross as an organization. Following this, a description of how the media reported and described Bengt Westerberg's remuneration is provided, as well as a description of how this publicity was handled by the organization. Following this is our analysis of the different ways of viewing confidence employed by media and the organization and their different opinions regarding the actions providing legitimacy. Finally, the consequences of media reporting for confidence levels in popular movements (*folkrörelser*), as a model for organizing and governing activities in civil society, are discussed.

The Swedish Red Cross

Based on the questions we have posed, it is important to understand the Swedish Red Cross as an organization, along with its prevailing logic in civil society. The Swedish Red Cross is notable as a nonprofit or voluntary organization and is part of a civil society with a long-standing tradition of popular movements (*folkrörelsetraditionen*). In Sweden, the popular movement model has been the dominating solution for how to organize nonprofit and voluntary activities since the beginning of the twentieth century (Wijkström and Einarsson 2006). The core of the popular movement organizations comprises its members; they manage and govern the organization through democratic processes. The members finance a large proportion of the operations through membership fees (and not primarily through donations) and they usually participate in the work of the organization as active members (and not primarily as volunteers). The form of these organizations differs from traditional charities or fundraising organizations of the Anglo-Saxon type, which normally do not have a large membership formally involved in the governance structure (Wijkström 2011). According to the logic of a Swedish popular movement (*folkrörelse*), member influence, democracy, and independence in relation to external actors are central components.

In terms of organization, the Swedish Red Cross rests on two pillars. One is the membership organization, which, in 2010, had some 200,000 members organized in local associations or chapters spread across the entire country, as well as the approximately 30,000 volunteers affiliated with the organization. In addition, the Red Cross has an administrative structure of 450 employees, the majority being located at the organization's headquarters in Stockholm. The highest representative of the membership is the chair of the board who, at the time of the study, was Bengt Westerberg, a high-profile former Swedish politician. The secretary-general is responsible for the administration and, at the time of the study, this position was held by Christer Zettergren. The highest decision-making body of the membership is the National Meeting, which is usually held on a biannual basis.

There are, however, nuances in the strength of the logic of the popular movement tradition as it is experienced within the Red Cross organization.

In recent years, employees have preferred to describe the organization as a "humanitarian network," rather than a popular movement. Another example of these differences within the organization is provided in the Red Cross's 2010 annual report, in which the chair and the secretary-general address the organization, on opposite pages of a double-page spread (Red Cross 2010a). The chair, as the highest representative of the membership, talks about members, associations, and voluntary leadership. He also writes about confidence-enhancing efforts directed at the organization and its members. The secretary-general (Ulrika Årehed Kågström, who replaced Christer Zettergren in 2010), however, does not use the same terminology. Instead, she addresses recipients, fundraising matters, and how the organization can improve its performance. She describes the organization as flexible, modern, and dynamic. In our view, the chair and the secretary-general are addressing, partially, very different groups: members versus donors and popular movement versus charity.

The Construction of a Crisis of Confidence

On June 2, 2009, the communications director of the Swedish Red Cross, Johan af Donner, was reported to the police by his employer. During the spring, suspicious circumstances were brought to the attention of the board of directors by numerous employees, leading the board to suspect that Johan af Donner had, in fact, fraudulently authorized false invoices that had resulted in Red Cross funds being diverted into his own pocket. When information on this fraud reached the outside world, af Donner's supposed guilt was immediately taken for granted by the media. For the Red Cross, the autumn of 2009 was characterized by media attention, and public disgust with the incident that was associated, to a very high degree, with the Red Cross and its management.

The questions raised included the following:

- Why had the management of the Red Cross failed to detect the irregularities much earlier?
- How close were the personal relationships between the members of the board of directors?
- Had they, in fact, protected af Donner?
- How can you trust an organization raising money for those in need that is, then, robbed of millions?

In the Red Cross, many employees felt that the organization was under fire and that the criticism was unfair, considering the fact that the organization had actually uncovered af Donner's fraud and, further-more, reported it to the police. Surely, it was the Red Cross who had been betrayed? Court proceedings against af Donner would commence in mid-January 2010 and, within the organization, it was hoped that the legal proceedings would follow their due course and that the media interest would soon fade.

The Chair of the Board and His Fees

However, this was not the case. In the spring of 2010, negative head-lines continued. This time, however, they concerned the chair of the board, Bengt Westerberg, and his remuneration. On January 16, the businessman, Roger Akelius, announced that he had donated kr100 mil-lion to SOS Children's Villages, Sweden. According to a statement by Akelius, one of the reasons for him choosing this organization had been that SOS Children's Villages does not pay remuneration to its board of directors. In an interview, Westerberg commented on Akelius's state-ment and argued that members of boards should receive a salary if they work full time (*E24.se*, January 19, 2010). The same article included Akelius's response to Westerberg in which he stated, "The boss of the Red Cross receives a salary which is double the amount of the salary of the boss of SOS Children's Villages. It would be fairer of the Red Cross to advertise using the text: If 10,000 people each text SEK 100, we will be able to pay Bengt Westerberg."

Akelius's criticism was reiterated in all major media, forcing Bengt Westerberg to defend his fee and the Red Cross Remuneration Policy. In articles titled, "Westerberg Costs the Red Cross 100 million" (*Realtid. se*, January 19, 2010), "Boards of Directors Should Receive No Pay" (*SvD*, January 19, 2010), and "A Shadow Falls over the Management of the Red Cross" (*DI*, January 22, 2010), the inability of Westerberg to defend his remuneration was criticized. Some weeks later, articles about Westerberg's other sources of income were published with titles such as "A Profitable Side Job—the Red Cross Chair Earns a Full-Time Salary and Cashes in Even More from His Other Assignments" (*DN*, January 31, 2010) and "Westerberg Earns a Million from His Side Job" (*Expressen*, January 31, 2010).

During the period in which Westerberg's remuneration was criti-cized, 30 percent of all articles published were opinion pieces—lead-ers, columns, debate articles, or letters to the editor. "The Red Cross Won't Get Any of My Money," wrote columnist Johanne Hildebrandt (*Aftonbladet*, January 24, 2010). Even private individuals backed

Akelius's criticism and, in a letter to the editor of *DN*, Westerberg was urged to waive six months' pay. Other letters to the editor from previous and current employees criticized the culture within the Red Cross. During the same period, *Expressen* repeatedly wrote about the luxurious lifestyle of af Donner in an article in which Westerberg's remuneration was mentioned and these two factors were regarded, in combination, as having caused an "alarming situation" and a "deep crisis of confidence in the organization" (February 6, 2010). When, at the same time, two members of the board resigned, Westerberg blamed time pressure. Journalists, however, linked the resignations to the handling of the scandals (*SvD* and *DN*, February 7, 2010).

The Red Cross's Communication Strategy Fails

Initially, employees in the Red Cross thought that the number of articles on Westerberg's remuneration would subside. Akelius's comparison and reasoning were regarded as unfair, incorrect, and simply stupid. The level of Westerberg's remuneration had been determined in accordance with the type of regulations and democratic principles that form the basis of any Swedish popular movement. In practice, this means that the ultimate power lies in the members' hands. The members make the crucial decisions at the annual meeting or congress. The popular movement meets the definition of a bottom-up organization.

In addition, the organization operated an established policy of paying better wages than many other fundraising organizations, in order to compete for employees with the best competence. According to employees, the operations and organization of the Red Cross differ significantly from those of SOS Children's Villages. The latter is a pure fundraising organization, while the popular movement Red Cross conducts far-reaching operations and is established all over the country. Initial, internal discussions at the Red Cross can be summarized in the statement, "People must understand these differences."

However, the media storm showed no signs of abating. The management soon discovered that the situation was so severe that it was necessary to inform the board of directors, and a report was compiled. The Secretary-General Christer Zettergren wrote, "Many employees now feel that the criticism directed towards the Chair's remuneration is of such a nature that it has become a hindrance to their work." Zetterberg also concluded that the strategy of focusing on operations in all external communications did not work: "Previously, discussions regarding the level of fees have always been over as soon as we have communicated our operations. Now, laying our operations bare in order to regain confidence in our organization does not seem to be enough" (Red Cross 2010b).

What had initially been regarded as, essentially, incorrect criticism developed into the perception that the organization was facing a crisis of confidence. Red Cross management discussed various strategic alternatives. The conclusion reached was that problems would not be solved by the chair resigning or accepting a reduced salary. Instead, management argued for maintaining the status quo and for putting the representatives of upper management in charge of communicating with the media, not Bengt Westerberg. No one should have to defend his or her own salary in public. It was further stated in the crisis report that it was not possible for the Red Cross to communicate its way out of this crisis. "There is a difference between being convinced about being right and actually being right in the eyes of the public," Zetterberg wrote. He concluded the report by summarizing that 2,200 members had, at the start of the year, chosen to terminate their memberships and approximately 400 more members had written letters of complaint expressing their criticism of the management. What is more, the proportion of people using the payment card sent through the Red Cross's magazine, *Henry*, had decreased from 52 percent to 45 percent in January 2010 (Red Cross 2010b).

Within the Red Cross, people were practically paralyzed by the criticism in the media and the frenzy that followed. Pressure on the press service, reception, and the membership service unit were regarded as particularly severe. The most threatening letters and phone calls were reported to the police. Other parts of the organization were also affected by this media storm. Various high-level personnel, who had nothing to do with communications, described how their work was brought to a halt as the management, including the chair, the secretary-general and the deputy secretary-general, were completely occupied by the state of affairs. "It was simply impossible to gain access," one of the employees stated. Finally, it was decided to hold a member meeting so that members could comment on the fees issue and an Extraordinary National Meeting was called in May 2010, which was to resolve on the level of remuneration to be paid to the chair. This was communicated externally and the Red Cross hoped for a little peace and quiet.

New Critical Headlines

However, it was neither more peaceful nor quieter after the decision to hold an Extraordinary National Meeting had been announced. In the media, reports were published on the manner in which the Red

Cross was trying to repair the shaken public confidence in the organization, something that provided journalists with the opportunity of repeating, once again, the story of Westerberg's fees. The large salaries paid to other employees in the Red Cross were also reported in the media. Akelius reentered the debate and wrote that Westerberg was a burden to the organization. *Aftonbladet* examined the expenses claimed in conjunction with Red Cross conferences and described the organization's training center as a drinking club. The sharpest criticism against Westerberg's fee and the actions of the Red Cross as regards the matter was found, not surprisingly, in the tabloids. The daily newspapers *DN* and *SvD* also joined in, albeit with slightly less sensationalist headlines and news angles. *DI* differed from the others by publishing news with a more neutral and, sometimes, even positive angle as regards the Red Cross.

Bengt Westerberg was offered the opportunity to provide his take on the matter in an interview in *Aftonbladet*, in addition to which he wrote, on his own initiative, a debate article in *DN* (February 28, 2010). In April 2010, *Aftonbladet*, again, published articles critical of Westerberg's fee levels.

Within the Red Cross headquarters, people felt frustrated with the situation. The objective of the Red Cross was to be professional and to be the "best" within the charity industry, without losing its special character as a nonprofit organization. However, as expressed by one of the communicators: "How can we defend our salary levels by stating that we are more professional, when we, the organization and the board, have been completely fooled by an imposter as Johan af Donner in the management? How professional is that?" Through conversations with managers and employees, it also became clear that the issue of remuneration was already a matter for discussion prior to the media getting wind of the issue. Red Cross policy was to offer competitive salaries; however, some employees regarded the defense of the high level of remuneration in the media as problematic. "The media have adopted the rule that, in a nonprofit organization, you work for little or no money," one official stated. The same individual also thought that the media defined the Red Cross as a nonprofit or voluntary organization, but did not take into account the fact that it was also a self-determining membership-based organization. Thus, the employees in the Communications Department clearly departed from the traditional member-driven logic of a popular movement, and evidenced acceptance of the media's definition of the type of organization the Swedish Red Cross was, or ought to be.

During the crisis, there was a mutual lack of confidence between the Communications Department and the management, not least between the department and Bengt Westerberg. Interviews demonstrate that the department and Westerberg did not cooperate, and that their sharing of information was weak during the period in which the organization was dealing with media reporting on Westerberg's fees. For the Communications Department, the situation was also made more difficult by the fact that the role usually responsible for managing this type of crisis, the communications manager, was a role that had, until very recently, been filled by af Donner, who had since been arrested. The allocation of responsibilities and work tasks, as well as the organization of the communication officers, was unclear. The fact that there was no reporting in the media about the Red Cross's actual operations and activities was the most frustrating issue. No journalists expressed any interest in operations. One employee from the Communications Department summarized the events of the previous months and their consequences for the Red Cross as follows:

> We were caught completely unaware. For years, we were the best and the biggest. We were not prepared for anything else. We thought that we would just have to explain ourselves and the public would say "OK, we'll support you." We had missed the small, symbolic issues that had been wheedling their way in for the last ten years. And it is evident that journalists had no interest in finding out what the situation really was. And that is sad. They have a pent-up need to crush our fair, kind organization which only wishes everyone well.

The Press Conference

On May 8, 2010, the Extraordinary National Meeting took place in Stockholm. The meeting lasted for hours and a press conference was held late in the afternoon. The chair of the Nomination Committee, Stig Andersson, opened the conference and announced that the organization had voted in favor of appointing a working chair, whose salary would correspond to the level of a Swedish member of Parliament. Thus, Westerberg's monthly payment was lowered from kr68,000 to kr55,000. Andersson emphasized the popular movement tradition of the organization and made sure to point out that 89 percent of the members had, directly or indirectly, participated in the decision on the tasks and salary of the chair, which, according to Andersson, meant that the decision had a clear democratic foundation and legitimacy. At the same time, he presented the new secretary-general, Ulrika Årehed

Kågström (the former secretary-general Christer Zettergren had decided to leave for a new position at the Swedish National Migration Board), along with the two newly appointed board members, Elisabet Perttu and Bo Hermansson.

Bengt Westerberg then spoke and made some initial comments on the intensive press coverage, stating that it would have been more exciting to receive the same degree of attention toward the Red Cross's actual operations: "This is especially directed at *Aftonbladet* because I see that you are here and your reporting has been extremely negative." He further expressed his satisfaction with the decision regarding remuneration for the chair and, above all, with the fact that there was now a logical principle for the organization to follow. The journalists and photographers present posed the same remuneration-related questions to Årehed Kågström and Westerberg. When the press conference was over, the representatives of the Red Cross heaved a sigh of relief. Surely, it was now over.

The next day, the media reported that Westerberg's remuneration had been reduced; however, it was still high. The article in, for example, *Expressen* (May 9, 2010) also included critical comments from readers:

> I sent a text message which cost SEK 50 to the Red Cross once. After these scandals, my donations have come to an end. (*Kentha*)
>
> Westerberg is happy to give up SEK 13,000 a month. The Swedish people are more than happy to give up Bengt Westerberg. (*Hurven*)

Later in the same month, *Aftonbladet* published an article (May 20, 2010) titled "Red Cross bluff," in which the journalist claimed that Westerberg's fees had not been reduced as previously announced but had, in fact, been raised.

> The salary fight at the Red Cross ended positively for Bengt Westerberg. The organization has drummed into the public that fees had been reduced—but in reality, the Chair's remuneration was increased by SEK 7,000 per month.

Aftonbladet reporter, Richard Aschberg, also claimed that members of the Red Cross, who had wondered whether total remuneration had actually been reduced, had contacted him.

Bengt Westerberg Does Not Stand for Reelection

At the end of May 2010, Johan af Donner was sentenced. In conjunction with the reporting on this matter, the issue of Westerberg's fees was addressed once more in the media. In an article titled, "Thousands of Members Leave the Red Cross" (*Aftonbladet*, May 27, 2010), Westerberg responded to the criticism and hoped that the fundraisers could deal with the insults and unfair accusations by standing up for the fact that they have a working chair who is paid with their own membership fees. According to the new Red Cross communications director, Westerberg was a burden on the organization in the spring of 2010 because of the negative tone of the media coverage. As a result, the Red Cross decided to publish a press release as soon as it became clear that Westerberg would not be standing for reelection. This was in contrast to the previous routines of the organization, as traditionally information was shared to the public only after the democratic work undertaken by the Nomination Committee had been completed. The reason for this course of action was, according to the communications director, that the Red Cross might have been forced to distance itself from Westerberg since they could not win against the media—the damage could only be limited.

On October 22, 2010, a press release from the Red Cross announced that Bengt Westerberg had chosen not to stand for reelection. The same information was later published by the major dailies *DI*, *DN*, and *SvD* in short notices. *Aftonbladet* and *Expressen* turned the event into something even bigger. *Aftonbladet* emphasized, "The Red Cross has lost one fifth of its membership due to the scandals," and continued, "Now Bengt Westerberg has accepted his responsibility and resigned." When asked about a potential successor in one of our interviews, an employee joked wearily and said that she was hoping that the next chair of the board would be "a rich guy who doesn't need a salary." She hoped that the organization would not have to deal with this difficult issue, and the resultant media circus, in the future.

Construction of Confidence in, and Concerning, the Red Cross

The media reporting on the crisis of confidence in the Red Cross gained pace as the communications director, Johan af Donner, was found by the court to have illegally embezzled millions. Around the same time as the trial against him began, a second round of crisis reporting on the Red Cross occurred, this time regarding the fees of the chair of the board. The fact that there had been a criminally greedy director in the organization certainly contributed to the continuous reporting about the chair of the board. In our view, however, the issue of remuneration has an enormous symbolical value for the way in which confidence is built, or lost, according to different logics. The fees issue formed the basis of the critical reporting, as well as of the organization's reaction to, and management of, the negative publicity. In the following section, we will account for the development of events on the basis of the fact that the Red Cross and the media are impacted by different logics regarding the actions considered to be legitimate for a nonprofit or voluntary organization, as well as being impacted in different ways by factors affecting confidence in an organization. In popular movements, the logic concerning what constitutes legitimate action is different to that put forward by the media. The issue was further complicated for the Red Cross as, even among the employees of the organization, there were those who accepted the logic of the media. There is a different approach in the media to the Red Cross as it is, and to how it ought to be, and thus to the actions that are considered legitimate and viable in these contexts.

Media Reporting Challenges the Logic of Popular Movements (folkrörelselogiken)

Our findings show that all of the media we studied had adopted a common standpoint as regards the issue of fees in charity organizations (it is noteworthy that these are not defined or understood as traditional membership-based popular movement organizations). The level of remuneration of the chair of the board is regarded by various actors in the media, and by the media, as *morally* reprehensible. According to their view, Westerberg's salary represented excessive compensation, which is the central issue in all of the reporting.

Media reporting is always tuned to its audience. In this case, it appears that the media views its audience primarily as *donors* to the Red Cross and not as, for example, members (and thus the owners) of the popular movement portion of its operations. The media, thus, assumes the role as representative of the donors, which has consequences for the issues that are chosen to be addressed and also as regards the angles in which the questions are posed: "The Red Cross won't be getting my money," writes, for example, Hildebrandt in her column in *Expressen*. The donors ought to receive value for their donated money. Nor is any significant distinction made between the membership fees paid by members and the financing generated by fundraising. High levels of employee remuneration, particularly in comparison with other nonprofit or voluntary, fundraising organizations, are provocative, and are viewed by the media as an illegitimate action.

The donors' perspective is very compatible with a professional charity or fundraising organization in which people work as volunteers, in which a large portion of operations are financed through donations from the public and in which the organizational structure is based on a hierarchy, with top-down decision-making processes, but this perspective is not really compatible with a membership democracy. By using this approach, reporting in the media will strengthen their logic of how confidence should be built up, at the expense of the methods inherent in how traditional popular movement organizations build confidence.

The Red Cross's management made the decision to confront the media crisis in a manner that, from the perspective of the popular movement logic and that of the organization's membership, builds legitimacy—that is, a return to the democratic process and the announcement of an Extraordinary National Meeting. In accordance with this logic, the members will, in the framework of the membership organization, together, discuss and resolve on the way in which the issue of the position of chair is to be solved, and will then take a democratic decision that is subsequently disseminated to the media. This may be interpreted as the logic of a popular movement still prevailing internally and, consequently, Westerberg's remuneration level is not viewed as a moral problem. Westerberg, himself, agrees that he has received an extremely positive response from members and employees and, although he has also received many negative emails, he would estimate that "non-members of the Red Cross" have written 75 percent of those. He clearly does not ask himself about how the reasoning of the nonmembers is constructed. The members have appointed him for the assignment and he is a strong supporter of the logic of popular movements. The media is, however, not interested in the mechanisms of popular movements, neither as an explanation nor a defense of the level of the fees paid to the chair. It is simply not regarded as relevant from their perspective. The media ignores the membership perspective and hardly pays any attention to the members' role, or to their influence. The members and their governing and management structures, which are, in fact, at the center of the organization, remain unseen in media reporting.

At the press conference, it becomes clear that the perspectives of the Red Cross and the media are based on different logics, implying that their expectations as to how the Red Cross is to act in order to be regarded as legitimate also differ. The popular movement organization sees to it that one of its most important figures in these matters—the chair of the Nomination Committee—talks for 20 minutes about the formal process and the results. The chair of the Nomination Committee oozes pride over what has been achieved in good democratic order within the organization. A total of 89 percent of the members of the organization have participated in the discussions. Of the members, 69 percent have voted in favor of a model with a working, paid chair of the board. According to traditional Swedish *folkrörelselogik* (the logic of popular movement), this process possesses strong, democratic legitimacy. It is, consequently, clear that the issue of fees is also legitimately accepted, and, therefore, confidence ought to be restored—or in any case, be well on its way to being restored.

However, from a donor's perspective, the media makes the news-arena evaluation that the internal processes and approaches of the organization are not significant. The media represents the donors' perspective, based on which Bengt Westerberg is still overpaid and there still is no reason for this to be so. Moreover, media interprets the fact that his fees were reduced, as an indication that the organization has listened to the criticism and has, thus, also—implicitly—accepted their perspective on what is an acceptable fee level. As the media are not primarily interested in the popular movement and its processes, they are not particularly keen to listen to the chair of the Nomination Committee. The people and positions catching the media's interest are the upper management of the organization, its chair and the secretary-general, who are the guarantors of operations vis-à-vis the rest of the world. Confidence among the broader public has, thus, not been restored. The Red Cross has attempted to rebuild the public's shaken confidence on the basis of a logic that has not been heard in the media and, as a result, the Red Cross message also falls on deaf ears.

Based on these events, it is clear that the Red Cross is presented in a manner to which many individuals in the organization are probably not accustomed, and which they do not recognize themselves. In addition, numerous relationships and interactions between various actors, taken as a whole, form the image of the organization projected externally—something that is difficult for the organization to control or even deduce and that is a consequence of the varying logic and trust regimes of differing organizations. It is clear in the reporting, that the media, in its analyses, does not take an active interest in the popular movement type of organization at least previously embodied by the Red Cross. The Red Cross is tacitly more or less understood to be a fundraising organization acting in a tradition of charity.

In our view, the fact that many people within the organization regard themselves as representing a classic, Swedish popular movement (*folkrörelse*) is absolutely crucial to understanding the way in which the organization responded to the remuneration issue and the media criticism. However, this is never clearly accounted for in media reporting, and the differences in approach are also, presumably, one important cause of some of the clashes between the organization and the media.

The Media as a Catalyst for Organizational Change

As stated in the introduction, the logic of a popular movement has been, to a certain extent, challenged in certain parts of the Red Cross. The media reporting, with its one-sided perspective on the organization, functioned as a catalyst to highlight the conflict between the various notions of the type of organization the Red Cross is, or ought to be.

The communications officers perceived that the media did not "buy" the Red Cross's argument about member-financed fees or democratic processes, everything that reflects the logic of popular movements. Instead of persisting with arguments founded on the logic of popular movements, they advocated *an adjustment* to the media's worldview, based on the notion that it is reality that counts. In addition, the new communications director suggested that the press release on Westerberg not standing for reelection be communicated as soon as possible as a means for the organization to distance itself from its chair. An employee of the Communications Department hoped for a "a rich guy" who does not need any remuneration, to succeed as chair, that is an altruistic representative of a charity organization, so that they could avoid having to handle the difficult clashes arising when the logic of popular movements meets the media.

The communications officers thus appear, within the organization, as carriers of the idea that it is important to adjust to the media in order to be able to work in peace, and even earn legitimacy. From their perspective, the media can be understood as a type of legitimate control function in society to which the organization must adjust itself, even if they disagree with its ethos. In the organization's opinion, the criticism expressed regarding remuneration was unfair and essentially incorrect; however, the fact is that the media has formulated reality, the reality to which the organization must adapt itself. As the communications director puts it, "you can't win against the media"—the only thing you can do is to focus on damage control to reduce negative effects. According to the logic of popular movements, it is up to the members to decide how they wish to govern and manage their organization, thus also remunerate the chair of the organization. As the members of the

Red Cross reiterate, it is they, not *Aftonbladet* who determine whether their chair should stay or go. The media is, thus, allocated different roles depending on the perspective from which the organization of the Red Cross is viewed.

According to the logic of a traditional charity organization, the media comprises an external actor who monitors, examines, and, to a certain degree through its monitoring function, also contributes to ensuring that everything is carried out in a correct manner. In this type of organizational form, the media comprises a part of the external management structure working on behalf of the public and the donors. However, according to the logic of popular movements, the media do not have a legitimate control function for the internal matters of the organization; media functions are reporting the decisions of the membership, describing the operations of the organization and operating as an arena for opinion building on important issues.

Our results show that the reporting in the media clearly emphasizes, or take its departure from, one particular civil society logic—that of charity—at the expense of the other—that of popular movement. Reporting in the media ignores the membership perspective (the logic of popular movements) while instead highlighting the donor perspective. This appears to impact the organization by exposing and intensifying differences of opinion among employees.

Media Impact and Consequences for the Organization

In summary, it can be stated that the media holds the power to form and create a crisis of confidence in an organization. Our study has shown that the media and the Swedish Red Cross are governed by different logics in terms of the patterns of behavior considered legitimate in nonprofit or voluntary organizations and also, as a consequence, in terms of that which contributes to the construction of confidence in the organization. To a certain degree, this clash implies a conflict in terms of the manner in which confidence in, and legitimacy-creating actions within, an organization can be understood. According to an organizational analysis of the events in the Red Cross, the traditional model of popular movements in Sweden, whereby confidence is primarily built through the membership and their structures and principles for managing and governing their organization, is threatened. Instead, another organizational model in civil society—the fundraising organization of classical charity type—is beginning to make itself known and is also gaining legitimacy. This model is, in the case in point of the Swedish

Red Cross, strengthened by reporting in the media, without the media necessarily being aware of the process.

Furthermore, it can be concluded that, in the case of the Red Cross, the media's creation of a crisis of confidence in an organization has an effect on parts of that organization's understanding of itself. The communications officers, in particular, wished to adapt to the media's description of reality and, in this way, increase the distance with the dominating logic of popular movements. In addition, one consequence of the clash with the media is the increased levels of demand imposed on the organization's communication, competences, and experience of understanding the media, and on them being able to act according to the logic of the media. In our view, this provides an example of the ongoing professionalization of nonprofit or voluntary organizations.

This case of the media's crisis reporting regarding the Swedish Red Cross should, in a broader perspective, be viewed as an example and as a result of a societal development in which confidence is constructed—built and maintained—in a different manner than previously was the case. We believe that this occurs in many steps and intertwined processes.

First, the media has gained greater scope and influence over time. In addition, over the last decade, more numerous, louder voices have been raised in favor of increased external transparency in society's various institutions and organizations. This applies to the media, to public opinion, as well as to regulations for private companies, authorities, and other organizations. External transparency of internal processes has become an important component in the building of legitimacy. Organizations must constantly convince the public, their target groups, and markets of the fact that they are trustworthy. Closed forms of organizations do not fit well into this type of public spirit. Consequently, the classical model of popular movements, as a method of organizing operations within civil society, is also under attack. One could pose the question whether it is possible, with such a trend underway, to build confidence in businesses and organizations without acknowledging and adapting them to the media and it's reporting?

Civil society organizations are becoming ever more visible in today's society and thus attention to and interest in the media has also increased. In our view, it is likely that the media's interest in, and examination of, organizations in civil society will increase and also shift focus (as shown in our analysis) as the trend continues. In the case of the Red Cross, one impression is that the media examined the Red Cross wearing its "normal" set of lenses, that is, rather than taking into account the previous distinctive character of the Red Cross as a traditional Swedish popular movement, it is, instead, regarded to comprise a charity-based fundraising organization.

The media imposes requirements characterized by economization, as well as by a demand for transparency and professionalism. It is not easy for a traditional popular movement organization to fulfill these requirements and demands as they are actually more enclosed in nature, relying on their members and their confidence in order to conduct operations. Is the popular movement model a completely impossible route to take for an organization wishing to build confidence through the media today?

This story can be understood as the crossing of institutional borders. The institution of the popular movement, and its logic, is being challenged by the institutional logic of the media. The latter advocates not just a different way of interpreting events and another base from which confidence is built, but also has a great advantage in and of interpretation of public debate.

The case of the Red Cross thus provides a good illustration of how organizations, in their work to build confidence, are dependent on how other organizations depict them. Among these organizations, media organizations appear to be particularly important as they shape ideas among fundraising organizations on how voluntary work should be organized and communicated. There, the border crossing is rather about the tensions that arise when media convey divergent images of how such popular movement contra the Anglo-Saxon charity is a more legitimate form of organization. From this, we learn that the construction of confidence is an intricate interaction that takes place in the meeting between institutional logics and in the crossing of institutional borders. Due to its role and mission, the media institution is, of course, a common occurring player in these transorganizational activities.

The case of the Red Cross discussed above opens up a series of questions for further research and analysis. Here, the Red Cross has also served as an example of the consequences that may arise whenever more media-dependent organizations operating in what could be understood as a "trust industry" are to build up or maintain confidence.

References

Friedland, Roger, and Robert R. Alford. 1991. "Bringing Society Back In: Symbols, Practices, and Institutional Contradictions." In *The New Institutionalism in Organizational Analysis*, edited by Walter W. Powell and Paul J. DiMaggio, 232–263. Chicago: University of Chicago Press.

146 • P. Petrelius Karlberg, M. Grafström, and K. Windell

McCombs, Max. 2004. *Setting the Agenda*. Cambridge, UK: Polity Press.
Petrelius Karlberg, Pernilla 2011. *Medialiseringen av ideella organsationer: en studie av Röda Korset*. SSE/EFI Working Paper Series in Business Administration, 2011:9.
Red Cross. 2010a. *Röda Korsets årsredovisning 2010* [The Swedish Red Cross Annual Report 2010]. Stockholm: Swedish Red Cross.
Red Cross. 2010b. *Rapport till Centralstyrelsen för svenska Röda Korset den 3 februari 2010* [Report to the Central Board of the Swedish Red Cross, February 3, 2010]. Stockholm: Swedish Red Cross.
Thornton, Patricia H., and William Ocasio. 1999. "Institutional Logics and the Historical Contingency of Power in Organizations: Executive Succession in the Higher Education Publishing Industry, 1958–1990." *American Journal of Sociology* 105 (3): 801–843.
Wijkström, Filip. 2011. "Charity Speak and Business Talk. The On-Going (Re)-hybridization of Civil Society." In *Nordic Civil Society at a Cross-Roads. Transforming the Popular Movement Tradition*, edited by Filip Wijkström and Annette Zimmer, 27–71. Baden-Baden: Nomos.
Wijkström, Filip, and Marianne af Malmborg. 2005. "Mening och mångfald. Ledning och organisering av idéburen verksamhet." In *Civilsamhället. Några forskningsfrågor*, edited by Erik Amnå, 74–100. Stockholm: Gidlunds Förlag.
Wijkström, Filip, and Torbjörn Einarsson. 2006. *Från nationalstat till näringsliv? Det civila samhällets organisationsliv i förändring*. Stockholm: Stockholm School of Economics.

CHAPTER 8

Trust in the Monitoring of Publicly Funded Services: A Case Study of Two Outsourced Care Homes for the Elderly

Eva Hagbjer, Johnny Lind, and Ebba Sjögren

Welfare Services: A Matter of Trust

In any society, citizens must be able to trust that publicly funded services, for example, health care, education, and social care, are of a high quality. If the citizens' trust declines, their willingness to pay taxes and fees will also decrease, undermining the financial basis of the publicly funded social welfare system. For society to function and prosper, it is essential to secure the citizens' trust in the ability of the state, municipalities, and counties to fulfill their commitments. This implies a problem if publicly funded services, such as elderly care, are found to be of poor quality. Such criticism not only constitutes a problem for those individuals who have suffered inadequate care, but also for the wider public, who pay for the services, as the general public's trust in society's institutions may decline. A well-functioning monitoring of the actors delivering publicly funded services is an important means of both lowering the risk of recurring failings in the quality of the services, as well as increasing the general public's confidence in society's ability to guarantee high-quality public services.

The Complex Monitoring of Publicly Funded Operations

Monitoring of publicly funded operations has become more complex in recent decades as external providers deliver an increasing number of public services. This is a result of demands, in the last 20–30 years, for increased efficiency in the public sector in Sweden and other Western countries. One common solution for increasing efficiency has been to make the conditions for public sector operations similar to the conditions assumed to apply to private sector companies (Hood 1995). Sweden was one of the nations to embrace the so-called New Public Management (NPM) in the 1990s and the country is now an established NPM context (Olson and Sahlin-Andersson 1998). In Sweden, the reform of the public sector has meant that municipalities have, to a greater degree, entered into agreements with external providers for the delivery of services, such as care homes for the elderly. The procurement procedure has resulted in the day-to-day provision of these services being assigned to external organizations, while continuing to be publicly funded. However, under the Social Services Act (2001:453, Chapter two, Section one), Swedish municipalities remain ultimately responsible for the care provided to users, even when the operations have been outsourced. Consequently, should something go wrong, the municipality, too, would be held publicly accountable for the operational shortcomings of the external provider. As a result, the externally provided services straddle the boundary between two institutional fields: the public sector and the commercial market. These two institutional fields operate with different taken-for-granted understandings of appropriate behavior.

It follows that municipalities need to have insight into the services delivered by external providers to ensure both its own ability to guarantee the quality of the services and the general public's confidence in that ability. Well-functioning monitoring can meet these two requirements (Seal and Vincent-Jones 1997; Seal et al. 1999) and bridge both the institutional boundary between the public and commercial sphere and the boundary between the municipality and the care provider as separate organizations. The municipality's need to be in control of events taking place at the external provider is met, as the monitoring contributes to their knowledge of the services being provided in the care homes. This can be achieved either by monitoring the operations from a distance, using questionnaires and standardized measurements, or by visiting the care homes. Receiving information about the local circumstances allows the municipality to establish trust in the external provider.

The need to create trust in public services that span institutional and organizational boundaries is satisfied when the monitoring of the services is regarded as being objective, and when the municipality, through the monitoring process, can show that they have control over the services provided. In this way, monitoring can both create interorganizational, actor-based, trust and contribute to creating system-based trust among the general public. Figure 8.1 provides an overview of the actors involved and the two forms of trust.

The aim of this chapter is to contribute to an increased understanding of the role of monitoring in building actor-based and system-based trust. The chapter will first describe the way in which monitoring is organized in the relationship between one Swedish municipality and two private providers who have been charged with operating care homes for the elderly, and the way in which this structure can contribute to creating actor-based trust across interorganizational boundaries. The manner in which monitoring is organized will, subsequently, be related to the need to build system-based trust in a setting with multiple institutional demands.

The chapter is structured as follows. The next section describes the way in which interorganizational, actor-based trust can be created through monitoring. This is followed by a description of the context and implementation of the study, and of the way in which the monitoring of the two care homes is organized. The conclusion discusses the way in which the described monitoring system contributes to building interorganizational, actor-based trust for each of the operations as well as system-based trust for the delivery of publicly funded services that

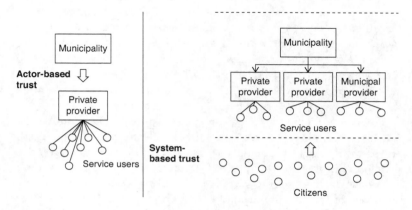

Figure 8.1   Actor-based trust and system-based trust across organizational and institutional boundaries.

straddle institutional boundaries. In addition, we point to the challenges involved in the future development of monitoring systems for publicly funded operations.

Actor-Based Trust and Monitoring across Interorganizational Boundaries

When a municipality outsources operations to an external provider, the municipality remains both legally and morally accountable to the users of the services and other citizens for ensuring that the quality of the services delivered is satisfactory. Assigning external providers to manage care homes for the elderly on a contractual basis creates a need for the municipality to trust that particular provider to deliver a service of good quality. One way of creating this actor-based trust is for the municipality to monitor the operations of the external provider as a way of crossing the organizational boundaries between them (Seal and Vincent-Jones 1997). At the same time, this assumes that there is trust in the monitoring per se. There are different ways of creating trust in the monitoring itself. One principle, which is generally regarded as desirable, is that the monitoring is designed to be independent and impartial. Another principle is that the monitoring should be designed to guarantee that the subject of the monitoring is relevant, in the sense that it adequately accounts for what is considered to be of interest to the intended recipients of the monitoring information. These two principles may conflict. In general terms, this implies that the party monitoring the operations must balance the need for distance and proximity to that which is being evaluated.

The literature on accounting often emphasizes the importance of ensuring that operations are monitored and evaluated by an *organizationally independent* party (Sikka and Willmott 1995). Avoiding formal ties to the operations under review creates the conditions necessary for the reviewing party to manage its task in a correct manner, and not to hesitate to report any irregularities. The formal structure of the monitoring is expected to ensure that the outcome can be trusted.

When a municipality reviews an external provider, the municipality will, by definition, be organizationally independent in relation to the provider managing a particular care home. In this chapter, interest will, therefore, be directed toward the efforts to create trust in the monitoring by achieving an *operational independence* between the reviewer and the reviewed in the monitoring process. The objective is to ensure that the content of the monitoring—ultimately, the judgment of good or poor performance—is determined in a manner that inspires confidence.

Power (1997) describes two general methods for achieving operationally independent monitoring. One is to apply a common standard. This means that the operations being monitored are assessed on the basis of fixed measures that clearly define what constitutes good, or poor, performance. This makes it possible to compare the same operations over time, and to compare different operations that are monitored according to the same standard. The common standard ensures a reliable monitoring process by making the supervision independent of the party performing it. One example of such monitoring is the ranking of primary health care clinics undertaken by a number of Swedish county councils since the implementation of the Choice of Care reform (*vårdvalsreformen*) in 2009. These comparisons use standardized metrics to follow up various features, such as telephone accessibility, attitude, and the patients' willingness to recommend the provider. Porter (1994) employs the term "mechanical objectivity" to describe the knowledge gained through the application of a standard.

The alternative to monitoring based on a common standard is that the supervision is undertaken by individuals with particular knowledge of the type of operations being monitored. Their experience enables them to evaluate and make qualified assessments of the performance of the operations through independent observations. On occasion, the Swedish National Board of Health and Welfare undertakes site inspections in conjunction with an investigation of a complaint under the Patient Safety Act (2010:659, Chapter three).[1] This type of monitoring produces knowledge which Porter (1994) refers to as *disciplinary objective*. The trust in the accuracy and relevance of the knowledge is based on an appropriate individual making a qualified assessment on the basis of personal expertise and common sense.

Thus, both methods for the creation of operationally independent monitoring aim to build trust by ensuring that reliable information is compiled in the monitoring process. The objective is that the users of the monitoring results will trust that a positive outcome is correct and that the operations which have been reviewed function well. There is a depiction ideal for the monitoring process: the content of the operations being monitored should be reported in a manner that is as fair and relevant as possible.

Elderly Care as an Example of Public Sector Care

Elderly care in Sweden is an area in which the general public's trust has been negatively affected by reports of improprieties. Consequently, it has been considered essential to restore the general public's system-based trust for the quality of elderly care through, for example, a greater amount of more efficient monitoring.

In this chapter, we describe the monitoring of two care homes for the elderly, located in two different regions within the municipality of Urban and managed by two separate contractors. One of the regions, East, had extensive experience of procurement and managed only a few care homes under its own auspices. The other region, North, had several care homes under municipal management at the start of the study and had relatively limited experience of contracting out services. This chapter shows the manner in which different types of monitoring were applied to build trust in the two providers. The monitoring has been studied on the basis of observations of evaluation meetings between the providers and the regions, supplemented with interviews conducted with the providers and the municipality, as well as a study of documents.

Figure 8.2 shows a simplified chart of the provision and monitoring of outsourced publicly funded care for the elderly in the municipality of Urban. Due to its size, the municipality was divided into a number of decentralized regions, each of which was responsible for, among other things, social care and care for the elderly. The ongoing monitoring

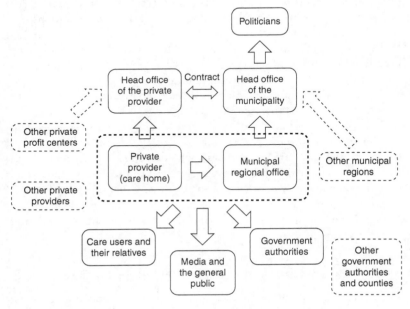

Figure 8.2 Implementation and monitoring of outsourced municipal services.

process was primarily conducted within the boundaries of the focal relationship between the municipal region and the private provider's local profit center, which was usually an individual care home for the elderly. The head office of the municipality also conducted a degree of centralized monitoring and information compilation, and was responsible for reporting to the politicians in the municipality.

Since 2008, a new central procurement unit had been responsible for the procurement of new providers of elderly care. Thus, the head offices of the municipality and the provider interacted directly during the procurement processes, which could include several care homes from different regions. The users and their relatives, in turn, were directly linked to the focal relations. Other central actors included the media and the general public, as well as government authorities with a supervisory responsibility within the sector.

Monitoring Processes in Urban

The monitoring of care homes for the elderly in Urban was characterized by an increasingly extensive and standardized performance measurement undertaken by various parties, in combination with inspections primarily carried out at local level in each region.

Surveys and Other Standardized Measurements

Both the regional offices and the head office of the municipality gathered information regarding the quality of the care for the elderly using standardized performance reports. The two regional offices requested certain basic quality statistics on a monthly basis, and conducted a more extensive monitoring of the care homes' health care and medical care annually. This data was analyzed at the local level, at each regional office, in order to quickly discover any negative trends such as a higher than average incidence of broken bones among the residents in any particular care home. At central level, the unit for elderly care at the municipal head office had developed two templates for monitoring, which the regional offices were responsible for submitting on an annual basis. One of these was designed to monitor the general quality of the care for the elderly, while the other was designed in 2009 to specifically monitor the medical aspect of the operations. Together, these reports were intended to provide the head office with an overview of the quality of the care homes in Urban.

The centrally commissioned evaluation reports were incorporated, together with a national quality assessment and user survey conducted by the Swedish National Board of Health and Welfare, into an annual report on quality, which was delivered to the regional offices. Initially, this report was also submitted to the municipal council; however, from 2010, the municipal council only received the financial and operational key ratios regarding care for the elderly, which were included in the regions' annual administration reports and Urban's aggregate annual report. A less detailed version of the aggregate annual report was also uploaded onto the municipality's public website. The regional offices leveled some criticism at the two central monitoring templates. Both were difficult to interpret and it was, for example, unclear whether certain key ratios were intended to include residents who had passed away during the year, or how the question of whether or not all staff "had a good command of the Swedish language in speaking and writing" was to be addressed. The general monitoring template was also criticized for tracking relatively trivial aspects of the care, such as the number of staff members wearing name badges, or extremely basic characteristics, such as the procedures for secure storage of care documentation. A perceived consequence of the overly basic monitoring was that the template captured only those cases in which the quality of the care was extremely poor.

A more general problem, according to care home management representatives, was that there was a partial overlap between the various monitoring reports from the head office and the regional offices. Dental care and dietary measures were addressed both in the regions' health care statistics and in the general monitoring by the head office, while staff training was reported both in the general monitoring and in the annual administration reports of each region. In an attempt to coordinate the information, East had developed its own monitoring system based on existing data. The aim was to focus on the outcome of the care rather than the activities undertaken. However, this monitoring was not reported to the head office of Urban either.

An important task for each regional office was to oversee the specific agreements that had been concluded during the procurement process. It was while overseeing the conditions stipulated in the contract that the municipality had its strongest position vis-à-vis the private provider. When Urban's head office took over the procurement process, they required the tenders to more clearly specify and quantify the services the company intended to perform. The regional offices noted that one disadvantage of this was that it was not always possible to measure the factors that were regarded the most important for good care. For example, measures such as staff training and the number of social activities per week were used in an attempt to assess the quality of care and daily life of the residents. Nor was there a system for reporting to the head office the degree to which the providers fulfilled the terms of the contract; as a result, there was no system in place to draw on the regions' experience in future procurements. Another disadvantage expressed by the regional offices was that the municipality published the type of commitments they rewarded already prior to the procurement, as the assessment process had to be described in the request for tender. The effect was that the contracts led to increased standardization.

This development was in contrast with the provider contract in East, which was procured prior to the centralization of the procurement function to the municipal head office. The local procurer for East intentionally avoided specifying the content of the tender, other than certain general categories, such as, describing the way in which an active way of life would be ensured for the residents. The reason for this was that a tender formulated by the provider was perceived to be more honest and allowed the provider to come up with its own suggestions for how the care would be provided. East also chose to not set out any requirements regarding the quantification of the care, as such requirements were considered to force a specification of the relative weight of quantifiable and nonquantifiable factors in the evaluation of the tenders. This would have been problematic, as the quantifiable aspects of care for the elderly were regarded as only a minor part of the whole.

Another method, which was used both centrally and locally by the municipality in order to guarantee the quality of the care, was to demand internally conducted quality assessments and user surveys from the providers. The results of the internal monitoring, which focused on similar areas of evaluation to those addressed in the municipality's quality assessments, were reported to the regions on a voluntary basis; however, they were not requested by the head office of the municipality.

In addition, both Urban's head office and the care providers collected the opinions of residents on the care through user surveys carried out by independent opinion research institutes. The results of the head office survey were incorporated into the annual quality report and were made available for current and future users on the Internet.

Inspections and Evaluation Meetings

In addition to the standardized assessments, the regional offices in East and North carried out both announced and unannounced inspections a few times a year. The purpose of the inspections was to make a general assessment of the care. Among other things, inspectors were able to see whether the providers' routines were being followed in practice or whether the residents were left sitting alone in front of the TV. They also inspected the care documentation, the handling of medicines, and other security aspects of the care. At the same time, the providers criticized the inspections for taking up time and interrupting the normal activities of the care home, particularly if the inspectors arrived in the middle of a meal.

The way in which inspections were organized varied between the regions. East had a designated monitoring function with personnel who monitored the elderly care on a full-time basis. The two quality inspectors from North carried out the inspections in addition to their normal duties, as health care manager and manager of a care home within the municipal care system for the elderly, respectively.

The regions' monitoring process and, in particular, the inspections and evaluations of contracts, constituted the basis for the evaluation meetings between the regions and care providers, which took place two to three times a year. At the meetings, complaints and operational incidents were discussed, along with the actions to be taken by the providers to solve the problems. The meetings also provided an opportunity to discuss and interpret the contract and the obligations of the providers, such as whether teenagers who organized social activities could be considered members of staff. Between the meetings, the providers and regional administrators maintained telephone and email contact whenever an acute situation arose, for example, in the event of a complaint from a resident or criticism in the media. The monitoring conducted through meetings, discussions, and inspections was, thus, a dynamic process, the outcome of which was difficult to compare between different regions. Nor was the information obtained from this part of the monitoring process passed on to the head office or the municipal council.

There were also a few quality inspectors at the elderly care unit at head office, who, on an annual basis, inspected a number of regions. The results of these inspections were passed on to the regions that had been inspected, and were also summarized in a report that included both good examples found in the yearly inspections and areas in need of improvement. The report was presented to the political majority and all regions in Urban, and was published on the website of the municipality. However, it was not submitted to the municipal council as a whole. Another centralized source of nonstandardized information was Urban's "Ombudsman for the Elderly," to whom the elderly could turn for information or to make a complaint. The commissioner for the elderly drew up a summarizing annual report, which was also submitted to the political majority and all of the regions, and was published on the website of the municipality.

Many Actors, Who Monitor the Operations in Different Ways

Seen as a whole, the empirical description of the official monitoring of two commercial, private sector providers of care to the elderly in the municipality of Urban demonstrates an extensive monitoring by a number of organizationally independent parties. The systematic monitoring of individual care homes is undertaken at both the central and local level within the municipality. The operations are also overseen by government authorities. The monitoring consequently needs to bridge both organizational and institutional boundaries.

The study shows that the contents and focus of the monitoring differs. This chapter describes a number of different standards employed for assessing the operations in North and East. The head office of the municipality gathers statistics on, among other things, dental care, the level of education and training among staff, and staffing levels. At the local regional level, statistics are also gathered regarding the operations at the care homes. In addition, both regions undertake site inspections, which are carried out by individuals with special competence in elderly care. Regular evaluation meetings are also held between representatives from the municipality and representatives from the care homes, in which operative matters are discussed in more depth. Both of the strategies for ensuring the operational independence of monitoring described in the literature are used: the application of standards and the use of professional expertise and judgment.

Figure 8.3 demonstrates a clear leaning toward monitoring procedures that are intended to create trust through the use of mechanical objectivity—monitoring that is associated with fixed standards. There are also indications that this type of monitoring is increasingly prevalent. The number of standardized reports has increased, and new reporting requirements have been added since 2008.

A more in-depth analysis of the level at which each type of monitoring is undertaken is presented in figure 8.4 and shows that monitoring based on a disciplinary objective assessment of operations is more common at the local level in the municipality. At the central level, various standards-based forms of monitoring are applied. The fact that there are such notable differences depending on where the various forms of

Mechanical objectivity	Disciplinary objectivity
Information on equality	Inspections
Health care statistics*	Report from the commissioner for the elderly
General monitoring of quality	Evaluation meetings
Key ratios in the budget	Telephone calls and email
User surveys	
Recurrent healthcare and care statistics	
Quantitative monitoring of the contract†	
Coordinated monitoring system* (only in the East regional office)	

* In use since 2009;
† In use since 2008.

Figure 8.3 Different forms of operationally independent monitoring of procured care homes for the elderly in the municipality of Urban.

	Operational independency	
	Mechanical objectivity	Disciplinary objectivity
Local level	Recurrent health care and care statistics	Inspections (the region)
	Health care statistics (the region)	Evaluation meetings
	Coordinated monitoring system (only in the East region)	Telephone calls and email
	Quantitative monitoring of the contract	
	Health care statistics (the elderly care unit)	Inspections (the elderly care unit)
	General quality monitoring	Report from the commissioner for the elderly
Central level	Key ratios in the budget	
	User surveys	
	Information on quality (the Swedish National Board of Health and Welfare)	

Figure 8.4 Organizationally independent monitoring at local and central levels.

operationally independent assessments are conducted, is particularly interesting against the background of the observed differences regarding the way in which the results of the monitoring are distributed. The disciplinary objective monitoring is not normally passed on from the local, regional level in the municipality. The mechanically objective monitoring in the form of standardized metrics, is, however, more widely distributed, both within and outside the municipality.

Conclusions

The conclusion that there is extensive monitoring of the procured care homes for the elderly, with many parties involved at both the municipal and government level, can be understood against the background of previous research, which stresses the importance of monitoring in providing greater control over the operations (Roberts and Scapens 1985). Due to the fact that the municipality does not have any hierarchical means of control over the procured care homes, the monitoring plays an important part in the municipality's ability to influence the operations of the care homes and to guarantee their content despite the organizational boundaries between them. Securing this actor-based trust can serve both to guarantee good quality and to avoid public criticism. Previous research suggests that the existence of a monitoring process may, in itself, contribute to increased system-based trust (Seal and Vincent-Jones 1997), meaning that an extensive monitoring system may also serve to raise the level of trust of the general public in publicly funded care for the elderly as a whole. This may be particularly relevant when the provision of the services spans across multiple institutional fields, which have different taken-for-granted understandings and codified standards for evaluating quality.

At the same time, extensive monitoring may also contribute to increased complexity. For example, we found that different parties request similar information, but that there is no discernible coordination of the collection or analysis of the data. In other words, the multiple organizational boundaries that the data must cross constitute a dilemma. This suggests that a greater degree of monitoring activities cannot be said to automatically lead to a better understanding of, or insight into, the operations. Instead, there might be a potential conflict between the aspiration to build system-based trust through an extensive monitoring process involving multiple organizations and organizational units, and the need to achieve interorganizational, actor-based trust through a relevant review of the content of the specific operations.

The fact that there are a number of different types of monitoring can be understood on the basis of the need to manage the benefits and shortcomings associated with each type's ability to build actor-based trust. This study describes a number of benefits and shortcomings, both of the standard-based, mechanically objective monitoring and of the disciplinary objective monitoring based on professional expertise. These benefits and shortcomings confirm the findings of previous research (Boland and Schultze 1996). Briefly, a mechanically objective monitoring process means that operations are assessed against a certain standard and can be compared with each other. However, questions may arise regarding the precision of the measurements.

In this study, for example, care home management representatives were critical of the unclear meaning of certain measures, such as a command of the Swedish language. This criticism suggests that it is not always clear what should be measured. However, this room for interpretation, which occurs when the standardized form is put into use, is not apparent as the results are passed on. Instead, the information appears as an unambiguous and precise depiction of reality. In comparison, monitoring based on disciplinary objective knowledge allows greater room for interpretation, a fact that reduces the level of comparability and the apparent accuracy. At the same time, there is a wider opportunity to make the potential interpretation problems visible. For example, during evaluation meetings or inspections, it is possible to discuss the practical content of both the requirements of the various monitoring standards and of the operational outcomes.

It follows that both forms of monitoring contribute different types of knowledge regarding the content and outcome of the operations. In doing so, they also contribute different bases for trust in the monitoring of operations. The mechanically objective knowledge obtained through a quantitative monitoring can credibly claim to show, for example, negative deviations from a predetermined minimum level. The consequence, however, is that it is not self-evident that an outstanding performance will be made visible and encouraged. Conversely, the disciplinary objective information obtained in the ongoing qualitative monitoring process is less successful at showing whether the operations are conducted in an appropriate manner, other than in the context of the specific conditions prevailing in the care home itself. The fact that mechanically and disciplinary objective monitoring processes provide different types of information regarding the contents of the operations shows the importance of applying both forms of monitoring in building actor-based trust.

In addition to this difference in depicting operations and thereby contributing to actor-based trust, there are also differences in the conditions for communicating both forms of monitoring. This is important for the way in which the monitoring contributes to building system-based trust. The disciplinary objective monitoring is based on local knowledge that is difficult to transfer beyond the municipal region level. The results of the assessments made by knowledgeable individuals are clearly linked to a certain local context and are, thus, more difficult to report to other units. The inherent uncertainty behind the assessments made within the context of disciplinary objective monitoring is, at the same time, more apparent. This may raise doubts regarding the ability of the monitoring to depict the content of the operations, as there is no way to assess the reliability of the implementation of the monitoring (Lonsdale 1999). This is different from the results of the mechanically objective monitoring process. The metrics resulting from a mechanically objective monitoring are easy to pass on to actors far beyond the context of the individual operations. At the same time, any uncertainty in conjunction with the metrics is not visible to the recipient.

Researchers have described these two characteristics as contributing to the fact that mechanical objective information is considered more reliable by actors who are organizationally further away from the operations and who lack in-depth knowledge as to the factors that may have been taken into account in the production of knowledge (Mackenzie 1990). For such actors, for example, members of the municipal management or individual citizens, the mechanically objective monitoring may, thus, be particularly powerful in building system-based trust. In a situation where the provision of the services extends across the boundaries between different institutions, mechanically objective monitoring becomes even more attractive. Where different institutions might have different taken-for-granted understandings and codifications of who qualifies as a knowledgeable individual and therefore can conduct disciplinary objective monitoring, the mechanically objective monitoring is valid in both institutions despite the distance in knowledge and space between them. At the same time, research shows that mechanical objective monitoring does not always capture relevant differences in quality (Bevan and Hood 2006), while the disciplinary objective monitoring is successful in recognizing "soft" values (Slagsvold 1997). Given the importance attached to the care users' experienced quality, for example, in the form of security and responsiveness, the long-term system-based trust could also be said to assume a monitoring process that allows this form of scrutiny.

In conclusion, this suggests that it is important to use both monitoring methods in order to create a functioning control system that contributes to the creation and maintenance of both actor-based and system-based trust across the organizational and institutional boundaries. Consequently, there is a problem if increased requirements for mechanically objective monitoring result in disciplinary objective monitoring being supplanted. In the case study, there were certain indications that the standard-based monitoring was becoming increasingly prevalent (see also the discussion in the chapter by Gustafsson and Tamm Hallström in this volume on the trend toward increased regulation).

Another development that may, in the long term, prevent the municipalities from conducting a satisfactory monitoring process, is the requirement to outsource operations. There is a question of what consequences this will have for the internal competency of the regions to assess how good operations should be conducted. The importance of this competence is the most obvious for monitoring where the relevance and usability of the monitoring is based on a disciplinary objectivity. Internal competence may also contribute to increased trust in the quantitative monitoring, which enables management from a distance. The reason is that professional knowledge can provide an understanding for the considerations taken into account in the production of mechanical objective knowledge.

One way of ensuring an internal operational competence is for the municipality to manage care homes for the elderly under its own auspices. However, Swedish municipalities are currently encouraged to outsource all or a majority of their operations to external providers. In one of the regions studied, the municipality managed the daily operations of care homes only as an exception to the norm. In these cases, it is essential that the municipalities secure their long-term operational competence. This chapter has identified some of the risks involved when the municipality is stripped of such competence over time. In the long term, the municipalities risk becoming less knowledgeable and competent, both as customers and as regards their ability to make demands. In other ways, the organizational and institutional separation between the public and private organizations risks growing wider.

This does not per se change the possibility for undertaking mechanically objective monitoring to build actor-based and system-based trust. However, the disciplinary objective monitoring, which has particular advantages for building actor-based trust and thereby contributing to the general public's system-based trust in the long term, is made more difficult. Such a development does not inspire confidence.

Note

1. Under the Patient Safety Act (*patientsäkerhetslagen*), care staff have a duty to inform the Swedish National Board of Health and Welfare if a patient has suffered, or been exposed to a risk of suffering, a serious injury or illness in conjunction with health care.

References

Bevan, Gwyn, and Christopher Hood. 2006. "Have Targets Improved Performance in the English NHS?" *British Medical Journal* 332:419–422.

Boland, Richard J., and Ulrike Schultze. 1996. "Narrating Accountability: Cognition and the Production of the Accountable Self." In *Accountability: Power, Ethos and the Technologies of Managing*, edited by Rolland Munro and Jan Mouritsen, 62–81. London: International Thomson Business Press.

Hood, Christopher. 1995. "The 'New Public Management' in the 1980s: Variations on a Theme." *Accounting, Organizations and Society* 20:93–109.

Lonsdale, Jeremy. 1999. "Impacts." In *Performance or Compliance? Performance Audit and Public Management in Five Countries*, edited by Christopher Pollitt, Xavier Girre, Jeremy Lonsdale, Robert Mul, Hilkka Summa, and Marit Waerness, 171–193. Oxford, UK: Oxford University Press.

Mackenzie, Donald. 1990. *Inventing Accuracy: A Historical Sociology of Nuclear Missile Guidance*. Cambridge, MA: MIT Press.

Olson, Olov, and Kerstin Sahlin-Andersson. 1998. "Accounting Transformation in an Advanced Welfare State: The Case of Sweden." In *Global Warning! Debating International Developments in New Public Financial Management*, edited by Olov Olson, James Guthrie, and Christopher Humphrey, 241–275. Oslo: Cappelen Akademisk Forlag.

Patient Safety Act. 2010:659 (*Patientsäkerhetslagen*).

Porter, Theodore M. 1994. *Trust in Numbers: The Pursuit of Objectivity in Science and Public Life*. Princeton, NJ: Princeton University Press.

Power, Michael. 1997. *The Audit Society: Rituals of Verification*. Oxford, UK: Oxford University Press.

Roberts, John, and Robert Scapens. 1985. "Accounting Systems and Systems of Accountability—Understanding Accounting Practices in Their Organizational Contexts." *Accounting, Organizations and Society* 10:443–456.

Seal, Willy, John Cullen, Alec Dunlop, Tony Barry, and Mirghani Ahmed. 1999. "Enacting European Supply Chain: A Case Study on the Role of Management Accounting." *Management Accounting Research* 10:303–322.

Seal, Willy, and Peter Vincent-Jones. 1997. "Accounting and Trust in the Enabling of Long-Term Relations." *Accounting, Auditing and Accountability Journal* 10:406–431.

Sikka, Prem, and Hugh Willmott. 1995. "The Power of Independence: Defending the Jurisdiction of Accounting in the United Kingdom." *Accounting, Organizations and Society* 20:547–581.

Slagsvold, Britt. 1997. "Quality Measurements and Some Unintended Consequences: Can Quasi-quality Be a Consequence of Quality Standards?" In *Developing Quality in Personal Social Services*, edited by Adalbert Evers, Riitta Haverinen, Kai Leichsenring, and Gerald Wistow, 291–310. Aldershot: Ashgate.

Social Services Act. 2001:453 (*Socialtjänstlagen*).

CHAPTER 9

The Grammar of Trust as Ethical Challenge

Bengt Kristensson Uggla

In the last few decades, many have stressed the fundamental significance of trust for people and organizations, politics and economics. The observation that the presence of trust between people comprises an entirely critical condition for humans to be able to share their existence with each other, has led K. E. Løgstrup to develop a complete philosophy of life as well as an ethical theory through the fact that we normally meet each other with trust as point of departure (Løgstrup 1956/1997). In a similar manner, Niklas Luhmann has argued in favor of the importance of trust in reducing social complexity and in creating scope for human action transcending time by claiming the future in advance (Luhmann 1979). In the wake of Francis Fukuyama's distinction between *low-trust* and *high-trust societies*, it has been argued that the growing economic significance of trust for complex postindustrial knowledge-based societies is increasingly supported by flexible networks. If people cannot trust each other, cooperation will only occur within the framework of systems of formal rules and regulations, resulting in increased transactional costs. But in efficient organizations of a "high-trust society," there is, on the contrary, little need for contracts and legal regulations due to the presence of mutual trust (Fukuyama 1995). In other words, a "higher level" of trust appears as something that is supposed to be "good" for the wealth of nations. Similarly, Robert D. Putnam has argued that seemingly trivial meeting places, such as bowling clubs, Bible study groups, football teams, and choirs can contribute to developing social capital, making society as a whole function better. If people trust each other after having socialized informally and after having interacted in equal relationships through these types of activities, other forms of interpersonal interaction are also facilitated—hence, the transaction costs in society decrease and, to put it simply, we achieve much more with less effort. Social trust, it is said, not only benefits economic growth, but also promotes political democracy and the general well-being of people as it presupposes social bonds characterized by mutual trust. And the other way around, if social capital of trust is eroded, this will have severe consequences for society (Putnam 2000).

As a result of this attribution, and with an increasing significance of the capacity to evoke trust, changes in the level of trust have developed into one of the prime bases for the most commonly used measurements and evaluations of politicians and executives in the mediatized public sphere. The growing number of different kinds of "trust barometers" testifies to the fact that government authorities, as well as companies and organizations, are highly dependent on the existence of trust in order to operate. However, a fundamental prerequisite for the media's presentation of how much the level of trust has "increased" or "decreased" for everything from different occupational groups and institutions to currencies and politicians—as well as a prerequisite for the "high" trust levels as being positive and the "low" trust levels as being negative—is that the trust in question is measurable and comparable.

Aside from the general questions that can be raised as regards the broader perspectives of these transformations in association with the rise of an *audit society* (Power 1997), I will, in this chapter, argue that there are other, considerable reasons for questioning the sustainability, as well as the relevance, of indiscriminately advocating the benefits of a "high level" of trust, together with the significant one-dimensionality associated with the audit society's preference for metrics and ranking. The mania for trust in our time is not without complications and serious ethical challenges. One way of showing the flaws that are connected with talking, without clear distinctions, about the need for "more" trust in people, society, and organizations, is to point out the simple fact that mafia organizations, drug cartels, terrorist networks, and other criminal activities are actually, also, characterized by strong "cultures of trust." Within these contexts, any attempt to "increase" any form of undifferentiated trust is scarcely a solution, but will rather have devastating consequences. Despite these critical objections, the particular reasons for these complications have, nevertheless, not been properly explained. The criticism has mainly consisted of ironic comments and objections, but has failed to expand the understanding of the concept of trust, as such.

The objection might also be raised that both "too little" and "too much" trust may appear to have the capacity to undermine trust among people (Kristensson Uggla 2002, 402–404). Moreover, from this background, the benefit has been argued in favor of "trust 'in moderation'" as it is not only a lack of trust that, in some circumstances, can lead to laziness, hubris, blindness, foolishness, and carelessness, but excessive confidence can also have unwanted effects, in the form of idleness, carelessness, foolishness, blindness, and hubris (Rombach and Solli 2006, 412).

In other words, it is not that peculiar that today there exists a great need to problematize and expand the understanding of that which comprises trust. In contrast to the dominating one-dimensional perspective, I will argue for the necessity of a multidimensional, hermeneutical perspective of the inner complexity of the concept of trust, taking my point of departure in two concrete case studies, two examples of trust crises. As a further expansion on Robert D. Putman's speech about how trust can function as both "superglue" and "oil," I will try to describe how trust has to be organized in different ways in different contexts, so that the different forms of trust, in dialogic and institutional relationships, is simultaneously *bound together* and *kept separate* (Putnam 2000). I will, then, use this differentiation of the concept of trust—with its implied multidimensionality—to demonstrate the necessity of introducing an element of negation and critical distancing in each relationship of trust in order to cope with the ethical challenges associated with the "conflict of interpretations" also inevitably related to the phenomenon of trust. In the absence of absolute knowledge, unequivocal and simple solutions, trust as an ethical problem challenges us to cope with contrasting interpretations in a creative, critical, and responsible way (Ricoeur 1969/1974). Thus, the journey of trust, from theory to practice, transgressing the boundaries between different contexts, progresses through a labyrinth where we have to, align with Aristotle, develop a well-informed judgment in every concrete situation through use of the practical wisdom—*phronesis*.

When Dialogic Trust Turns into Corruption

The photograph, that received the Swedish award "Picture of the Year" in 2007, depicts a man and a woman in a bar. They are kissing each other and caressing in a manner indicating a loving and passionate relationship. Encountering this scene during an evening in a bar is not entirely uncommon and discomforting; it may even evoke a sense of empathy. The kiss has admittedly, as a cultural expression, an ambiguous history associated with hypocrisy, cheating, and treachery, although our spontaneous reaction likely testifies that it is something beautiful, a sign of affection and trust. In this particular situation, however, the kiss proved to be part of a far more complex story.

The photograph in question was taken on the evening of October 23, 2007, and the two individuals seen kissing in the Stockholm restaurant *Judith & Bertil* were not just usual members of the public. The man was a prominent political reporter, Anders Pihlblad, from TV4 in Sweden, who, on this particular evening, was dining with Ulrica Schenström, state secretary working for the Swedish prime minister, Fredrik Reinfeldt, and who had specific responsibility for staffing, planning of domestic issues, and communication within the prime minister's office. At the time, she was also one of the central figures in the transformation of the Moderate Party into the New Moderates. What happened on this evening in October 2007 proved to be the beginning of a turbulent process that would soon result in the ruin of both their personal lives and their careers.

The very next day after the restaurant visit, the scandal burst onto the public arena in Sweden's largest tabloid, *Aftonbladet*, which published the story with the headline "All-Nighter: Reinfeldt's Right Hand Woman Partying with TV4's Political Reporter" (October 24, 2007). A photograph "revealing" that a leading political journalist had privately met—and, in addition, appeared to have been physically intimate with—the top political official of the government offices, as well as a leading Moderate Party politician, is, in no way, favorable. Moreover, this situation occurred only a few days prior to the Moderate Party conference, and Pihlblad was the very person who had been assigned to monitor that event. Therefore, it was no surprise that the kiss incident had devastating consequences for both of these individuals: professionally, it meant that Schenström had to resign and also that Pihlblad was forced, for a while, to take *time out* from his work responsibilities. On a personal level, the negative impact was even greater for both of them.

How did the "Schenström affair" develop into such a nightmare for those involved, and, ultimately, for Sweden's prime minister Fredrik Reinfeldt? In order to understand this, the critical importance of trust for both political power and the fourth estate, the media, must be brought to the fore. When the Schenström affair rapidly became an affair of trust, it also developed according to the complex and delicate logic characterizing crisis of confidence. It is obvious that leading polit-ical officials of government offices should maintain a greater distance from the media—and it is true that Pihlblad, as a journalist, had come far too close to the very political power he had been assigned to monitor. At the same time, it is an indisputable fact that personal relationships are absolutely vital for anyone wishing to operate successfully within both the media and politics. Public press conferences cannot function in a void; they require pre- and postconference work in the form of trustful, informal conversations in different constellations between the spheres of media and politics. This relationship of dialogic trust, which Ulrica Schenström mastered to perfection, is critical for both journalis-tic and political operations. However, the power of the image, showing the kissing couple in a bar environment, generated an uncontrollable crisis of confidence. This crisis evolved irrespective of whether the issue was about whether a top official of the government offices was really sober and capable of managing emergency standby duty or whether it was about the ability of the same official to maintain an objective dis-tance in her relationship to the media, whose purpose is to critically scrutinize the government.

The Correct Institutional Coldness of Civil Servants—an Alternative?

The Schenström affair raises important questions about the nature of trust. Why is it that friendship between people who are on first-name terms with each other—something that, spontaneously and out of con-text, should surely rather be viewed as an expression of trustful relation-ships—can, through a certain contextualization, suddenly ignite such outrage and generate such a rapidly accelerated crisis of confidence? How can dialogic trust turn into corruption? Is it not "good" to have a "higher level" of trust? Or are we not talking about "the same" type of trust in these contexts?

Is the only conclusion of the case study above to imply that close dia-logic relationships are a threat to trust and that trust in this context can only be maintained through the icy distancing and factual formalism characterizing institutional relationships? Is the only alternative in poli-tics and media to entirely avoid informal relationships built on dialogic trust and, instead, to focus, exclusively, on an institutional perspec-tive? In order to clarify that a distanced objectivity does not solve all problems, we will take a closer look at an opposite case study, demon-strating what happens when dialogic trust, characterized by friendship relationships on first-name terms, is completely marginalized in favor of an institutional perspective—all with the good intention of counteracting the form of corruption with which we were confronted above, yet which still produced devastating results.

The second case study has its origins in the official assignment given to the Swedish agency Krus, Swedish Council for Strategic Human Resources Development, by the government minister, Mats Odell: the formulation of an "ethos for civil servants." This assignment resulted in the publication, *Shared Values for Civil Servants* (Krus 2009), which contains a "compilation" of the shared value system of civil servants, developed through a selection of laws and regulations considered to "reflect" the governmental foundational value system. The point of departure for this value system is that government officials are employed in the service of the citizens, a broad idea that is, then, further divided into different principles on how public administration should be built on and supported by democracy, human rights, and the rule of law while, at the same time, offering efficient operations with a distinct citizen perspective.

The assignment asking for an articulation of a common value system must be understood from the crisis considered above and it is possible to say that a lot of the institutional dimension of trust, which the players in the Schenström affair were lacking, is articulated in the report produced by Krus—but consider carefully that the alternative presented by Krus is a correct and pure version of institutional trust, which gives no consideration to, and, in fact, fully excludes all the informal aspects characterizing dialogic trust. It is of significance, that the ice-cold formalistic tendency and the pure juridical focus of the texts are strongly contrasted by the living, organic plants that have been chosen to adorn the cover of the report, without this ever being problematized. One dilemma is solved, however, at the expense of a new dilemma arising.

A consistent concept in *Shared Values for Civil Servants* deals with protecting trust in the government, which implies, negatively, that receiving gifts, benefits, or other types of conflicts of interest are not allowed; however, the positive implication of protecting trust can be said to be the discipline, reliability, honesty, and impartiality of the civil servants' actions. The word "trust" appears frequently in the text, but is exclusively linked to an institutional objectivity that is seen to be unquestionable. Civil servants must strictly abide by legal clauses and frameworks. Within this "legal clause machine" to which I am referring, the fundamental democratic principle is not connected, to any degree, with dialogic relationships; instead, ideals, such as efficiency and housekeeping, are brought to the fore, for example, when it is emphasized that the established goals for the operations in question are to be met with an appropriate input of resources and within the given economic framework. However, it is at the same time possible to state that the ethos for civil servants, as developed by Krus, due to the one-sidedness of that ethos, is characterized by a problematical type of "institutional coldness." As a result, on the one hand, civil servants surely behave correctly from a strict institutional perspective; however, on the other hand, they do not seem capable of relating dialogically with citizens in accordance with a democratic "spirit." Justice, as a virtue, implies a clear requirement of factuality extending beyond the dialogicity of friendship—however, do these two, justice and friendship, really rule each other out in this manner?

Against the background of these critical objections, it seems to be a doubtful strategy to, first, "compile" a stable foundation in the form of a "value system," in order to, then, allow civil servants to utilize that same value system in the form of a simple implementation process. In reality, conflicts can be found right from the start and the complications and dilemmas that they give rise to are, from a hermeneutical perspective, in fact, constitutive for trust as a multidimensional problem.

Interlude: Antigone's Dilemma Is Also Our Dilemma

Even if Krus, in *Shared Values for Civil Servants*, in passing, states that it must be possible to expect personal responsibility from a civil servant, as well as their own ability to make ethical choices, the legal and institutional aspect of the value system—the striving for the rule of law—is completely overshadowing. The aspects that are constantly brought forward are justice, the rule of law, and consistency that "like cases be treated alike" in a world without dialogic accounts or trust, where serious legal or ethical dilemmas do not, in fact, seem to exist, nor do any conflicts exist at all between these various value systems. It seems to be implicitly assumed that ethics and law are the same thing or, alternatively, that ethics can be ignored or simply reduced to a subdivision of law. In any case, there is no understanding of the fact that ethics and law can be said to comprise only *partially* overlapping problems and that trust is a multidimensional problem in which genuine dilemmas must be constantly managed, requiring an awareness of how to cope with inevitable conflicts of interpretations in order to develop critically reflected convictions.

However, when the presentation addresses the manner in which the principle of public access to official documents is to be combined with the obligation to preserve secrecy, a real problem arises and, for once, a gap in the formalistic facade can be seen. The fact that a discussion of the freedom of sources and whistle-blower protection—described as a "security valve"—is, in a seemingly unproblematic manner, included in secrecy requirements, it implies a conflict of norms, but this dilemma is not taken seriously into consideration to any degree. Instead, formalism assumes the dominating position, so that the dilemmas are erased and no questions, whatsoever, are posed regarding the manner in which these different requirements can be coordinated. The conflicts are made invisible and, thus, it becomes impossible to manage them from this one-dimensional perspective.

In one of the most well-known tragedies of ancient times by Sophocles, with the title of the main character, *Antigone*, a significantly more complex reality is articulated, in which various values, instead, inexorably clash with each other. When Antigone returns to Thebes, she is forbidden to bury one of her dead brothers, Polyneices, because he has been deemed an enemy of the city. However, Antigone defies this prohibition by burying her brother and is, therefore, sentenced to death. Antigone is imprisoned in a vault where she commits suicide, which entails another series of tragic circumstances for those involved. However, in the story Antigone never denies, in any manner, her (legal) crime; instead, she questions the morals of the regulations, which also contributes to her being sentenced to death. In contrast, she chooses to act according to morals instead of the law, fully aware of the consequences this may bring.

Without going into the details of this multifaceted plot, which I have brought in inspired by the Paul Ricoeur's "interlude" in chapter 9 of *Oneself as Another* (1990/1992), it is possible to observe that Krus, in its presentation of foundational values for civil servants (Krus 2009), does not take into consideration that these types of value conflicts between morals and legislation, in fact, may arise; instead, the issue is reduced to an instrumental question of implementation. A contributing cause for this is likely to be, that trust is one dimensionally dealt with from a pure institutional perspective, which does not take into account the multidimensional—and, thus, inherently conflict-filled—nature of trust. The challenge that is described in the case studies above does not, at the same time, constitute a problem that can be said to be possible to "solve," but rather a genuine dilemma: How is it possible to understand that which may constitute a virtue in dialogic relationships (friendship) may, at the same time, be regarded as corruption at institutional level? Or vice versa, how is it possible that virtues, such as justice and the rule of law, which are absolutely necessary from an institutional perspective, are insufficient to maintain trust in dialogic relations? In order to address such issues, it is required that the unambiguous and "perfect" model of formalism is abandoned and that conflicts generated by the great number of possible contextualizations, based on the multi-dimensionality of trust, are taken seriously.

In Sweden, this challenge is brought to the fore each year by the annually recurring "Almedalen Week," which brings together politicians, representatives of public authorities and business managers, lobbyists, and journalists to meet and interact with the public through a nearly incalculable number of activities on the agenda. From having been more of a "politicians' week," this incredibly informal event, which takes place during the first week of July in Visby, Gotland, has developed into an arena for initiatives, discussions, conversations, and late-night mingling. This has aroused suspicion and criticism, as the scope and extent of these activities, which include very informal meetings and friendly, spontaneous conversations between representatives of different sections of society, is often far greater than that seen in the Schenström affair. It is therefore, from the exclusive perspective of institutional trust, easy to draw the conclusion that these activities are illegitimate and should cease. I believe, however, that such a simple approach would be too hasty a solution, as one would then have to ask if democracy and the rule of law would function better if such contacts were avoided, and a purely institutional approach was pursued instead. The number of informal meetings during Almedalen Week is, in fact, good for democracy, which has assumed an ever more purely institutional character, while at the same time democracy as a way of life has been overshadowed. In addition, Almedalen Week very likely reduces the "transaction costs" in society as a whole, as it decreases the number of meetings, as well as initiates processes enhancing both efficiency and prosperity in society. However, one absolute precondition to ensure that the activities taking place during Almedalen Week do not lead to corruption is that those who participate are "socially robust," and have the integrity to manage their various roles. In order to cope with the ethical challenges associated with the multidimensionality of trust, the people who participate require a hermeneutical awareness that may support the formation of critically reflected convictions.

The Grammar of Trust—between Friendship and Justice

Although the question of trust was of little interest within philosophy for a long period of time, this has changed (Lagerspetz 1996, 1–14). In order to elaborate on what kind of contribution philosophy may offer when coping with the multidimensionality of trust, and the connected ethical challenges, I would like to return to the proposition that trust within societies and organizations can function both as "superglue" and as "oil," in the sense that it both *binds together* and *holds apart* our world. I will use this proposition as a departure point for a hermeneutic discussion about the relationship between the dialogic and institutional dimensions of trust.

The particular problem that I want to tackle starts with the seemingly simple question, which Paul Ricoeur deals with in the introduction of *Oneself as Another*: How is it possible, that I am actually able to understand a personal address to myself, when someone says "you," or identify a "me," when spoken of in terms of "him/her"—or merely in terms of a neutral statistic data—and yet still understand that this is all about "myself"? The fact that it is fully legitimate to refer to "me" by shifting personal pronouns, not only by "me" speaking in first person, but also through indentifying "me" in both second, as well as in third person, says something essential about the fundamentally reflexive structure that characterizes our configurations of identity. The shift in roles, made possible through the use of various personal pronouns still referring to one and the same person, reveals a reflective, communicative structure that relates the *self-understanding* (of a "me" in first person) to a *dialogic understanding* (in a "you" of second person) and *objectifying explanations* (in terms of a "him/her/it" in third person).[1]

With this argument from the philosophy of identity, inspired by the linguistic, practical, narrative, and moral determination of selfhood in Ricoeur's *hermeneutics of the self* as a resource of philosophical thinking, it becomes possible to develop a more complex, multidimensional notion of trust in which trust is seen as a fundamentally relational phenomenon. And through this *grammar of trust* (Kristensson Uggla 2002, 406–411), it becomes possible to show how the communicative phenomenon of trust requires that we create a connection between the three distinct dimensions of trust, as articulated in the first, second, and third personal pronouns. In this triadic context, every person's self-confidence (in first person) can be seen as a necessary requirement for dialogic relations and institutions in order to function at all. Trust also requires the dialogic relation (in second person) between people meeting face-to-face, which is based on the insight that our lives ultimately rest in the hands of others. However, in the long run, trust can never be maintained only through self-trust or dialogic relationships. These dimensions of trust also imply the existence of an institutional dimension (in third person), which cannot be fully understood in terms of an extended dialogue, since these relations, to an anonymous "every man" in the third person, extend beyond the close relationship that we maintain face-to-face with another "you." At the same time, it is obvious that institutions without any relationship to dialogic relationships or self-trust are, in the end, seen as insufficient with their interpersonal indifference and cold objectivity.

With this "grammatical" structure of trust—based on the *hermeneutics of the self* developed by Ricoeur by the use of "mixed" and "unstable" discourses—as a starting point, trust cannot, in other words, be limited solely to self-strengthening measures, dialogic intimacy between an "I" and a "you," nor can it be reduced to something simply related to rules and anonymous institutions. The grammar of trust, instead, is seen as a sociocultural infrastructure making it both possible and legitimate to *speak*, to be *spoken to*, and to be spoken *about*, according to the articulation with the different personal pronouns.

What radically increases the complexity of this grammar of trust is the simultaneous *continuity* and *discontinuity* between the three dimensions articulated in terms of the three separate pronouns. Thus, the relationship between dialogic and institutional relations is characterized by a remarkable *discontinuous continuity*; there exists, so to speak, a dichotomous relationship as well as a complementary relationship in meeting as an "I" and a "you" in a friendly interpersonal relationship, face-to-face, and acting within the framework of an institutional relationship where "every man" is treated fairly and with equality. Ricoeur describes the institution as "a structure which cannot be reduced to interpersonal relations, yet is connected to them in a remarkable manner" (Ricoeur 1990/1992, 194). Thus, if we want to cope with trust in a responsible way, it appears as if we have to face the challenge of having to both *bring together* and *hold apart* dialogic and institutional trust. In Ricoeur's terminology, one could say that the challenge regarding connecting the dialogic and institutional dimensions of trust is about establishing a bridge between "the prose of fairness" (where one argues) and "the poetics of love" (where one does not argue), or in other terms, between "the formal rule" and "the hymn" (Ricoeur 1990, 40).

From Theory to Practice—a Vulnerable and Provisional Dialectic of Trust

Against the background of a hermeneutically informed multidimensional view of trust, one could argue that neither successful organizations, nor democratic societies, can either be without, or be completely reduced to, anonymous institutions for representation; dialogic relationships are also necessary, as well as self-respect among citizens who are able to mutually break their own convictions in favor of another. Societies and organizations, thus, can neither be reduced to formal, anonymous entities, nor to informal personal networks of relationships. From this perspective, trust seems to belong to a discourse characterized by risk rather than security—and the task can never be to offer a solely theoretical solution to the dilemmas that one confronts. Because of the fundamental disproportion existing between dialogic and institutional trust, a *practical* mediation between these two dimensions can only assume the shape of a *vulnerable* and *provisional* dialectic. However, this disproportion also implies that friendship and justice coexist in practical life—at the same time, as they have to be separated, as they follow two separate logics of trust, they are mutually related.

This relationship has its counterpart in the field of ethics, because here also it seems a necessity to both retain an ethics of proximity and simultaneously exceed the limitations of a phenomenological ethics in order to affirm the ideal of justice that can only be articulated at an institutional level in connection with a legal discourse. How this abstract argumentative social morality, which consistently remains indifferent to friendship relationships by being based on the responsibilities of the institutions toward "every man," can be related to more concrete ethical beliefs found in the mutual relationship between an "I" and a "you," is a starting point for the conflicts generating many of the contemporary crises of confidence. This complex articulation of an ethical vision based on discontinuous continuity between its different parts we find in the "little ethics" that Ricoeur presented in Chapter 7–9 in *Oneself as Another* summarized as "the aim for the good life, with and for others in juste institutions" (Ricoeur 1990/1992, 172).

Based on the specific examples that we here have placed on the agenda, it becomes obvious how complicated it can be to claim, without establishing any clear distinctions, that we in general need "more" trust in society and organizations. Trust appears, instead, to be what Don Ihde has named a *multistable* phenomenon (Ihde 1986). Trust capital is a *shared* capital, which presumes multidimensional perspectives, a dialectic approach, and an interpretative ability, so that it is possible to both keep together and differentiate between the shape of trust in dialogic and institutional relationships. Only against this background, will it be possible to comprehend how something that appears to be a virtue in dialogic relationships (friendship), could imply corruption at an institutional level—and why institutional virtues (such as justice) are far from sufficient to maintain confidence in dialogic relationships. Trust is, in fact, a value that is already on the right side of the rules, in the same way as it also continues to travel beyond the limit of the validity of the rules—how can we keep together and set apart these dimensions?

Trust certainly cannot exist in the long run without institutions, formalized structures, and regulations—however, neither can confidence be completely reduced to something that can be formalized and regulated. Considering the complexity of the grammar of trust, we are confronted by the necessity to develop a concept of confidence that shifts from blind trust to reflective trust (Kristensson Uggla 2002, 402–406; Rombach and Solli 2006, 417). When we travel from theory to practice, it becomes apparent how complicated and multidimensional the concept of trust really is. It is, indeed, impossible to live and survive without trust, but, at the same time, based on everyday experience, it is similarly impossible to live together with other people without becoming disappointed, as trust is being constantly betrayed. Therefore, it is not only reasonable, from the perspective of trust, to develop a critical mind, but also impossible to maintain trust without also incorporating a substantial degree of mistrust and suspicion.

Criticism should not, in other words, be considered an external threat to trust. A sound level of suspicion and skepticism constitutes, instead, an absolutely indispensable part of a reflective trust. This is an aspect that neither organizations nor communications, neither politics nor the business world can exist without—also in order to be able to distinguish between the different dimensions of the grammar of trust. Democracies, companies, organizations, and markets cannot survive if trust is configured as blind trust. A profound grammar of trust assumes a critical distance, otherwise, one is forced to cope with the false alternative to choose between dialogic confidence and institutional confidence, friendship relationships and justice and legal security—as if, this was a question of mutually exclusive alternatives. In the end, trust relies on *practical wisdom*, where situation-based judgments and robust personal convictions have to accompany each other.

As conflicts are inevitable when coping with the problem of trust, there can be no clear-cut theoretical solutions; instead, the "solutions" must be concrete and practical, and must be carefully contextualized in each specific situation. We may, therefore, together with Ricoeur, interpret *Antigone* as an appeal to "deliberate well," as it is not only impossible but also dangerous to imagine the existence of both societies and organizations without such conflicts. If we want to defend a true democratic society, we are condemned to live with a fundamental uncertainty, due to the fact that democracy, as a way of life and as a system, accepts its contradictions to a degree to which it institutionalizes conflicts. However, functioning markets and business relationships also assume that it is possible to manage the complexity of simultaneously holding together and separating dialogic and institutional relationships of trust. This means, that we can preserve trust in all its complexity only through the ability to simultaneously keep together and differentiate between friendship and justice, as we need both dialogues and institutions, and cannot dispense with either of them. However, for the shift from theory to practice to become characterized by a profound reflective trust, and not by blind trust, interpretative competence is required, which makes it possible to deal with the multidimensionality of trust in societies and organizations.

Note

1. My inspiration for this discussion about trust, and my construction of the *grammar of trust*, comes from the fourfold (philosophy of language, action, narrative, and morals) determination of the self, which Paul Ricoeur presented in his study of identity problems. Throughout the study, he experiments with a triad structure, emanating from three different personal pronouns in first, second, and third person (Ricoeur 1990/1992; Ricoeur 1992, 203–221). The "good" (perfect, complete) life, as referred to by Aristotle, appears, therefore, as a tripartite multidimensional structure. In his book from the turn of the Millennium (Ricoeur 2000/2004), a fifth determination of the self is being added: human memory.

References

Aftonbladet. October 24, 2007. "All-Nighter: Reinfeldt's Right Hand Woman Partying with TV4's Political Reporter."
Fukuyama, Francis. 1995. *Trust. The Social Virtues and the Creation of Prosperity*. New York: Free Press.
Ihde, Don. 1986. *Experimental Phenomenology. An Introduction*. Albany, NY: State University of New York.
Kristensson Uggla, Bengt. 2002. *Slaget om verkligheten: Filosofi, omvärldsanalys, tolkning*. Stockholm; Stehag: Brutus Östlings Bokförlag Symposion.
Krus. 2009. *Den gemensamma värdegrunden för de statsanställda*. Stockholm: Kompetensrådet för utveckling i staten [Krus].
Lagerspetz, Olli. 1996. *The Tacit Demand. A Study in Trust*. Turku: Department of Philosophy at Åbo Akademi University.
Luhmann, Niklas. 1979. *Trust and Power*. Chichester: J. Wiley.

Løgstrup, Knud Eijler. 1956/1997. *The Ethical Demand.* Notre Dame: University of Notre Dame Press.

Power, Michael. 1997. *The Audit Society: Rituals and Verification.* Oxford, UK: Oxford University Press.

Putnam, Robert D. 2000. *Bowling Alone: The Collapse and Revival of American Community.* New York: Simon & Schuster.

Ricoeur, Paul. 1969/1974. *The Conflict of Interpretation: Essays on Hermeneutics.* Evanston, IL: Northwestern University Press.

———. 1990. *Liebe und Gerechtigkeit / Amour et Justice.* Tübingen: J. C. B. Mohr. Mit einer deutschen Parallelübersetzung von Matthias Raden, herasugegeben von Oswald Bayer.

———. 1990/1992. *Oneself as Another.* Chicago: Chicago University Press. English translation by Kathleen Blamey.

———. 1992. "Approches de la personne." In *Lectures 2. La contrées des philosophes,* 203–221. Paris: Seuil.

———. 2000/2004. *Memory, History, Forgetting.* Chicago: Chicago University Press.

Rombach, Björn, and Rolf Solli. 2006. "Om nyttan av lagom förtroende." In *Värdet av förtroende,* edited by Inga-Lill Johansson, Sten Jönsson, and Rolf Solli, 385–417. Lund: Studentlitteratur.

CHAPTER 10

The Historical Incubators of Trust in Sweden: From the Rule of Blood to the Rule of Law

Lars Trägårdh

The previous chapters in this book highlight the many ways in which concrete organizational practices that aim at creating, capitalizing on, and manipulating trust, rely on, but often also undermine, stretch, and cross, different types of boundaries in society. If, however, we lift our gaze above and beyond the immediate landscape of the organizations that form the basis of our societies, we are confronted with the more fundamental question: What makes people trust one another in the first place, and what is the reason the degree of basic trust toward other people and toward societal institutions varies strongly between different societies? What historical and institutional factors tend to determine the quality and intensity of mutual trust within a society?

This chapter's primary empirical focus is Sweden and more specifically how we are to understand the conditions under which a high degree of social trust and confidence in institutions have developed in this particular society. The objective is to discuss the Swedish experience from a comparative perspective that allows us to think theoretically about the historical incubators of trust, thus extending the relevance of this experience beyond the confines of Sweden itself. Sweden is, it will be argued, of interest not simply because it is a high-trust society but also, and more significantly, because it embodies many of the aspects of modernization that often have been linked to a decline in trust. Thus, the chapter seeks to identify and briefly explore a number of dimensions that appear to be historically linked to—and presently sustain—trust.

The Specter of Mistrust

In the wake of James Coleman's (1988) and Robert Putnam's (1993) influential research, interest in the issues of social trust and social capital has increased dramatically since the early 1990s. However, one can trace the interest in social trust much further back in time, indeed all the way back to the birth of modern social science. A typical example is the moral philosopher Sissela Bok. In a book from 1978, she argued that trust is essential for the proper functioning of society and that, conversely, when "trust is destroyed, societies falter and collapse" (Bok 1978, 26).

This ominous tone is rather typical for trust researchers for whom trust is a precious and also vulnerable resource: easy to squander, difficult to recover. A few scholars, for example, Russel Hardin, stress that a certain degree of mistrust, particularly in relation to the state, but also in relation to other institutions, companies, and individuals, is also essential in order to avoid constructive trust to turn into naive gullibility (Hardin 1999). However, the dominant position among economists, political scientists, sociologists, psychologists, and other researchers is that trust functions as a form of social glue, holding together families, communities, organizations, companies, and nations. In instrumental terms, trust is also perceived as a crucial asset that reduces transaction costs, not only in economic terms, but also in the political system and, more generally, in the daily social relations between people (e.g., Fukuyama 1995; Seligman 1997; Bordum 2001).

While the trust literature agrees on the fundamental importance of trust and its positive role, a variety of researchers theorize the genesis of trust and its essential nature in ways that, at least at a superficial level, appears to be contradictory. On the one hand, we have the researchers, such as Erik Erikson, who argue that general trust is deeply rooted in the individual's basic character, which is formed early in a child's life and which, once childhood socialization is complete, is subsequently stable and relatively insensitive to external influences (Erikson 1993). Along the same lines, but with an emphasis on the societal rather than the individual level, Eric Uslaner (2002) argues that trust is a social fact, a "sticky" structure that is very stable over time within its delimited social space (country, society, nation). For both Erikson and Uslaner trust thus constitutes a "moral foundation," for the individual and for society.

This association of trust with childrearing and the subsequent rein-forcing socialization in school, work, civil society, and interactions with public institutions, appears to be a plausible explanatory model in the analysis of a society, such as the Swedish one, where the level of trust is not only high, but also stable over time—at least until the present time. However, in other countries and in other periods, the question of trust has been raised against a far more somber backdrop, where the primary issue facing the researchers has been very low levels of trust or a marked tendency toward a decline in social trust. In this context, the focus has not, understandably, been on the durability of trust but, rather, on its fragility. In our time, this particular view on the problem of trust is associated, first and foremost, with trust-related research in the United States and especially with Robert Putnam and his acclaimed book *Bowling Alone* (2000). Putnam marshals a wide range of statistical data demonstrating a downward trend in social capital, a component of which is social trust (along with a measure of civic engagement in voluntary associations). Putnam suggests that this trend is linked to other changes in American society, such as the decline of the traditional family, a decrease in religiosity, an excessive amount of time spent alone in front of the TV, an adversarial legal culture in which people sue each other rather than talk their way to solutions, and other negative aspects of a modern, individualistic, and pluralistic market-based society.

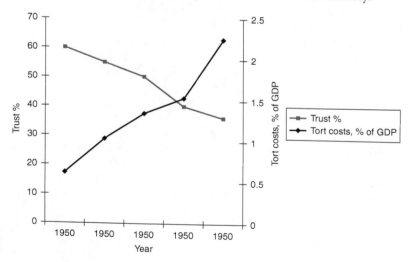

Figure 10.1 US tort costs versus trust 1954–1998.
Sources: World Values Survey (WVS) and Towers Perrin (2006).

Putnam's alarming analysis of the collapse of American communities aligns well with the data to which we have access measuring the level of overall trust in the United States. This data suggests a reduction from an excess of 60 percent who claimed to trust others around 1950 to 32 percent, according to the latest survey conducted by the General Social Survey (GSS).[1] This can be contrasted with data that measure the increase in tort costs, a proxy measure for distrust and conflict in society. This data demonstrates an opposite trend of a steadily increasing level of cost. From around 1950 when this figure was equivalent to 0.5 percent of GDP, tort costs are currently five times higher, equivalent to 2.5 percent of GDP (see figure 10.1).

Globally, comparative national studies demonstrate that trust levels have declined in Southern and Eastern Europe since the late 1980s and, if we move away from Europe and North America and other Anglo-Saxon countries, such as Canada, Australia, and New Zeeland, the tendency suggests that trust is low even if we do not always have access to fully reliable data, especially data that captures changes over time.[2]

Trust and Modernity

This is one of the reasons why the current literature on trust reflects such an angst-ridden tone of voice. However, it should be noted that the contemporary preoccupation with the decline and presumed fragility of social trust has a long history. Prominent thinkers, like Marx, Durkheim, Simmel, Weber, and Tönnies, who effectively created modern social science, took as their starting point a position that equated modernity with an unhealthy individualism that distanced man from the community and weakened the relations of trust that characterized traditional society. In the wake of the new freedom of the city and the anonymity of mass society followed alienation (Marx) and anomie (Durkheim), a shift from *Gemeinschaft* toward *Gesellschaft* (Tönnies), and life trapped in an "iron cage" (Weber). The individual was caught between, on the one hand, the modern, bureaucratic state, which weakened organic community ties, and, on the other, a market society that promoted consumer narcissism and materialist egoism (Sztompka 1999 for a discussion of trust and early sociology).

This association of modernity with social malaise has ever since been a recurrent trope among both politicians and social scientists, in recent times especially in the United States. Indeed, it at times appears as the history of modernity coincides with a parallel and constantly repeated

anxiety that the intrinsic logic of modernity itself with inexorable necessity undermines the very bonds of trust, which, over time, are essential to
keep a society together. Echoing the concerns of the seminal figures cited
above, David Riesman achieved major success in the 1950s with his book
The Lonely Crowd (1950), in which he analyzed the loneliness at the heart
of modern American mass society. A few decades later, Christopher Lasch
(1978) bemoaned the "narcissistic individualism," which, he argued, had
undermined local communities and resulted in the decline of the traditional family. In our own time, this rhetoric of imminent social collapse
has been expressed using new vocabularies but, in substance, the analysis and the gloomy conclusions remain the same. Some observers have
remarked upon the dangers lurking in the "risk society" characteristic of
our new age (Beck 1992). Others have described an increasing threat to
the "lifeworld" or have raised the alarm about declining "social capital"
(Habermas 1996; Putnam 2000). What is common in these depictions
is a concern that the trust between people and the confidence in institutions is steadily, and constantly, decreasing.

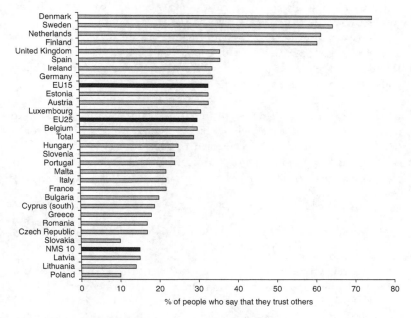

Figure 10.2 Social trust in international comparison. EU15 refers to the original 15 member states, EU25 refers to the extended 25 member states, and NMS10 refers to the 10 new
member states.
Source: WVS.

However, the well-established dystopian discourse regarding the negative aspects of modernity notwithstanding, we have, in recent decades, been afforded access to new and extensive empirical evidence measuring and comparing social trust in nearly all of the countries in the world. While these data have been criticized as problematic in many respects (Lundåsen and Pettersson 2009, for a critical analysis of trust-related data), it is nonetheless clear that this empirical evidence forces us to address a number of new—and significant—challenges with respect to how we theorize the genesis of trust and the conditions under which it thrives or declines.

To begin with, social trust varies dramatically from country to country, as figure 10.2 demonstrates. There is, furthermore, no general, or universal, tendency toward a decline in trust. Not only do Sweden and other Nordic countries have a comparatively high level of trust today but also the level has increased, rather than decreased, over the last 20–30 years. This implies that even if we look only at the relatively rich and modern Western world, it is obvious that modernity, itself, cannot explain the large differences in trust existing between Sweden and other modern countries, such as France and the United States.

Moreover, this variation is structured in a manner of additional theoretical interest. Specifically, if one looks more closely at the countries that exhibit high levels of trust it immediately becomes clear that these countries present fundamental problems for the classic theories associating modernity with the dissolution of social ties and decreased social trust. There are a few countries in which the majority of people claim to trust others, a group that includes Sweden and the other Nordic countries. But one would be hard-pressed to accept a description of these countries as being more traditional and less modern. Indeed, if there is one epithet that can be and has been applied to Sweden, it is precisely "modernity."

Modernity and the Radical Individualism of the Swedes

The notion of Sweden as the "prototypical modern society" has deep historical roots.[3] As Arne Ruth observed in an influential essay from 1984, politicians from Right to Left, since the late nineteenth century, have embraced the idea that Sweden is particularly progressive and forward looking. This idea was further strengthened after the famous Stockholm Exhibition in 1930, which came to be associated with modern design and utopian social engineering. Moreover, the Swedish Social mocrats came to embrace this legacy. An election campaign poster from

Figure 10.3 Swedish Social-Democratic election poster from 1936 [*Framtidsfolket röstar med Arbetarepartiet*].
Source: Arbetarrörelsens Arkiv.

the 1940s, figure 10.3, captures this view very well: the Worker's Party identifies itself with the Swedish people as "the people of the future."

However, modernity was not only a question of an imagined national identity or lofty political rhetoric. If by modernity we mean, for example, a desire to move away from traditional social and economic structures and to embrace a modern market society in which individual freedom and autonomy are at the center, Swedish modernity was, also, remarkably concrete and expressed in social practices and institutional reality. The Swedish welfare state has increasingly served to both create and develop the values and practices maximizing individual autonomy in the context of a peculiar, even extreme "social contract," according to a moral logic I have called the Swedish "statist individualism" (Trägårdh 1997; Berggren and Trägårdh 2006). This becomes particularly visible when looking at figure 10.4, which is a map of values based on data from the WVS. This map captures the various countries' position in relation to the two value dimensions measuring the degree to which societies are traditional or modern. Sweden and other Nordic countries seem extreme in their prioritizing of personal liberty and rational values at the expense of traditional values, such as religion, nation, and family. When studying figures 10.2 and 10.4, it appears that this comparative data points to a positive link between a more modern, individualistic social order and a high level of trust, rather than the reverse (Inglehart 2006; Inglehart and Welzel 2005).

Societies with a more traditional view of the family, nation, and religion, developing countries in Africa, Asia, and Latin America as well as some modern market societies, such as the United States, which are characterized by more communitarian values, do not stand out as countries with high trust, on the contrary. Sweden's radical difference in a comparative perspective, combined with the fact that Sweden and the other Nordic countries form a special group with shared characteristics, suggests that an analysis of conditions of trust in Sweden is, in fact, of particular interest. Could it be that a specific Nordic variant of modernization, where the individual's liberation from the traditional and thick community ties of family, clan, community, and faith-based institutions, has played a decisive role in the development of cooler, but more widely shared, social trust?

The debate about and the study of trust has, not surprisingly, been much more intense in those contexts in which trust has been absent, very limited, or in decline. Putnam's groundbreaking book—*Bowling Alone*—referred to these concerns in its very subtitle: *The Collapse and Revival of American Community*. For a long time, however, the study of trust was more limited in countries such as Sweden, where the majority of the people claim to have solid, basic trust in others. However, this imbalance is now in a process of being corrected.

For example, the writings of Bo Rothstein and his colleagues regarding trust and social capital can largely be seen to constitute a criticism and corrective of existing, above all, American, theory from a Swedish empirical perspective (Rothstein 2003; Rothstein and Stolle 2003). In addition, the growing body of comparative data provided by large population surveys has made an increasing number of researchers aware of the fact that the Nordic countries are of particular interest for the analysis of the conditions under which trust appears to thrive.

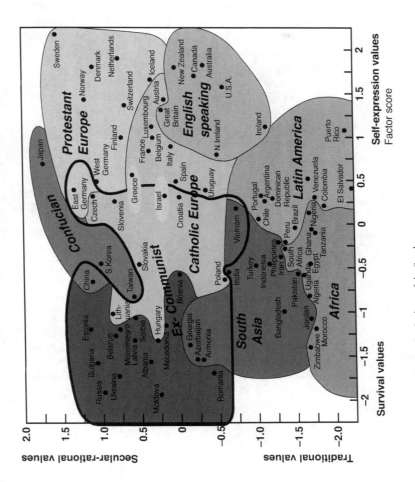

Figure 10.4 The radical individualism of the Swedes.
Source: WVS, fourth wave (1991–2001). See also Inglehart and Welzel (2005).

What these data show is that Sweden and other Nordic countries play a special role not only in terms of social trust (see figure 10.1) but also as regards a number of other attributes. High trust correlates with socio-economic equality, relatively low levels of corruption, and the adherence to the rule of law. This is, in turn, associated with modern values, such as individualism, as discussed above, gender equality, the acceptance of divorce, gay rights, and young people's relatively autonomous status. The same association, or correlation, is found with respect to other measurable variables, such as economic prosperity, education, trust in common institutions, a high degree of secularization, and others.[4]

Overall, from these data the Nordic countries, and particularly Sweden, emerge as a special case of rather radical difference. In their analysis of such data, Thorleif Pettersson and Yilmaz Esmer therefore concluded that Sweden could be labeled *Landet Annorlunda* ("the Outlier Country"), a society occupying an extreme position in a global comparative perspective in terms of basic values (Pettersson and Esmer 2005). Other researchers, working with the same or similar data sets, have tried to identify the social and cultural conditions that appear to correlate with a high degree of social trust. In this spirit, Jan Delhey and Kenneth Newton have written about a Nordic "exceptionalism" when it comes to social trust (Delhey and Newton 2005). Their starting point was to compare the degree of social trust reported in the WVS with other data measuring wealth in terms of GDP per capita, economic equality in terms of income, quality of democracy and governance, ethnic homogeneity, and the degree of Protestantism in religious communities.

Delhey and Newton drew several conclusions from their data analysis: first, that trust covaried with other factors and second, that the pattern was much stronger in the Nordic countries. Furthermore, when the Nordic countries were left out of the equation, the correlation with Protestantism disappeared completely and the other correlations also became much weaker.[5] The question was, Delhey and Newton suggested, whether high levels of trust were so closely connected to the Nordic countries that one could only with reservation, under qualified conditions, theorize more generally, in global terms and within a general explanatory model, when it comes to what "variable" correlates with—let alone causes—high levels of social trust (Delhey and Newton 2005, 320–321).

The preliminary conclusion of this analysis can be narrowed down to the need to examine the high level of trust in the Nordic countries in a broader context. Following Delhay and Newton, it may be posited that trust is, perhaps, best understood as part of a cultural complex, where a number of factors interact and where the precise causal relationships are, as yet, unclear. In accordance with this logic, we will therefore turn next to what I argue are a number of fundamental factors or aspects of Swedish and Nordic culture with respect to trust.

To begin with, I would like to discuss the transition from a tribal society steeped in the rule of blood to a society built on law, a development that is intimately linked to a positive view of the state, public institutions, and the Swedish type of "cool" but broad trust. Second, I want to emphasize the peculiarity of Swedish civil society, both in internal structure, moral logic, and relations to the state. Third, I would like to introduce the Nordic marriage pattern and family culture as a central dimension for the comparative study of trust. Fourth, I will connect the analysis of family culture and rule of law to my thesis regarding a specific form of Swedish individualism, what I call statist individualism. However, let us begin by briefly considering a fifth dimension that is closely related to the others, namely, the Lutheran legacy and the role it has played to strengthen and legitimize central values and practices such as statism, universalism, equality, and individualism.

The Lutheran Legacy

Anyone who has watched a sufficient number of Ingmar Bergman's films or pondered Greta Garbo's desire to be left alone would recognize that the Lutheran Church's stark view on the relation between the solitary man and a mysterious and at times cruel God has left its mark on modern Sweden. The legacy of the Swedish state church entails both national community and social security, on the one hand, and loneliness and unbending individualism, on the other. In order to understand the existential dimension of the Swedish social contract, which assigns so much importance to solidarity and a sense of security for all, but which also promotes individualism leading to both independence and solitude, the analysis of the Lutheran heritage is not only a useful but also an essential starting point.

Even if Sweden is today a largely secular society, it is still profoundly marked by its Lutheran heritage. The value patterns and social practices associated with the Lutheran state church deserve particular attention at a time when increased immigration makes the question of Swedish culture rooted in a particular Christian tradition more relevant than perhaps ever before. Religion and religious institutions play a crucial role in the socialization of the individual, and thus the creation of trust versus distrust, in much the same way that the family, the school, and relations with other public institutions has an influence. In this perspective, we should ask the question as to what extent the Lutheran legacy has left its mark on modern Sweden in at least two crucial ways: first, through its emphasis on individual autonomy and equality before God; second, by affording the state a central role in ensuring that these ideas have universal reach within the country. In this perspective, the modern welfare state can be viewed as a secular extension of the Lutheran state both as an instrument for individualization and as an expression of national community anchored in the firm institutional framework of the state.

It should also be noted that the role of religion can be analyzed in several dimensions. On the one hand, it is a matter of individual faith and values, and on the other, it is a question of organization and social networks. In the latter case, one might include the analysis of, in a broader discussion, the role of civil society in creating and sustaining trust—a matter that I will shortly return to. In the former case, the questions about religion and religiosity touch on matters of great current concern, namely, immigration and ethnic and religious diversity. Religious identity and ethnicity are connected to the question of how trust is related to increased cultural diversity. If the old Lutheran state church is, as I argue, an important incubator of the modern social contract in which the state, the individual equality, and universalism are central, then the emerging religious diversity is connected to communitarian visions of a pluralistic and a more unruly civil society. An important question then becomes if such a development will undermine the cool but broad social trust in favor of more inward, limited, bonding, and "hot" relations of trust confined to subnational communities, characterized by more or less distrusting relations to the state. Or, alternatively, if it will lead to a social order more tolerant of deep differences united by a common interest to "live and let live."

From Rule of Blood to Rule of Law

In present day research, several scholars have attempted to analyze the question of whether a more lawful society is more or less characterized by trust. One possibility is that modern society, with its individualism and tendency to juridify all human relationships and to take all social conflicts to court, undermines and destroys the "natural" trust that is said to prevail in more traditional societies. As mentioned before, Robert Putnam, for example, promotes the thesis that the decreasing level of trust in the United States must be understood against the backdrop of the increasing use of lawsuits and other juridical forms for managing conflicts (Putnam 2000, 145; see also fig. 10.1).

However, if one exposes this thesis to a more systematic evaluation, the picture becomes considerably more complex. In a thorough analysis of how trust and law are related to each other, the American law professor, Frank Cross, reaches a diametrically opposed conclusion. With the support of quantitative, as well as qualitative empirical data, he claims to be able to show that both individualism and rule of law covary with trust (Cross 2005). Cross, however, also suggests that it is important to differentiate varying kinds of trust. The modern law-bound society, based on individualism, is associated with a cooler, less emotional, more rational trust than the hot, emotional, and irrational trust characterizing tribal and clan societies, where blind trust and loyalty to a family can lead to blood feuds and honor killings.

The central historical question refers to when, how, and why certain societies, such as the Nordic ones, moved from honor to law, from blood vengeance to courts. This is a major question that we are unable to resolve in this chapter. However, we can point to a number approaches and key questions. To begin with, it is apparent that the relationship between the Nordic family culture and the growth of provincial laws and courts should be the center of attention. Laws and courts came to replace conflict resolution based on family honor and blood vengeance. Where a social order based on rule of law grows and prevails, the culture of honor and the rule of blood take the back seat.

In Sweden and the other Nordic societies the classic saying, "The country shall be built with law and not through violence," has its roots in the old medieval laws, as well as in the provincial courts—the *Ting*—in which 12 chosen men from the district both created and adjudicated the law. Although it was the church that compiled and spread these laws in written form, the laws were written in the vernacular, in Swedish, and not in Church Latin. This is because the law, as it was stated in the Law of Uppland of 1296, was established "to serve as guidance for all people, both rich and poor."[6] In other words, the old district courts were simultaneously courts and legislative assemblies, the free peasants were subject to the law but they also created and administered it. Not even the king, following the establishment of the Swedish unitary state, was, over time, able to set himself above the law, neither in principle nor in practice.

The interesting thing about the emergence of Swedish society was its beginnings as a decentralized but law-bound social order, which did not become a state until much later (for a more detailed discussion, Trägårdh 2007). Modern theories on the state, which define the state in terms of having a monopoly on violence and force, tend to miss this characteristic. The great legitimacy of the law and the state in a country like Sweden is closely related to the fact that the law is not imposed from above but is, rather, a product of many centuries of negotiation in a society in which the peasants remained free, and where the relative degree of social and political equality was great. Even the royal absolutism, which characterized Sweden of the great power era during the seventeenth century, was based on a protodemocratic political order, culture of negotiating rather than a cult of action, as the historian Eva Österberg has so eloquently described it (Österberg 1993, 145). The law and, above all, compliance with the law, became internalized and transformed into social norms with major legitimacy. On this foundation, a cool but, broad, social trust could evolve based on a regime requiring minimal police action, where citizens voluntarily followed the laws, rules, and regulations.

The State, Civil Society, and the Public Institutions

In modern times, this heritage has found new forms. The positive view of the state, the law, and the public institutions has found new expression in the modern, democratic welfare state and its fundamental legitimacy among the citizens. With respect to the study of trust, this has led Swedish researchers to challenge theories derived from American empirical data and normative assumptions, which have tended to stress the role of civil society and local communities within a normative tradition that views the federal state with suspicion. Not least is the Swedish political scientist Bo Rothstein associated with this critique of Robert Putnam and other American scholars. Thus, Rothstein argues that the role of associations has been exaggerated and he instead has pointed to the role played by the institutions of the public sector, especially those that are associated with the legal system and the universalist welfare state. Where Putman, the American, views the state more as a necessary evil than a precondition for trust and community, Rothstein, the Swede, points to the fair and incorrupt institutions of the state as the incubator for the fragile social trust. According to this logic, we learn to trust our fellow citizens thanks to habits and mores acquired through our dealing with our public institutions.

This view of Sweden as part of a Nordic cultural cluster characterized by a "state friendly" welfare state has also found expression in attempts to capture the specific character of the Nordic "model" in comparative regime-type theories. Thus, a number of researchers have attempted to thematize differences between, for example, Anglo-American (liberal), Continental (conservative), and Nordic (social-democratic) welfare regimes (Esping-Andersen 1990; Janoski 1998; Schofer and

Fourcade-Gourinchas 2001; Jepperson 2002). These analytical models are interesting and relevant in terms of trust research. For example, it is often stressed that Sweden and the Nordic countries have a long tradition of consensus and compromise, a relationship that naturally ought to promote (or ought to be based on) trust between interest groups, political parties, and the citizens they represent. Similarly, as discussed above, researchers such as Rothstein have promoted the thesis that egalitarian and universal welfare policy plays an important role in the emergence and maintenance of widespread social trust and a high level of confidence in social institutions.

At the same time, many of these regime theories misunderstand the dynamics underlying the Swedish social contract. Above all, this applies to the relations between state, individual, family, and civil society. Rather than view Sweden as a corporatist state ruled from above, there are good reasons to describe the system as a democratic model in which the outstanding feature is the close relations between the agents of the state and the representatives of civil society. Without doubt the state plays an important role, but it is also impossible to understand the Swedish variety of democratic governance without taking into account the part played by the organizations in civil society, especially when it comes to the input side of the political process.

This is further underlined by empirical research that shows that even if the public sector in Sweden is large, it is characterized just as much by its extensive and vital civil society.[7] Indeed, in so far as institutions matter for trust creation, these include not only the public institutions of the (welfare) state but also private ones, from for-profit corporations to nonprofit organizations and voluntary groups. From a trust perspective, it is significant that the Swedish form of governance is based on the interweaving of civil society and state in which a number of formal and informal channels link organizations with public administration and democratic institutions. The epitome of this idea is the Swedish system of government commissions, public inquiries, and the related referral system that are unique to Sweden and, to some extent, the Nordic countries (Trägårdh 2007, for a discussion regarding the role of public inquiries).

This is a theme that has for a long time been central to Swedish political science research, where the idea of Sweden as a state-dominated corporative society is set against the image of Sweden as an "associative democracy" where, instead, the members of civil society—"from below"—play the first violin (Heckscher 1946; Johansson 1952; Rothstein 1992). In this perspective, it is not particularly fruitful to oppose public institutions and civil society organizations in the manner that has at times been the case in the debates between Rothstein and Putnam. Instead, they ought to be viewed as kindred institutions that both have the potential to either undermine or build trust depending on the degree of corruption and arbitrariness versus openness and fairness.

To understand the role of civil society in Sweden, we should therefore not only analyze it in quantitative terms, but also in terms of its moral logic. What makes Swedish civil society interesting and different is that—like so many other institutions in Sweden—it is based on certain fundamental principles as regards both order and internal structure, the principles that we have already mentioned: individual autonomy, social equality, democratic process, voluntary participation, membership, and a culture of negotiation. Where, for example, American civil society to a great degree consists of hierarchical and undemocratic institutions—foundations, religious organizations, charities, nonprofit companies—Swedish civil society has historically stressed a struggle to emancipate individuals from traditional, often hierarchical and patriarchal, institutions such as the traditional family, philanthropic organizations, and charities.

Instead, one can observe a historical development away from charity toward social rights founded on the idea of an alliance between state and individual, institutionalized in the social and family policy of the welfare state that to a great extent has sought to underwrite the autonomy of the individual. In other words, if civil society plays a decisive role on the input side of the Swedish political system, the output end is then rather a matter of a direct relation between state and individual. To understand the moral and existential basis for this emphasis on the individual, social equality, and gender equality, we now turn to another crucial dimension: the Nordic family culture.

The Nordic Family and Marriage Model

The fact that the autonomy of the individual in relation to the family is much larger in Sweden and in other Nordic countries has been long pointed out by researchers (Gaunt 1983). Moreover, it has also become apparent that the Swedish family's special character is not the result of any recent efforts on behalf of the welfare state's meddling social engineers. It is important to stress this, partly due to the fact that so many scholars are researching trust focus on the welfare state, partly because more conservative critics of modern Sweden blame the alleged decline of the Swedish family on the welfare state (Popenoe 1988, 1991). Rather, modern Swedish family policy is essentially the most recent manifestation of practices and norms with a very long history. To understand this Nordic peculiarity, one must analyze Swedish and Nordic marriage patterns, family structures, and socialization practices in a comparative and historical perspective.

In analyzing the genesis and variation of trust in various Western European countries, the political scientist Gerry Mackie speculates that differences in marriage strategies and family cultures play an important role (Mackie 2001). Building on John Hajnal's and Peter Laslett's theories about the different marriage patterns and family structures that can be identified in Europe, with roots as far back as the thirteenth century, if not longer, Mackie suggests that a comparison between the differences in marriage patterns described by Hajnal and Laslett and the data we now have on the variation in social trust exhibit striking similarities (Hajnal 1965; Laslett 1983). Countries in Northwestern Europe, characterized by a high level of trust, are also the countries having a special, and globally unique, marriage pattern. Briefly summarized, the researcher notes three distinctive tendencies: first, women marry late; second, new couples move from their parental homes to form new independent households and nuclear families; third, it was common that the children were sent away to work in other households who needed extra help (Mackie 2001, 259).

This marriage pattern can be seen to be related to a number of phenomena of significance from a trust perspective. The higher age of women at marriage is linked to a higher degree of literacy and with higher equality within the family. According to Mackie and other researchers, these patterns are, in their turn associated with a higher level of equality as well as with a higher degree of individualism. Children are raised to be independent and form significant social relationships outside the family, which are based on the individual's reliability and mutual social trust. This encourages a cooler, but also a broader, sense of community and who can and should be trusted. In contrast with countries in Southern Europe where both family honor and blood vengeance remain deeply rooted, the higher equality and individualism associated with the Nordic countries results in a cooler trust, based on a system that is focused on the individual and which is not family based.

The Nordic marriage pattern and family culture has, in time, found expression not only in family practices, but also in legislation. According to the historian Christina Carlsson Wetterberg and her colleagues, it is possible to distinguish a specific Nordic marriage model with deep historical roots (Melby et al. 2006). This model is, according to Carlsson Wetterberg, characterized by an emphasis on the individual's freedom, state friendliness, and the importance of gender equality

(Carlsson Wetterberg 2006). Even if other countries over time also came to reform their marriage and family law, this was generally undertaken at a much later point in time and without the same radical and systematic approach. The conclusions of the Nordic researchers agree well with international comparative research regarding family and marriage, such as theories on various marriage patterns discussed above (Gaunt 1983; Bradley 2000; Ronfani 2001; Bradshaw and Hatland 2006).

Swedish Statist Individualism and the Future Prospects for Trust

To conclude, this chapter argues that the interplay between state, family, civil society, and the individual is the key to the mystery of high trust in Sweden. This is not to suggest that Sweden is unique. The Swedish social contract should be viewed as but a local, if specific, solution to a universal dilemma that human beings are constantly caught in a force field whose poles, on the one side, are the desire for individual sovereignty and, on the other side, the inexorable necessity of belonging to a society. Our basic assumption is that the modern Swedish welfare state has offered its citizens maximum freedom without necessarily jeopardizing the fundamental social order. The solution is called, as mentioned earlier, Swedish "statist individualism" and is an alliance between the state and the individual based on social equality and personal autonomy, as well as on the state's role as the guarantor that these values are realized and maintained.

"Statist individualism" is, however, not a simply a modern invention but is, rather, a logical development of historically rooted values and practices. Among these, we find the principles already discussed in this chapter—individualism and pathos of equality rooted in a special family culture and special marriage patterns and a positive view of the state that may ultimately be traced to a law-abiding system with deep roots in Sweden.

In this perspective, it is not surprising that Sweden is characterized by a low degree of corruption and a high degree of social trust. According to the majority of researchers, trust seems to be correlated precisely with equality, gender equality, individualism, and a regulated system. It is, however, important to emphasize that this concerns a particular type of trust that we have chosen to call "cool trust." Swedes live in a world where cool trust, independence, and solitude coexist and are, to some extent, closely linked with each other.

To be sure, this is an order of things that some may well find to be abhorrent. Sweden is a country with a record number of single households, a large number of divorces, a country where children are in nurseries, and elderly care is largely managed by public institutions. When the Swedish journalist Sanfrid Neander-Nilsson asked the question "Is the Swede human?," he was alluding to the social coldness that he experienced in Sweden compared with what he experienced in his beloved Italy (Neander-Nilsson 1946). He wrote in the 1940s, long before Putnam and other researchers had arrived at the point at which they compared the corrupted, low-trust society of Italy with the law-abiding, individualistic high-trust society of Sweden.

And Neander-Nilsson's preference was for the hot, passionate Latin form of love, not the bloodless Swedish variant. Nor is he the only one to spontaneously recoil in first experiencing the special Swedish combination of statism and individualism. Even today, many people look with strong distaste upon modernity in which the family and other close community ties are subordinated to an atomistic individualism allied with anonymous market forces and the state's chilly formalism. The late nineteenth century's Gemeinschaft's supporters have their counterparts in today's communitarian thinkers and political movements, from Left to Right. These individuals and organizations speak highly, in various forms, of the family and of civil society's associations and communities as constituting more human, warmer alternative ways of living. The choice between a broad, but cool, form of trust and a hot, but narrowly focused one, is not, it would appear, easy.

Nor is it clear that the Swedish social contract is sustainable. As indicated above, the current trends toward increased cultural diversity constitutes a direct challenge to its fundamental values and institutionalized practices. At the same time, it would be unwise to write, too quickly, its obituary. Neither should the lure of individual freedom in the context of social security be underestimated, nor should the appeal of traditional communitarian institutions be overestimated. If we look at the previously cited WVS data over time, one thing becomes clear. While Sweden looks extreme and thus possibly both irrelevant and vulnerable, it is also true that the long-term trend over time is that the world at large is moving in the general direction of Sweden.

Notes

1. The trust level figures are from 2010. GSS data can be found on http://sda.berkeley.edu/cgi-bin/hsda?harcsda+gss10.
2. See Wollebæk (2011, 77) for a comparison of 22 European countries based on the data from WVS, European Values Surveys, and Eurobarometers. Analyses show a decrease in the proportion of those who agree that "most

people can be trusted" from 1988–1990 to 2006–2008 in Italy (34% to 28%), Spain (34% to 27%), Portugal (21% to 17%), Poland (35% to 28%), Russia (38% to 26%), Bulgaria (30% to 20%), Slovakia (23% to 13%), Hungary (27% to 21%), Ireland (47% to 39%), Northern Ireland (44% to 31%), and the United Kingdom (44% to 31%). Levels are stable in Belgium, France, the Netherlands, and the Czech Republic. Trust increased in Denmark (58% to 76%), Norway (65% to 75%), and Iceland (44% to 49%). In Sweden, the level of trust decreased in conjunction with the crisis taking place at the beginning of the 1990s. From 1988–1990 when the level was 66 percent, the figure dropped to 60 percent in 1994–1996 but it, subsequently, increased to 71 percent in the latest survey. Finland demonstrates a similar pattern. In Germany, Latvia, and Estonia a slight increase in trust level can be noted.

3. Quotation from the title of Thomasson (1970). See also Ruth (1984) and Jenkins (1986).

4. Much of the WVS data is analyzed in Inglehart and Welzel (2005). See also discussion on Sweden as an exception in Pettersson and Esmer (2005).

5. It should be noted that one of the factors that Delhey and Newton mention, ethnic homogeneity, has been studied later in more detail by other researchers. Putnam (2007) created quite a stir with an article that pointed to the strong negative correlation between trust and ethnic diversity. Hooghe, Reeskens, Stolle, and Trappers (2009) came later to the conclusion that any connection between ethnic heterogeneity and lower degree of trust cannot be verified on the basis of their data. Putnam based his conclusion on the US data and some scholars have questioned whether the US data can be extrapolated to Europe. Since then, interest in the possible links between trust and ethnic diversity has been great, for obvious political reasons. The same applies to the links between trust and socioeconomic equality. For a discussion of this literature and the results from a large study of local community trust in Sweden, where the emphasis is on precisely the relationships between trust, ethnic diversity, and socioeconomic equality, see Trägårdh, Wallman Lundåsen, Wollebaek, and Svedberg (2013).

6. See Spangenberg (2009), which is also the source of the quotation from the Law of Uppland.

7. For the scope of Swedish civil society and its composition, see Wijkström and Lundström (2002), as well as Jeppsson Grassman and Svedberg (2007).

References

Beck, Ulrich. 1992. *Risk Society: Towards a New Modernity*. London: Sage.
Berggren, Henrik, and Lars Trägårdh. 2006. *Är svensken människa: Gemenskap och oberoende i det moderna Sverige*. Stockholm: Norstedts.
Bok, Sissela. 1978. *Lying: Moral Choices in Public and Private Life*. New York: Pantheon Books.

Bordum, Anders. 2001. "Tillid er godt! Om tillidsbegrebets værdiladning." In *Det handler om tillid*, edited by Anders Bordum and Søren Barlebo Wenneberg. Frederiksberg: Samfundslitteratur.

Bradley, David. 2000. "Family Laws and Welfare States." In *The Nordic Model of Marriage and the Welfare State*, edited by Kari Melby, et al. Copenhagen: Nordic Council of Ministers.

Bradshaw, Jonathan, and Aksel Hatland. Eds. 2006. *Social Policy, Employment and Family Change in Comparative Perspective*. Cheltenham, UK; Northampton, MA: Edward Elgar.

Carlsson Wetterberg, Christina. 2006. "När äktenskapet blev ett modernt kontrakt." *Svenska Dagbladet*, September 9, 2006.

Coleman, James S. 1988. "Social Capital in the Creation of Human Capital." *American Journal of Sociology* 94:S95–S120.

Cross, Frank. 2005. "Law and Trust." *Georgetown Law Journal* 93:1457–1545.

Delhey, Jan, and Kenneth Newton. 2005. "Predicting Cross-National Levels of Social Trust: Global Pattern or Nordic Exceptionalism?" *European Sociological review* 32 (4): 311–327.

Erikson, Erik H. 1993. *Barnet och samhället*. Stockholm: Natur & Kultur.

Esping-Andersen, Gøsta. 1990. *The Three Worlds of Welfare Capitalism*. Cambridge, UK: Polity Press.

Fukuyama, Francis. 1995. *Trust: The Social Virtues and the Creation of Prosperity*. New York: Free Press.

Gaunt, David. 1983. *Familjeliv i norden*. Stockholm: Gidlund.

Habermas, Jürgen. 1996. *Kommunikativt handlande; texter om språk, rationalitet och samhälle*. Gothenburg: Daidalos.

Hajnal, John. 1965. "European Marriage Patterns in Perspective." In *Population in History: Essays in Historical Demography*, edited by David V. Glass and David E.C. Eversley. London: Arnold.

Hardin, Russel. 1999. "Do We Want Trust in Government?" In *Democracy and Trust*, edited by Mark Warren. Cambridge, UK: Cambridge University Press.

Heckscher, Gunnar. 1946. *Staten och organisationerna*. Stockholm: KFs bokförlag.

Hooghe, Mark, Tim Reeskens, Dietlind Stolle, and Ann Trappers. 2009. "Ethnic Diversity and Generalized Trust in Europe: A Cross-National Multilevel Study." *Comparative Political Studies* 42:2.

Inglehart, Ronald. 2006. *Inglehart-Wenzel Cultural Map of the World*. www.worldvaluessurvey.org, accessed February 13, 2007.

Inglehart, Ronald, and Christian Welzel. 2005. *Modernization, Cultural Change, and Democracy: The Human Development Sequence*. Cambridge, UK: Cambridge University Press.

Janoski, Thomas. 1998. *Citizenship and Civil Society*. Cambridge, UK: Cambridge University Press.

Jenkins, David. 1986. *Sweden and the Price of Progress*. New York: Coward-McCann.

Jepperson, Ronald. 2002. "Political Modernities: Disentangling Two Underlying Dimensions of Institutional Differentiation." *Sociological Theory* 20 (1): 61–85.

Jeppsson Grassman, Eva, and Lars Svedberg. 2007. "Civic Participation in a Scandinavian Welfare State: patterns in Contemporary Sweden." In *State and Civil Society in Northern Europe: The Swedish Model Reconsidered*, edited by Lars Trägårdh, New York: Berghahn Books.

Johansson, Hilding. 1952. *Folkrörelserna och det demokratiska statsskicket i Sverige.* Karlstad: Gleerups.

Lasch, Christopher. 1978. *The Culture of Narcissism: American Life in an Age of Diminishing Expectations.* New York: Warner Books.

Laslett, Peter. 1983. "Family and Household as a Work Group and Kin Group: Areas of Traditional Europe Compared." In *Family Forms in Historic Europe*, edited by Richard Wall. Cambridge, UK: Cambridge University Press.

Lundåsen, Susanne, and Thorleif Pettersson. 2009. "Att mäta tillit: teori och metodproblem." In *Tilliten i det moderna Sverige. Den dumme svensken och andra mysterier*, edited by Lars Trägårdh. Stockholm: SNS.

Mackie, Gerry. 2001. "Patterns of Social Trust in Western Europe and Their Genesis." In *Trust in Society*, edited by Karen S. Cook. New York: Russell Sage.

Melby, Kari, Anu Pylkkänen, Bente Rosenbeck, and Christina Carlsson Wetterberg. 2006. *Inte ett ord om kärlek: äktenskap och politik i Norden ca 1850–1930.* Gothenburg: Makadam förlag.

Neander-Nilsson, Sanfrid. 1946. *Är svensken människa.* Stockholm: Fahlcrantz & Gumaelius.

Österberg, Eva. 1993. "Vardagens sköra samförstånd. Bondepolitik i den svenska modellen från Vasatid till Frihetstid." In *Tänka, tycka, tro*, edited by Gunnar Broberg, Ulla Wikander, and Klas Åmark. Stockholm: Ordfront.

Pettersson, Thorleif, and Yilmaz Esmer. 2005. *Vilka är annorlunda?, Integrationsverkets rapportserie, 2005:03.* Norrköping: Integrationsverket.

Popenoe, David. 1988. *Disturbing the Nest: Family Change and Decline in Modern Societies.* New York: Aldine de Gruyter.

———. 1991. "Family Decline in the Swedish Welfare State." *The Public Interest* 102 (Winter): 65–77.

Putnam, Robert D. 1993. *Making Democracy Work. Civic Traditions in Modern Italy.* Princeton, NJ: Princeton University Press.

———. 2000. *Bowling Alone: The Collapse and Revival of American Community.* New York: Simon & Schuster.

———. 2007. "E Pluribus Unum: Diversity and Community in the Twenty-first Century: The 2006 Johan Skytte Prize Lecture." *Scandinavian Political Studies* 30 (2): 137–174.

Riesman, David. 1950. *The Lonely Crowd.* New Haven, CT: Yale University Press.

Ronfani, Paola. 2001. "Family Law in Europe." In *The History of the European family, Vol 3: Family Life in the Twentieth Century*, edited by David I. Kertzer and Marzio Barbagli. New Haven, CT: Yale University Press.

Rothstein, Bo. 1992. *Den korporativa staten.* Stockholm: Norstedts.

———. 2003. *Sociala fällor och tillitens problem.* Stockholm: SNS Förlag.

Rothstein, Bo, and Dietlind Stolle. 2003. "Introduction: Social Capital in Scandinavia." *Scandinavian Political Studies* 26 (1): 1–26.

Ruth, Arne. 1984. "The Second New Nation: The Mythology of Modern Sweden." *Dædalus* 113:2.

Schofer, Evan, and Marion Fourcade-Gourinchas. 2001. "The Structural Contexts of Civic Engagement: Voluntary Association Membership in Comparative Perspective." *American Sociological Review* 66 (6): 806–828.

Seligman, Adam B. 1997. *The Problem of Trust.* New York: Free Press.

Spangenberg, Carl Gustav. 2009. "Land skall med lag byggas—men hur spreds lagarna?" http://www.jamombud.se/docs/carl_gustaf_spangenberg.pdf.

Sztompka, Piotr. 1999. *Trust. A Sociological Theory.* Cambridge, UK: Cambridge University Press.

Thomasson, Richard. 1970. *Sweden: Prototype of Modern Society.* New York: Random House.

Trägårdh, Lars. 1997. "Statist Individualism: On the Culturality of the Nordic Welfare State." In *The Cultural Construction of Norden*, edited by Bo Stråth and Øystein Sørensen. Oslo: Scandinavian University Press.

———. 2007. "Democratic Governance and the Creation of Social Capital in Sweden: The Discreet Charm of Governmental Commissions." In *State and Civil Society in Northern Europe: The Swedish Model Reconsidered*, edited by Lars Trägårdh. New York: Berghahn Books.

Trägårdh, Lars, Susanne Wallman Lundåsen, Dag Wollebaek, and Lars Svedberg. 2013. *Den svala svenska tilliten: Förutsättningar och utmaningar.* Stockholm: SNS.

Uslaner, Eric. 2002. *The Moral Foundations of Trust.* Cambridge, UK: Cambridge University Press.

Wijkström, Filip, and Tommy Lundström. 2002. *Den ideella sektorn. Organisationerna i det civila samhället.* Stockholm: Sober Förlag.

Wollebæk, Dag 2011. "Norge og Nordens sosiale kapital i europeisk kontekst." In *Sosial kapital i Norge*, edited by Dag Wollebæk and Signe Bock Segaard. Oslo: Cappelen Damm.

Contributors

Niklas Egels-Zandén is associate professor in business administration at the School of Business, Economics, and Law at the University of Gothenburg. His research field includes the integration of environmental and social issues into the strategic and operative processes of companies. Niklas's publications include academic articles in international journals, such as *Journal of Business Ethics*, *Business Ethics: A European Review*, and *Business Strategy and the Environment*.

Johan Fornäs is professor of media and communication studies at Södertörn University and chief editor of *Culture Unbound: Journal of Current Cultural Research*. With a background in musicology and cultural studies, his research primarily concerns the various types of media interactions through which identities are constructed. His publications include *Cultural Theory and Late Modernity*; *Consuming Media: Communication, Shopping and Everyday Life*; *Signifying Europe*; and *Capitalism: A Companion to Marx's Economy Critique*.

Maria Grafström is associate professor based at Stockholm Centre for Organizational Research (Score) at Stockholm School of Economics (SSE) and Stockholm University. Her research primarily concerns the mediatization of the business world and consequences of such mediatization, not the least in terms of the way in which the increasingly web-based media environment alters the preconditions for communication and news production.

Ingrid Gustafsson is a PhD student at the School of Public Administration at the University of Gothenburg. In her thesis, she addresses the issue of the increased inclusion of private sector standards in the public sector, with an empirical focus on Swedish Board for Accreditation and Conformity Assessment (Swedac) and its work with standards.

Maria Gustavson is research fellow at the Department of Political Science at the University of Gothenburg. She received her PhD in 2012 with a thesis titled "Auditing the African State. International Standards and Local Adjustments." Her research primarily concerns administrative reforms in developing countries, particularly in sub-Saharan Africa, and the significance of auditing for democracy and public sector performance.

Eva Hagbjer is a PhD student at the Department of Accounting at the Stockholm School of Economics (SSE). Her research addresses financial control and the allocation of responsibilities within and between organizations performing public services. In her thesis, she studies the management and follow-up of outsourced elderly care.

Kristina Tamm Hallström is associate professor at the Stockholm School of Economics (SSE) and works as research director at the Stockholm Centre for Organizational Research (Score). She has conducted extensive research on the legitimacy and authority in transnational standardization and third-party certification. She currently leads one research project on the control organization of certificates and ecolabels, and another one on the implementation of management accounting and control models in public sector organizations.

Bengt Kristensson Uggla is Amos Anderson Professor in Philosophy, Culture, and Management at the Swedish-speaking university in Finland, Åbo Akademi University, and among other things appointed associate professor (Docent) in faith and world views at Uppsala University. He is a distinguished expert on the philosophy of Paul Ricoeur and has developed a kind of cross-disciplinary hermeneutics in a great number of publications, such as *Ricoeur, Hermeneutics, and Globalization* (New York; London: Continuum, 2010).

Johnny Lind is professor in financial control at Stockholm School of Economics (SSE), where he also heads the accounting department. His research interests include accounting in interorganizational relationships and networks, covering both private and public sector organizations. His most recent books are *Innovation eller kvartalskapitalism* (with Lars Bengtsson, Stockholm: Liber, 2013) and *Accounting in Networks* (London: Routledge, 2010).

Pernilla Petrelius Karlberg is associate professor at the Stockholm School of Economics (SSE). Her primary interests include the mediatization of the leaders of the business world and organizations. Her PhD thesis (*Den Medialiserade Direktören*) was published at SSE in 2007. She lectures on organization and leadership at both undergraduate and postgraduate levels. She is also program director for SSE MBA Executive Format.

Marta Reuter is research fellow at the Stockholm Centre for Organizational Research (Score) at Stockholm University. She has recently completed a postdoctoral project at the Department of Political Science at Stockholm University, funded with a scholarship from *Riksbankens Jubileumsfond*. Her research interests revolve around civil society and its organizations, with particular focus on the transnational dimension. She was recently the first editor of a comparative special issue of the international journal *Nonprofit Policy Forum* (vol. 3, no. 2, Oct. 2012) on government-voluntary sector compacts.

Bo Rothstein is holder of the August Röhs Professorship in political science at the University of Gothenburg, where he is responsible for the research program, "The Quality of Government Institute." His latest publications include *The Quality of Government: Inequality, Corruption and Social Trust in International Perspective* (Chicago: University of Chicago Press, 2011) and *Good Government: The Relevance of Political Science* (Cheltenham: Edward Elgar Press, 2012).

Ebba Sjögren is assistant professor at the Department of Accounting at Stockholm School of Economics (SSE). Her primary research interest is the development and use of knowledge-based management tools in organizational control and decision making, particularly in the health care sector. She has studied, for example, the organization of geriatric inpatient care.

Lars Strannegård is professor in business administration at the Department of Management and Organization at the Stockholm School of Economics (SSE) where he is the holder of the Bo Rydin and SCA Chair in management. Lars is currently also vice president at SSE and leads a research program on aesthetics and economy, and on media, corporate leaders, and communication consultants.

Lars Trägårdh is professor in history at Ersta Sköndal University College. His research has concerned the Swedish social contract in a historical and comparative perspective with particular focus on civil society, trust, and individualism. His works include *State and Civil Society in Northern Europe* (New York: Berghahn Books, 2007) and *Civil Society in the Age of Monitory Democracy*, with Nina Witoszek and Bron Taylor (New York: Berghahn Books, 2013), and in Swedish *Är svensken människa*, with Henrik Berggren (Stockholm: Norstedts,

2006) and *Den svala svenska tilliten*, with Susanne Lundåsen Wallman, Lars Svedberg, and Dag Wollebaek (Stockholm: SNS, 2013). From 2011 to 2013, he served as a member of the Swedish government's Commission on the Future.

Filip Wijkström currently holds a position as visiting professor in business administration at Stockholm University while on sabbatical leave from his position at the Stockholm School of Economics (SSE). Since the early 1990s, he has studied and taught on civil society and its organizations, with focus on governance and strategy issues on which he has published extensively. Among his latest publications are the anthologies *Nordic Civil Society at a Cross-Roads* (Baden-Baden: Nomos, 2011; coedited with Annette Zimmer) and *Civilsamhället i samhällskontraktet* (Stockholm: European Civil Society Press, 2012).

Karolina Windell holds a PhD in business studies from the Department of Business Studies at Uppsala University. She is currently working as a researcher at the Swedish Agency for Cultural Policy Analysis and at the Stockholm Centre for Organizational Research (Score). Her research concerns the way in which ideas on corporate responsibility are developed, and the way in which the business media's increased monitoring of the business world contributes to establishing notions of responsible and irresponsible companies.

Index

212   •   Index

Printed in the United States of America